This book studies the importance of typographic shapes in French Renaissance literature in the context of psychoanalysis and of the history of printed writing. Focusing on the poetry of Clément Marot, Rabelais's *Gargantua*, Ronsard's sonnets, and the *Essais* of Montaigne, it argues that printed characters can either supplement or betray what they appear to articulate, revealing compositional patterns that do not appear to be under authorial control and fostering the elaboration of signs between their context and the reader or spectator.

Professor Conley shows that graphic forms are crucial for the development of complex interactions of verbal and visual materials in the early years of print-culture. Marot and Rabelais articulate a religious program through the letter; Ronsard conflates the arts in poetry of the French court in the middle years of the sixteenth century; Montaigne stages the birth of the self in print and inscribes political dimensions in the relationships between the letter and meaning. This unconscious, proto-Freudian writing has complex historical relations with verbal and visual practices in the media of the twentieth century.

Cambridge Studies in French

General editor: MALCOLM BOWIE

Recent titles in this series include:

A complete list of books in the series is given at the end of the volume.

Cambridge Studies in French

THE GRAPHIC UNCONSCIOUS
IN EARLY MODERN FRENCH WRITING

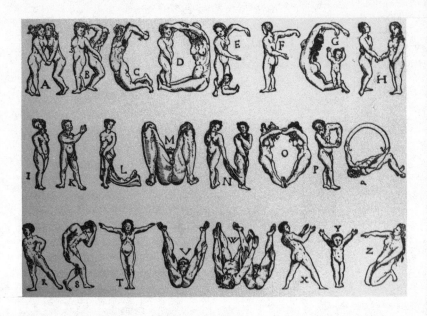

Replica of Peter Flötner, *Menschenalphabet* (ca. 1534), engraved by Martin Waygel (Augsburg, 1560). Munich, Hofbibliothek.

THE GRAPHIC UNCONSCIOUS IN EARLY MODERN FRENCH WRITING

TOM CONLEY

Professor of French,
University of Minnesota

CAMBRIDGE
UNIVERSITY PRESS

Published by the Press Syndicate of the University of Cambridge
The Pitt Building, Trumpington Street, Cambridge CB2 1RP
40 West 20th Street, New York, NY 1001-4211, USA
10 Stamford Road, Oakleigh, Melbourne 3166, Australia

First published 1992

Printed in Great Britain at the University Press, Cambridge

A catalogue record for this book is available from the British Library

Library of Congress cataloguing in publication data
Conley, Tom.
The graphic unconscious in early modern French
writing / Tom Conley
p.   cm. – (Cambridge studies in French)
Includes bibliographical references and index.
ISBN 0 521 41031 2
1. French literature – 16th century – History and criticism.
2. Type and type-founding – France – History – 16th
century.   3. Visual poetry, French – History and criticism.
4. Printing – France – History – 16th century.
5. Psychoanalysis and literature.   6. Reader – response
criticism.   7. Semiotics and literature.   I. Title.   II. Series.
PQ239.C67   1992
840.9'003 – dc20   91-33177   CIP

ISBN 0521 41031 2 hardback

A VERENA

CONTENTS

ILLUSTRATIONS

ACKNOWLEDGMENTS

I wish to thank Malcolm Bowie, who supported the idea of this project, and especially the Cambridge University Press readers, who offered constructive counsel at various stages of its writing. Katharina Brett, Nancy-Jane Thompson, Rosemary Morris, and staff at the Cambridge University Press have been instrumental in bringing the work to completion. Grants from the National Endowment for the Humanities, the American Council of Learned Societies, and the Graduate School of the University of Minnesota have sustained a good deal of the research and writing. David Buisseret, director of the Hermon Dunlap Smith Center for the History of Cartography at the Newberry Library, has generously offered texts and perspectives on the French Renaissance.

My greatest debt is to Alfred Glauser, whose inspiration and friendship have guided me through French literature of the sixteenth century. I am personally grateful to the late Donald M. Frame, whose vivid translation of Montaigne's *Essays* first led me in the direction of French studies too long ago. Others to whom this book is dedicated include Germaine Brée, Lucette Finas, Floyd Gray, and Douglas Kelly. The project began and, years later, has been completed at the Institute for Research in the Humanities. I wish to thank Loretta Freiling for unfailing support that spans two decades.

I owe much to graduate students at the University of California-Berkeley, the Graduate Center of the City University of New York, and the University of Minnesota. Their time and patience have been strained in courses and seminars taught with them on the Renaissance. In particular, I wish to thank Scott Fish, Christiane Zablith, and Kerry McIndoo, who have helped prepare the manuscript. My fondest expression of gratitude is to Verena Conley and our children, David and Francine, adepts of Rabelais and Montaigne, who know and savor good literature.

INTRODUCTION

In the conclusion to his recent *Pictorialist Poetics: Poetry and the Visual Arts in Nineteenth-Century France*, David Scott argues that two moments which have changed human perceptions of visual and textual elements in writing include the Renaissance and nineteenth-century France. Following Walter Ong, he ends by saying that in the Renaissance conditions of thought and communication are projected into space and are gridded according to diagrammatical reason.[1] The sixteenth and nineteenth centuries, two periods of "radical development," call into question the formatting, dissemination, and mediation of printed writing and pictures. Both periods show what happens when "complex interactions" of spatial and textual elements produce composite forms of literature. The nineteenth century, he continues, points to central concerns of art, literature, and criticism of our own time.

The work that follows can begin with the area that David Scott uses to background his *Pictorialist Poetics*. Like the nineteenth century, the Renaissance may be equally important for our understanding of similar interactions and their destiny in the media of our time. Because the French Renaissance seems distant from us, its manifestations of printed writing may appear so strange that we inherit them as if from the depths of an unconscious of history. A highly visual, even tactile sense of writing appears to mark early modern literature, but how the major texts articulate complex relations with graphic form still remains a mystery. They appear to be self-contained, complete, and without sign of stages of development outside of their inner causes. What follows cannot claim to include what lexicographers, historians of the printed book, or art historians have studied in detail in their respective disciplines,[2] but it does seek to find where graphic and poetic sensibilities produce identities through formal differences. The work may cause more problems than it solves. I wish to argue that the printed letter comprises an element crucial to pictorial and lexical dimensions in

1

sixteenth-century literature, and that it is basic to a general practice of verbal montage. Two problems ought to be addressed as we begin. The first entails typography and the study of sixteenth-century literature outside of French or European boundaries. Access to original documents and editions is limited in the western hemisphere. For many of us the field — the rich, vibrant, incomparable writing of the canon — comes not only across geographical distance but also through filters of ideology. Representations of the Renaissance in manuals and anthologies have, until quite recently, been motivated by a model of evolution towards classical ideals. We learn classical languages to discover a vernacular quite unlike contemporary French, and to gain an inkling of the mental structures that inform Renaissance literature, we train ourselves in history that requires extensive work in anthropology, economics, and other fields. Our lives can be done before we acquire knowledge enough to claim any understanding of the writing. The question of beginning or of transferring our attention from one age to another is laden with constraints that are both practical and ideological in design.

Secondly, because it attracts specialists of uncommon faith and endurance, *seiziémisme* can run the risk of celebrating itself for its own ends. Outsiders perceive the specialists of the *terroir* establishing self-enclosed agendas that tend not to ponder broader issues of literacy and the role of humanities in our own time or amidst a public weaned on contemporary culture. Renaissance scholars, especially those in the Americas, can find themselves knotted in a double bind. As *seiziémistes* we easily realize that our research hardly pertains to issues affecting the world of the next centuries. But from another standpoint, we know we are all involved in matters of form that enormously broaden our grasp of cultural history. The forms of the past we study have much to tell us about the strategies of control exerted upon us now. Since printed literature is indeed a shape of mediation, its past must continually be brought into the present.

For this reason we must ask how we can keep in view a sense of discipline and practice. One facet of the task, I believe, has to do with transmitting a literary canon of the Renaissance into the present for a public that perforce lacks extensive training or background in the liberal arts. The sixteenth century must be drawn into our own time with as little loss of specificity as possible as regards both its context *and* the conditions of our comprehension of the past. The opacities of its practices and their transmission can become a pleasure of investigation.[3] The delight we sense in contact with the materiality of early modern writing can be used to open a dialectic between our grasp of the sixteenth century and that of our own historical moment. I would like to suggest that typographical form may provide one avenue of appeal.

The approach may not in fact be without some parallel to that of the early Renaissance. In pedagogical literature of the 1530s, pictures are used to mediate vernacular and classical languages or serve as memory-aids to students of the trivium. Images are destined for those who have not been professionally tutored and aim at developing cognizance of various orders of knowledge through correlations of objects and languages. Typography serves a functional role as a ground and a shape that moves between one idiom and another. The pleasure that figural shapes can afford opens on to the disposition of early modern literature in general. Since it shares common lexical and pictorial properties, like D. W. Winnicott's famous concept of the "transitional object," the letter can mediate between our experience of language and that of the Renaissance. Both a verbal and pictographic hold on writing is assured, thus suggesting how composition of the period may be just as "transitional" (and also, transnational) as ours or any other into which all of us are born as users of language. With attention to the typographic character we can momentarily place ourselves in common material operations and experiments, at a time comparable to our own, when language and technology are in flux and in dialogue with oral cultures of earlier centuries.

In the sixteenth century, graphic display of writing seems to provide a way of juxtaposing and mixing present languages and regional cultures with materials revived from the classical past. Print culture seems to be something new in its production and classification of information but also very old in respect to the materials it inherits and reshuffles. The same notion of "transitional" forms can be developed in our relation to the sixteenth century. The period is often understood as a moment of transition from the Middle to the Modern Ages. But in its own time, print served as a form of mediation between vernacular and learned cultures. For the purpose of the study that follows, we can hypothesize that the Renaissance saw the beginning of technologies which inform our own experience of writing, that is, of mediated information. From this angle our world serves as a background for the study of the past. Thus imagined, the sixteenth century is not entirely isolated in a frame that scholars cultivate for professional agendas but is projected as a paradox of an immediate or timeless background in the workings of our own lives.[4]

Mechanical print no doubt changes the technology and imagination of letters in different ways and with various intensities in early modern times, but sooner or later it institutes a difference between voice and graphics. The latter is generally assigned the task of translating the former. Nonetheless, printed letters are traits endowed with spatial, figural and iconographic value independent of voice or of transcriptive functions. Printed writings represent ideas, but they also produce *other* meanings in their physical shape and in their movement on the page. When casually scanned, letters can leave impressions of motion. Forms appear, gain momentary retinal hold, and vanish. They come forth and recombine in ways suggesting to us that memory and sight work coextensively, and in modes sometimes unbeknown to consciousness. Letters convey meaning through the conventions associated with their contour in units of vocables, but their disposition also shows that relations between meaning and form have been, long before our "age of mechanical reproducibility," fortuitously conventional or even a product of our own desires. Despite what surrounding words may do to limit a context of meaning, letters can acquire horizons of their own and a syntax that is not explained by a context of grammar or logic.

The principle of analogy informs the letter with the axiom that resemblance of any given sign to another can generate numerous figures and dimensions of meaning. Because the process multiplies from the dialectic of form and substance, the increasing sum of meaning confirms the divine order of an expanding world. By way of analogy artists and writers reproduce the glory of universal creation, they reenact it, but when their creations take control of themselves, they even run the risk of rivalling with it.[5] Upon a cursory view, the texts that will be taken up in this study bear witness to a range of suggestion that is not immediately apparent to us. Many of the modes of analogy that generate them have receded from our view. Historians have shown that with the growth of the centralized state and eventual triumph of absolutism in seventeenth-century France the graphic dimension of writing lost visible and pictorial character. The formerly multiple possibilities of combinations of language at once resembling and reproducing the image and process of the world were stolen away when the presence of God became hidden.

When Montaigne remarks in "De la gloire"[6] that "le nom, ce n'est pas une partie de la chose ny de la substance, c'est une piece estrangere jointe à la chose, et hors d'elle" [The name is not a part of a thing, it is an extraneous piece joined to the thing and outside of it], he underscores a rift opened between names and things.

Because it is formulated as a declaration, the same statement suggests that names and things might possibly share certain homologies simply because the assertion is denying their existence. To deny is to affirm: thus the author of "De la gloire" can also remark in the next breath, in "Sur des vers de Virgile" (III, v), that, like Plutarch he sees "le langage latin par les choses" [Latin language through things]; in his own style, in his vernacular, "icy de mesme: le sens esclaire et produict les parolles; non plus de vent, ains de chair et d'os" [here the same: sense illuminates and produces words; not wind, but rather flesh and bone] (873). Montaigne demonstrates that he can transmute the most banal representation of a thing that has little to do with a name – a *chose* – into atoms of living matter (*chair, os*) when he uses graphic means to transform discourse into poetry. The letter assures a hidden analogy when common units are folded or mixed into each other.

The work that follows will seek to retrieve some elements of this manner of early modern literature. Readings will be aligned on the logic of resemblance and analogy that a good deal of recent criticism has studied.[7] But, I hope, with an orientation that studies the printed letter as a point of difference. If, as historians have noted, the language of the years 1530–1598 evolved in a direction that progressively lost its visibly significant texture,[8] the concealment of graphic presence might be a consequence of divisions – or studies and clefts – already written into post-incunabulum print culture. The visibility of the letter of Renaissance literature marks coextensive points of linkage and multiplication, but also of breakages of meaning. In this sense the letter can be understood as a graphic unit, locked into surrounding orders of syntax, that focuses attention at once on its visual and referential properties. The letter conveys ideas, but its shape, form and penchant for movement often play unexpected roles in the designs of meaning. Even when seen in context, the letter tells us that print is a form endowed with "tracks" that distinguish image from sound. Divided into autonomous functions but displaying an integral form, the letter is available to work within and outside of the syntactical orders it serves; it is subsumed by context but also gains independence from whatever control a context imposes, its form not always conforming to unilateral orders of meaning.

We can hypothesize that the letter of early modern French literature displays at least four properties that enhance its play of resemblance and analogy. First, as in most pragmatic areas of discourse, the letter figures as a *relay*. Part of a skein of inscriptions, it serves the cause of its writer or editor by appearing to convey ideals from a given origin, interlocutor, or group to others. An imaginary community of readers translates the material back into what had been emitted prior to the mediation of print. For the same literate public, the letter is seen as a mode of conveyance disappearing when the abstraction it carries acquires mental form among readers. Like the definition of prose that Sartre tenders in *Qu'est-ce que la littérature?*, discourse is assumed "transparent" whenever its intentions or uses are practical. Transparency of the medium assures passage and continuity of meaning.

In contrast to this function of relay, poetry tends to be literal and plastic. It draws the eye to the shape and play of its own form, short-circuiting communication wherever the reader's attention is directed to graphic configurations independent of meaning. In the early years of the Renaissance, when writers strove for a language that would resemble the world, their poetry followed Sartre's definition. It drew attention to itself, but in contrast to modern times, it also served as a relay. The letter offered a glimpse of a human microcosm reflecting the cosmic order of the world. Humanists never failed to underscore the efficiency of print in encouraging collective access to letters. The early Renaissance envisioned knowledge in passage free from the resistances they associated with inertia and the fatigue of manual transcription. A world of words like and unlike what Sartre ponders, the dream of an immediacy of mechanical communication, no doubt prompted an extraordinary resurgence of faith in the transparency of letters. Rabelais, we recall, satirizes Gargantua's scholastic instructors, unaware of print culture, who initiate the boy to rote memorization and the art of copying by hand. Why memorize when books can retrieve information in a flash or be glossed with other books on the same desk under one's eyes? Under enlightened instructions Gargantua accedes to a culture whose new sense of relay promises immediate access to the world's infinite meanings.

The unfettered relation with knowledge that the printed letter offers begat one myth inspired by typography at the dawn of Humanism in France. But if the technology of mechanical writing informed the art of reading, intellectuals of the Renaissance were cognizant of the modes of production that formatted the printed books they were reading.[9] Roman font of the 1530s constituted an unsolicited effect of difference. It recalled what it had just replaced, the fake effect of the manuscript in the *lettre bâtarde* or *lettre de forme*. While eliciting comparison with Gothic typography, the Roman letter was endowed with a sense of its transformative agency, thus begging its readers to take note of the figural history it was developing.[10] Surely the dialectic of Gargantua's "old" and "new" educations resembles the difference of "new" and "old" typographies insofar as print culture in the 1530s envisaged a coextension of the two at the same time. Humanists might employ a new mode of production, but it remained within the memory of others that preceded and ran concurrently with Roman font. Different cultural imaginations and codings of knowledge were working in the same space and time and yielded heterogeneous effects.

Our grasp of the mix of typographies might be compared to what today we are quickly imagining to be the paleolithic age of the typewriter. When our fingers glide over the keyboard of a word-processor, we shiver at the thought of how much labor we spent in typing manually with our fingers, handling carbon paper, erasers and, if we were fortunate, daubing ether-based correction fluid over our mistakes. Today we are experiencing a "screen-memory" by which the two technological "ages" of transcription − typewriting and word-processing − are momentarily superimposed upon one another. Our sense of pleasure in having emerged from that previous epoch derives from an illusion of time and energy saved.[11] A similar screening appears to hold in early print culture, when the letter was imagined as conveying in its form a history that bridged two or more cultures.

The dream of untold efficiencies of new letters is put in question when they are understood in a second way, in terms of *inscription*. Following this view, a typographic mark prompts memory of an initial percussion or of the impress of a divine or mechanical puncheon striking a page that receives it. The valleys and ridges of a printed page that the fingers touch thus reproduce as many remembered moments of inscription as there are characters alloted to its extension. This view is clearly an energetic one that does not depend on passage of information. It brings to light an erotic, generative and theological process that organizes and vivifies the world through mechanical reproduction.[12] The reader can envision a page of writing retracing memory of the congress of universal forces that emboss the page, give contour to extension, and that mime various biologies of generation. A reader's free attention isolates the letter to assign it a task that does not simply relay a meaning, but that inscribes *as* it means, in other words, that signals an action bearing force that exceeds the limits of what is being indicated through the letter as meaning. Inscription can thus remain foreign to or detached from what it produces.

Once separated from its practical role of sending information, the percussive agency of the letter can also acquire a didactic and sadistic cast. In the thirty years after the heyday of Humanism, during the Wars of Religion, inscription reflected practices associated with Kafkaesque techniques of torture: alphabetical marks were branded upon the body to imprint moral meaning encoded in their shape. The letter stamped its virtue on the flesh of the victim, striking home its meaning at the same time as percussion and violence drew out or neutralized the evil that was said to be within the victim's body. The tortured subject learned a spiritual value through the persisting figure branded on his or her body. In this dialectical system of exorcism, the physical impact of the letter was used for ideological purposes by any group that assigned a given meaning to a printed sign and used it emblematically in its system of propaganda.

Now thirdly, if the letter works as both inscription and relay, it allows a momentary fissure to be opened between form and meaning or cause and effect. The gap allows a reader to note the position of the letter in the rectangular frame that holds it. Adjoined to other letters in the groove of a line of type, the character mirrors in miniature the proportion of height and width of the printed page. Seen according to the art of composition in a printer's atelier, the font of each letter bears the square surround of a *picture*. From this standpoint, the letter signifies perspectively, in conjunction with an image or a figure. However "like" language they may be, the properties of visibility invested in letters cannot function in identity with the order of grammar. Letters may reproduce the figural sense of the sentence in which they are placed, but they also display their own autonomy. When endowed with figural shapes that enhance meaning, the form becomes linguistic material "joining" language to iconic representations of things. If it has no pictural traits, then, as Montaigne says in "De la gloire," the letter remains a "foreign object" having only a conventional relation to its referent.

Yet if the sound that the letter relays is associated with its pictural form, the combination produces a form resembling a hieroglyph,[13] a divinely endowed shape that is at once the cause and proof – as it were, the spitting image – of its own being in the cosmos. Its makes of print a language that shares much with the world of gods. At the same time, a Freudian dimension comes into play whenever inscription, picture, and relay are combined to produce a hieroglyph. Picture-writings or *Bilderschriften* are fashioned to beget an "unconscious" language that seals in movements of figure and meaning what grammar cannot readily express. Icons and discourse conflate in space; an order of revelation and enigma is restored in practices of writing that now display both "manifest" and "latent" dimensions.

To promote his *Champ fleury* (1529), following Martianus Capella and Isidore of Seville, Geoffroy Tory invented hieroglyphic conceits to make his new Roman characters proof of the universal design of sound and figure and of the perfect analogy of writing to the human body and the cosmos. The title is set in a decorative frame, and the subtitle is designed to summarize the reigning analogy of writing and visual form: "Auquel est contenu Lart & Science de la deue & vraye Proportion des Lettres Attiques, quon dit autrement Lettres Antiques, & vulgairement Lettres Romaines proportionnees selon le Corps & Visage humain" [In which is contained the Art and Science of the just and true Proportion of Attic Letters, otherwise called Antique Letters, & commonly Roman Letters proportioned according to the human Face and Body]. All letters possess allegorical virtue: projected into three-dimensional space, the I becomes Virgil's flute with as many stops as there are Muses and Liberal Arts. Turned on its side, the flute displays the O of its mouth, but also the rotund shape married to the linear bar of the I. It signals the myth of writing by analogy with Ovid's IO, the sacred cow whose divine memory and the orthogonal and curvilinear aspects of whose name, he argues, must be seen in the origin of every printed character. His capital A opens the way to the alphabet by a God-given stature that grants solidity to the two legs that arch up to its intellectual apex, a letter so virtuous that the crossbar delicately covers the pudenda of the outstretched athlete over whom it is cast. His conceits bear witness to what human alphabets – *Menschenalphabeten* – would shortly typify when bodies contorted themselves to resemble printed characters.[14] The Tory of 1529 was certainly not forgotten in 1583 when the ideals of his program were facetiously inverted in the chapter inaugurating Etienne Tabourot's *Bigarrures*, that glosses the same letter A as the point and the stylus that originate inscription, followed by Q whose coda offers a clue to what flows out of the lower orifice to which it is attached. In the passage of fifty-four years the world had been turned topsy-turvey. The letter that joined the mind, the body, and the world was now of a parodic order comparing ink to excrement. Yet even if meanings are inverted, the pictographic elements that Tory inaugurated held firm in the visual imagination throughout the passage of the century.

A student of Euclid, Tory drew his letters with a compass. He follows a compositional grid that equates the letter and the body according to a square surround. Each of his typographical units endows the letter with components of Italian perspective. The author implies that indeed a recessional order of space can be imagined within and about the letter, and that it moves between a denotative or transmissive form and a figural and spatial one. The letter legitimately becomes an area in which human maps are conceived in microcosm. Following the imagination of the *Champ fleury*, we can wager that most early modern literature merits reading with attention drawn to the synchronous perspectival revolutions taking place in the plastic arts. They may be invested concurrently into printed writing, allowing us to speculate that texts of the 1500s submit to visual torsions in painting and architecture that in France waver between medieval or Gothic models and those of the *quattrocento*. Northern or allegorical space mixes with the logical or Southern perspective within the confines of the letter and its virtue of analogy. In this respect Pierre Francastel has shown how the most apparently homogeneous works of the Northern and Italian Renaissances are signs of mixed creation and coextension of different cultural speeds and ideological impulsions.[15] The presence of two or more visual traditions in the letter seems to inhabit not only Tory, as both allegorist and geometer, but other French texts of the same period. Often hidden from us, the figural wealth born of the mix of systems might have been obvious to painters and designers under royal patronage who were transforming both decorative programs and the contours of printed matter.

In the Northern Renaissance and the later Middle Ages, Erwin Panofsky has noted, painting did not offer the illusion of a unified space as seen through a grid; its effects were conveyed through accumulation of details that reached an allegorical "saturation" which tends to lead the eye all over the canvas. Representation persisting from the time of the Van Eyck brothers and Roger Van Der Weyden constructed a densely fictive space through forms amassed that covered their surface with verbal and visual analogies. Details became totalities simultaneous with views offered by the greater picture. In the Italian Renaissance, the world was seen through a rectangular screen that multiplied the frame into formal subunits in accord with laws of perspective, determined by Alberti and others, that push the eye toward the illusion of a whole and integral volume.[16] The Northern tradition built itself from allegories that articulate space in a staged perception of the immediacy and infinite meaning of the world. A mystical dialogue was developed wherein painting and writing were imbued with an ocular experience concretized in shape, mass, color, and contour, while the Italian

Renaissance fabricated its sensations through a distance gained and held by perspective.[17]

In its beginnings the text of the French Renaissance appears motivated by similar problems. Like the Northern world or its own flamboyant Gothic style, it accumulated detail and "saturated" itself with allegory; its meaning developed anywhere and ramified everywhere, at once in its semantic fields, its visual configurations, and its cardinal or cartographic form.[18] The medieval vision of endless analogy that rewrote meaning from the congress of sight and sound was taken as proof of divine design; so elaborate is early modern literature that verbal and visual modes flow together and multiply through an ongoing process of division and unification. Like the detail of a Gothic edifice, a letter initiates a visual relation with the world but also leads a viewer's imagination into a labyrinth of sensuous forms.

With the imprint of Italian traditions in typography, a sense of distance is introduced into the world of analogy. Roman type offers new relations of center, vanishing point, and periphery in the world of printed characters. Bodies and letters are now proportioned according to the enclosing figure of the circle and square. A text is seen in terms of its aspect, and of the square units that fit letters according to the layout of moveable type. The early modern text offers at once a mystical relation of analogy in its own network of repeated inscriptions of framed space, and a critical and cognitive distance by virtue of its perspective. The Euclidean geometry that came to French workshops through Tory played with and against a process of analogy holding ground throughout the transition from manuscript to printed text.[19] Hence the advent of paradoxical literary works that encourage the reader to let attention meander freely so as, in his or her distraction, to encounter the infinity of their extension and to exceed the authors' own executions of their works. But no less present in them is a fixing, "fixating," or controlling perspectival design that converges on certain shapes or enigmas, like vanishing points, in the visual composition of language.

Here the subcategory of the pictural dimension of the letter extends in two directions. On the one hand, early modern writing appears to be constructed according to focalizing plans that lead discourse toward or about a letter or a mark conceived as a vanishing object or a crossing of verbal and visual design. A graphic trait will "spot" a juncture on which its picto-verbal allegory or its role as a hieroglyph will conjoin visible forms to invisible structures. As a perspectival figure, the letter reveals where mental schemes, discursive orders, and pictural compositions converge and evolve. On the other hand, the same site is, quite possibly, so favored in the classical rhetorical tradition that in an œuvre it reserves — like a crypt, a tomb, or a memory-place — a site for the inscription of a dedication, for a crucial concept or a hidden signature.

In both instances a psychoanalytical process informs the play of the letter. Since the entire century shows how personal names of subjects and of individuals came into being and how they gradually acquired both unique and collective histories, the place where the signature is identified — with a crypt or a contingent sign of origin or finality — allows the letter to be aligned with the notion of the "perspectival object." The writer projects his or her creation into posterity, but the operation works only through the inscription of the author's name or apothegm into the mathematical or spatial microcosm of the book or poem.[20] We shall see that Clément Marot puts himself at an axis that a letter or a rebus marks at the center of his *rondeaux*. By contrast, Rabelais invents a gargantuan hieroglyph that scripts his name by anagram and chimerical forms or grotesque figures of silence carved about *Gargantua*. Ronsard plays on visual centers in sonnets that he fills with graphic riddles. These strange shapes betray the graphic nature of his lyrics, his politics, and, above all, a will to build a verbal monument that will immortalize its author. Montaigne will craft an autobiography shaped according to double and triple ellipses in which letters figure as the links in an almost endless concatenation of inscriptions and emblems.

If perspectival, calligraphic, or hieroglyphic properties of the visible letter were used to structure literature of the time, its decipherment also offered poets and artists other avenues for transcoding meanings. A piece of type could become a landscape, a chimera, it could turn into what it was not — into a monogram, a cipher, a number, a vocable from a foreign tongue — all the while remaining a letter. Variously occult powers associated the letter with codes known outside of Roman or Gothic characters. These might be analogical dimensions of numbers, Roman numerals, or the figural shape of punctuation marks or chemical signs. Devices and characters from other alphabets also found their way into writing. Their presence may underscore the function of relay but also reroute or disrupt the passage of meaning. Wherever different modes of transcription combine, verbal noise or an artful interference is produced.

Thus, because many of the arcane dimensions of the letter project a relation with unknown forms, a fourth aspect of the letter seems to be the consequence of the first three. The sense of an *opaque object*, or a presence that is neither inscription, relay, nor picture, can be invested in the printed character. Endowed with an absence of meaning, the letter can resemble a code without a message or a shape that designates nothing of familiar aspect. In an era when the ostentation of knowledge was held as a virtue – we witness almost endless compilation in Belleforest, Thevet, Ravisius Textor – figures of the unknown stimulated renewed effort of decipherment and textual production that seems to follow a geometrical progression.[21] As a signless mark, a paraph detached from a signature, an enigma, or unknown quantity, the letter can spur investigation or elicit meaning from the very act of decipherment. The enigmatic shape of the letter has heuristic value, encouraging interpretation that cannot be completed. It may not have meaning in itself, but its configuration in the "tracks" that are coordinating its placement make the reader produce meaning where, in reality, there is none. In the same fashion, printed matter that does not relay codes of gender or number can impugn the erotic and generative powers of inscription. The neutral quality of the typographic impression can indicate an absence of code or a sign that is not of this world. The unknown qualities of the letter gain analogy with the fanciful image of flora and fauna that comes from the travel to the West, in pictures of the kind that punctuate travel books, guides, and compendia of marvels and monstrosities.

If the four traits of the letter adumbrated above – relay, inscription, picture, and enigma – serve to theorize some aspects of analogy in sixteenth-century literature, we should not forget that movement from one to another brings forth other questions concerning perception, framing, and relations of figure and ground. When it jumps from one function to another, the letter traces movement that runs along at least three axes. One is horizontal, where characters and spacings constitute *montages* of serial units that when scanned appear and disappear. For Montaigne, "l'alleure poetique, à sauts et à gambades" (III, ix, 994) [the poetic allure, that jumps and saunters] makes figures appear in letters just as they are evanescing. His poetics transcodes shapes and sounds across different combinations of vocables and printed units. His poetics sum up a process by which words mercurially slip out of each other, compress, or elide and divide.[22] A sublime, vagabond style is born of continuous metamorphosis of space and letter along the line of their printed articulation.

The same montage of shapes can occur along a vertical axis, when the page yields to acrostic and emblematic practices. Here the letter effects various *fadings* of meaning when a title in superscript disappears, lingers retinally or in memory, and recurs – like something once repressed – from the design of pagination. The linear operation of delay and of displacement turns into a vertical play of emblematic form.[23] Inscriptions can disappear and recur, they can dissolve and become reincarnate before vanishing again. For Ronsard of the *Amours*, the sonnets are placed under an enigmatic subtitle *Vœu*, which spells a dedication, but also places the capital V at a point that opens on to visibility and ocularity that will be avowed in figures of the eye in the poems that follow. The letters of his beloved's name, Cassandre, hover over the sonnets, then recur, recombine or redound to evoke a *cassure*, a breakage of enclosure and rapture, of fright and bliss, that comes with the return of the memory of her name in writing. She is enclosed and eternized in the volume, but the nagging presence of the seven digits of her name breaks and burns the poet, leaving his body in ashes (with the turning of *casse ... cendre*) in the urn of his book. The text flickers whenever titles are glossed before burning or atomizing into fragments of emblems allusively placed in and over the collection. A name and its components exchange discursive and figural roles. A movement ensues in which emblematics are subsumed in the flow of discourse.[24]

A third vector of movement, one that is more difficult to locate and more subjective in essence, follows from the eyes to the page and through the printed characters. We have already noted that as readers we often see meaning where there is none. We will be tracked – or tricked – into believing that a given word is attached to a definite signification. Throughout the Renaissance, the experience of reading and the space of memory shared between reader and writer are called into question. Two worlds slip over each other, then separate on a typographical interface. A letter may allude to an object distant in time, but it comes into an area between the reader and the text supplanting memory or the duration of retrieval needed for production of meaning. It asks the reader to compare his or her relation with that letter to those being articulated in print. Whenever two or more words are born from one, a relation of depth and ground is granted. A word is recollected that misrepresents what is there; distortion results, so that the characters of a name or a word are taken as simple marks, then shuffled so that one vocable emerges where another recedes and remains visible. A process of graphic screening is born, revealing and disguising figures in each another, that jump forth by means of multiple unveilings and repressions of forms. These constitute instantaneous *screen-memories* that function according to the suggestive analogies of the letter.

A screen-memory "surfaces long enough to draw attention to itself and to allude to a psychic change around it, but veils that element just enough to defy complete understanding."[25] Metamorphoses operate so quickly along all three axes that notions of sequence, progress, development, or procedure are severely tested. Textual time becomes that of an absolute present laminating past and future on to the surface of writing. We feel this present moment, Michel Jeanneret notes, when the tedium of exegesis or task of copying explodes into illumination.[26] Because movement in three dimensions turns the text into surfaces of forms in play, and because the allure of a self-generating process is glimpsed in passage, a general disruption accompanies articulation of meaning. Time becomes movement in space, where the graphic qualities of print arrest movement as they convey it.

Since its various traits convey sense and confusion at once, the letter cannot fail to be aligned with some of our own notions of the unconscious. In a roughly Freudian sense, known since the middle of the nineteenth century, it is defined as unbound force, as whatever resists control in the discourse of a speaking or writing subject. Like the Dora of the case history devoted to that name, it amounts to what the analyst cannot grasp, when he discovers that in the same utterance the patient says "yes" and "no" in the same breath. The unconscious *would prefer not to* do what it is told, and rejects all designs of control or interpretation placed upon it. Freud repeatedly states that the unconscious can be likened to time because it knows no time: no sense of historical continuity, of development, of age or season can be imposed upon it by a scholar, a critic, an analyst, or "the subject who is supposed to know."[27] For the amateur of the sixteenth century, the unconscious is glimpsed where writing couches often contradictory meanings in expressions that do not follow verbal orders that we practice today. Those who develop an unconscious writing – like the canon of Renaissance literature, but also what Freud seeks to retrieve in his essays blending art and science – create texts that do not transcribe speech in print, but use the virtues of the letter to multiply, betray, and redirect avenues of meaning. Writing of the sixteenth century appears to display an acute awareness of these dimensions of the letter, and to place the unconscious not in the depths of the psyche, but on the surface of things.

Three stages appear to mark the figural sensibility of French writing in the Renaissance. In the chapters that follow I shall first argue that in the 1530s an acute typographical sensibility inheres in Clément Marot's "adolescent" poetry, and that it raises questions of Evangelism. Topical religious matters, it appears, were also bound to the design of print culture. An autobiographical subject is born where the self is scripted into the changing characters of his verse. Marot's diligent readers are asked to discover the secrets of his talents in both poetic and theological aspects. Rabelais shares Marot's sense of silence in writing but constructs an unfinished work that deploys the analogical properties of the letter to multiply and engender new meaning. The style of *Gargantua* engages a politics of written discourse that marks the same period but that cannot be detached from the massive force and range of style. In a second stage, dating from mid-century, Ronsard elaborates a programmatic literature using print to articulate poem-pictures that set the author or his signature at vanishing points, assuring him of glory and eternity. The typographic aspect of the poem constitutes the space of a verbal world that the poet arrogates for himself. In a third and final moment synchronous with the Wars of Religion, we discover that Montaigne's self-portrait in the *Essais* figures in part as a creation of printed shapes, and that with an arcane sense of the letter his book is turned into a carefully crafted political object at play with forces in a time conceived to be eternal. In the three periods that are taken up – the Humanism of the 1530s, the Valois court, and memorial writing at the time of the civil war – our intention is not to distinguish one style from another but to retrieve a common and obsessively productive sense of poetics and printed writing.

1

A SECRET SPACE:
MAROT'S *RONDEAUX*

If any piece of literature can be called a transitional object, it is
Clément Marot's *Adolescence clémentine*. Published in 1532 in
Paris, the work soon became associated with Geoffroy Tory's
"new" typography. In assembling circumstantial verse that documents the formative years and apprenticeship of the poet, the work
marks a poetic and spiritual itinerary and a passage from youth
to the threshold of adulthood. Ten editions were printed up to 1537.
In 1538 Marot produced an augmented and definitive version.[1]
L'adolescence clémentine heralds an uncommonly graphic poetry
at the same time as it bequeathes a rich anthology of poetic forms –
epistles, complaints, epitaphs, ballads, *rondeaux*, and songs – that
are at once medieval and renascent, of Northern and Southern
traditions, whose sum shapes a composite, even latent autobiography
of an individual born into the Renaissance. With Marot a signature
and a proper name emerge from a collective and variegated past.
Marot owes much to his father Jean Marot, a great *Rhétoriqueur* of
the second generation, and to Jean Lemaire de Belges, of the same
school and the premier poet and historiographer of the French
court up to 1513. His renown is present in Thomas Sébillet's *L'art
poétique françoys: pour l'instruction des jeunes studieux, encore peu
avancés en la poésie française* (1548) that is based in part on the
Adolescence. A story of a poet born from other poets, Marot's
poetry also develops complex relations of graphics, of voice, space,
of discourse, and of poetic transmission.

This chapter will take up some of these elements in the *rondeaux*.
Seventy-seven poems make up the collection that is set approximately
in the middle of the volume and seems to tell of an inner itinerary.
Mirroring the plan of the book as a whole, dialogue is developed
through many voices (of men, women, male and female lovers,
ill-married wives, jealous husbands, the poet's friends, Marot's
autobiographical persona), while the apparently closed symmetry
of the medieval genre frames and controls the diction. The *rondeaux*

hark back to a form well known in manuscript culture. Marot had recently unearthed Villon, and his 1533 edition of the *Testament*, a work containing several *rondeaux*, was the first of its kind printed in Roman type. Marot admitted that Villon's language was difficult to decipher but said it was worth the effort for the revival of a unique voice and poetic tenor. Villon's *rondeaux* have an affinity with those of his contemporary Charles d'Orléans and other poets of the middle years of the fifteenth century. They also look forward to Jean Molinet, who would develop the genre quite graphically in the 1470s. Marot's sources are especially from his father Jean Marot's work of the early 1500s. The poems come at the end of one tradition and at the beginning of another.

From the fifteenth century onward the genre calls for a delicate play of abstract and technical closure with openings, recurring points, shifts of inflection, proportion, and variation. The initial words of the verse, usually the first four syllables of a decasyllabic line, return at the end of a central tercet framed by one quintain above and another below. Counting fifteen lines, the poem is grouped into the initial quintain, a median tercet, and a final quintain. A problem is announced in the incipit and recurs with its meaning modified at the end of the tercet and at the conclusion. The second quintain reproduces the shape of the first, but its fifteenth line ends, with the first four syllables of the first line and the last four of the tercet (of the ninth line). A delicate closure and freedom of symmetry results, in which a circular form is approximated by openings and returns, by the tercet "enclosed" by the two quintains, and by the fifteen units that suggest a division of the poem into two units on either side of the axis drawn by the eighth line. The initial formula in turn varies in inflection at least twice as the reading moves forward and turns back upon itself.

Marot provides a clue to the subtlety of the play of opening and closure in a figure common to the first and last *rondeaux* of the collection. The first is positioned as a response to a hypothetical poem above or before the title: "Rondeau responsif à un autre, qui se commençait: Maître Clément, mon bon amy" (I, 135) [Rondeau responding to another, that began: Master Clement, my good friend]. The poem recapitulates the rules of its poetics in its thirteenth line: "Clouez tout court, rentrez de bonne sorte" [Nail it right down, return as you should]. When the poem closes or turns on the nail of its pivot (*clouez*), the verb suggests that the poem describes a circle between a vocal axis and a written circumference. A play of disorder works within and at the edges of the geometry. "Tout court" follows *clouez*, that is, what closes immediately and crisply (*court*, as an adverb) and what can run or happen unconsciously (*court* as the verb having as subject *tout*, as in the expression *tout court*). When the poem retrieves its initial syllables in order to come to closure, it goes out again: "de bonne sorte" [in a good way] suggests that something good might exit (with a visual pun on *sortir*, seen in the present subjunctive, implying "rentrez, afin qu'on sorte de bonne façon," or "return so that you can go out properly once again."

In the field of equivocation, *clouer* acquires extended visibility by dint of the pattern of its recurrence, like a refrain, within and at the end of the seventy-seven poems. *Clouer* is printed twice in the last, or "perfect," *rondeau* that moves far from the didactic tenor of the opening poem of the itinerary. In his adieu Marot thanks his friends for having freed him from incarceration in 1526. Describing his plight he utters, "Mais en prison pourtant je fus cloué" (LXXXVII, lines 17–18, 216) [But nonetheless I was nailed down in prison], and soon remarks, qualifying the utterance, "J'eus à Paris prison fort inhumaine, / A Chartres fus doucement encloué" (lines 19–20, 216) [I had a very inhuman prison in Paris / In Chartres I was softly enclosed]. Along with the montage of alliteration (P**a**ris pr**i**son), the recurrence of the verb within the poem and across the span of the ensemble suggests a major change of inflection. At least three tones – historical, poetic, and structural – are struck. The first evinces a shift between pure poetry and the poet's entry into history. The inaugural *rondeau* responds to a Platonic, absent Ideal below the Roman numeral **I**. The last (77th) answers the first and is elaborated into a "perfect," doubled form that tells of the author's liberation from travail in the recent dispute over religious reform. From enclosure to release we follow a trajectory moving slowly from poetic to subjective dimensions. Formal or didactic closure turns into historical imprisonment whence the poet is liberated, but only as if he were emerging from the constraints of repression identical to the task of writing seventy-seven poems of a genre reputedly difficult to master. Here a mystical dimension is invested into the poetics of the *rondeau*, since the body of the writer is deemed at once present (*cloué*) and absent (*en liberté*, as the refrain notes three times) in the trace of circular writing. Structurally, then, the "freedom" Marot gains by escaping from the ideological center of the nation, Paris, will come only with the reiterated closure that the return of the verb confirms, buckling the collection across the distance between the first and last *rondeaux*.

Plate 1. Self-portrait in historiated letter ''O'' by Oronce Finé (1494–1555), mathematician, cartographer, and engraver, used in his *Protomathesis* (Paris: Simon de Colines, 1532). The initials of Finé's signature (O and F) on either side of his portrait draw attention to a play of interior duplication. The composition of Marot's *rondeaux* uses a similar analogy of letter and figure.

Concurrently, the modification of meaning seen in *clouer* loosens the fixity of the narrative and the poetic scheme. Already in the first *rondeau* the transitive verb can mean ''to close'' and ''to nail,'' thus conflating geometrical and theological connotations. *Clouer* cannot fail to refer to the nails of the Crucifixion, and it can be generalized to evoke confinement. A palette of meanings fans out when the word appears to recur according to a careful logistics of inscription and reiteration. *Clouer* is literally ''nailed'' into the verbal design so as to open and close a story of adolescence in the confines ... of the *Adolescence*.

Further, the verb oscillates between a perspectival role, as we have seen in the way it allows the text to be scanned, and a signatory function. *Clouer* spots the point where the typographic letter becomes a vanishing point or a microcosmic sign focalizing the form and overall itinerary of the *Adolescence*. A reader cannot fail to see the name of a celebrated painter of the poet's time, Clouet (who in fact executed a portrait of Marot), in the verb. The echo of the artist's name underscores the verbal and plastic representation in the verse. The verb becomes a mark or an indeterminate sign in a pattern that begins to emerge from the collection. In the eighteenth poem, Marot emits a volley of associations moving from letters to words to proper names.[2] Marot responds to a fairly pedestrian *rondeau* written as an epistle, addressed to Marot, from a certain "Etienne Clavier," that is, "Stephen Keyboard" or "Stephen Keyring."[3] *Clavier* is linked to cleavage, division, and to spatial closure since its relative, *claveure*, is a keyhole or a tiny aperture through which one looks. "Clavier" cannot fail to infer typesetting machines or the metal puncheons of a printing studio. Given the range of inference, in his response to Etienne Clavier, Marot types out his signature in association with the past participle of *clouer*. Apart from the first and last *rondeaux* of the collection, here is the only other inscription of *clouer*, set adjacent to the poet's proper name:

XVIII
RESPONSE DUDICT MAROT AU DIT CLAVIER

> Pour bien louer, et pour être loué,
> De tous esprits tu dois être alloué,
> Fors que du mien, car tu me plus que loues:
> Mais en louant plus hauts termes alloues,
> Que la Saint-Jean, ou Pâques, ou Noué.
>
> Qui noue mieux, réponds, ou C, ou E?
> J'ai jusque ici en eau basse noué:
> Mais dedans l'eau caballine tu noues,
>   Pour bien louer.
>
> C, c'est Clément contre chagrin cloué.
> E, est Etienne, éveillé, enjoué;
> C'est toi, qui maints de los très ample doues:
> Mais endroit moi tu fais cygnes les oues,   .
> Quoique de loz doives être doué
>   Pour bien louer.

RESPONSE OF THE SAID MAROT TO THE SAID CLAVIER

> To praise well, and then to be praised
> Of all minds you must be approved
> Except for mine, that you have overly raised
> By praising, avow, higher terms than allowed,
> With Saint John, or Easter, or Noël.

21

Who knows better, answer, C or E?
Until now I've swum in shallow water
But in Pegasian current you've been stroking
　　To praise well.

C, see Clement countering cloven chagrin,
E, esteem Etienne ever-even, evocative,
See yourself, to whom praise is amply due,
In honesty I say you make swans out of geese,
Though with glory you should be endowed,
　　To praise well.

The rhyme that depends on the capital letter and the vocable of the tenth and eleventh lines is lettered, or *lettrisé*. **C** leads to its voiced equivalent, *c'est*, that is the key, or *clé*, the clue to the enigma about *Clavier*. The two names not only betray each other, as the respondent lies to his interlocutor – *Clé ment contre Clavier* – but fit in the allegory of praise like a lock and key. The *lettrisé* verse produces a montage of rebus-forms that move horizontally (C...C...C/c...c...c) and vertically, in acrostic, where **CE** equals a "c'est" that identifies the initials *CM*, sewn and sown (as in *sème*) at the head of **C**lément **M**arot. The dialogic qualities of the verse are so graphic that voice seems to be congealed in a play of crisscrossed vectors:

　　　　　　C'*est* **C**lément

　　　　　　E

　　　　　　C'*est* toï

　　　　　　M

The "you" and the "I" of the poem conflate in the paragrammar of a visual syntax in which a montage of spacing or serial play destabilizes the semantic elements of the encomium graciously outdone by encomium:

　　　　　　Mais endroit moi tu

reads as if the "moi" and the "tu" are in the same place where Clavier is praised, such that he can make swans – but also signs (*cygnes/ signes*) – out of geese. The text also notes that the handsome bird is figured at this point for a second time in the poem, since the sixth line, "Qui noue mieux, réponds, ou C, ou E?" reads in three ways. First, the two letters encode the two Christian names; secondly, the scansion reveals *coue* (rhyming with *noues*, line 8) that marks the *cou* or serpentine neck of the swan; lastly, in the serial placement of the vowels and consonants in

22

ou C, *ou* E.

The poem opens its play of letters on to a general field of combination of graphs that are at once syllables and ideograms (such as CM = *sème;* C = *c'est, ces,* or *ses;* M = *aime;* R = *erre, air, aire,* etc.). If the logic of the *Champ fleury* is followed, the poem can be read as staging the congress and separation of straight and curved forms. The relation of the two shapes reflects that of the poet and his correspondent, Etienne Clavier, just as it will underscore the difference of gender in other poems that treat of love. One of the voices is rectilinear, an "I," while the other is rounded, in the form of an "O." One of the voices tends to be a visible mark, a consonant, while the other is a sign of *voice,* a vowel. The implicit difference of the I and O, the two "originary" letters of Tory's alphabet, forms a graphic component of the dialogic field of the verse.[4]

The text shows that other dialogic features of the *rondeaux* owe their vocal and chromatic wealth to the ways the printed letter destabilizes the fixed tenor of statements or even of words. We have seen that *clouer* establishes a careful relation of signature, space, enclosure, and recurrence. In fact, even the proper names of the *rondeaux* are both historical beings (Etienne Clavier was indeed, historians note, Marguerite de Navarre's secretary and one of Marot's friends who helped free the poet from confinement) and combinations of vocables and letters in a poetic hieroglyph.

Other letters function in cross-textual montages in which poems dissolve into each other. The poet ciphers certain words because their letters unsettle meaning. Typographic shapes split into autonomous "tracks" of voice and image. The consequence appears to be that the notion of dialogism, at least as we know its definition and its pervasiveness in Marot,[5] depends on the paradoxical *silence* of speech that comes with the sight of voice in graphic characters. The concept seems to be grounded in this moment of early print culture, when experiment with multiplicities of "points of speech" (in contrast to what we know as "points of view") coincides with experiment with different alphabets and visual signs. And the lettrism at least in its crucial presence in the first, the eighteenth, and the final *rondeaux,* where Marot displays his initials as an emblem of capital letters, promotes an equivocal movement of meaning. A supple and generative, indeed polyvocal, sensibility comes with verbal silence. Fixed oppositions that are needed for meaning begin to blur, just as words and letters fade into and emerge from each other.

The point can be shown when we follow one word through several poems. The tenth rondeau is typical:

X

DE L'ABSENT DE S'AMYE

Tout au rebours (dont convient que languisse)
Vient mon vouloir. Car de bon cueur vous veisse,
Et je ne puis par devers vous aller.
Chante qui veult, balle qui veult baller
Ce seul plaisir seulement je voulsisse.
　　Et s'on me dit qu'il faut que je choisisse
De par deça Dame qui m'esjouisse
Je ne sçaurois me tenir de parler
　　　　Tout au rebours.
　　Si respons franc: 'J'ay Dame sans nul vice;
Autre n'aura en Amour mon service.
Je la désire, & soubhaite voller
Pour l'aller veoir et pour nous consoller.'
Mais mes souhaits vont comme l'Escrevice,
　　　　Tout au rebours.[6]

[Completely backwards (whence I must languish)
Comes my will, for if I saw you in anguish,
Toward you I would hardly dare to advance.
Sing who may sing, dance who may dance,
This single pleasure would ever I wish.
And if they ever say I must make a choice
From herefore to have a lady make me rejoice,
I could barely keep myself from speaking
　　　　Completely backwards.
Should I avow frankly: I've a lady of my wish
And another for whom I will ever famish,
– I want her, and dream of flying.
To go and see her and to be consoling –
But my dreams go like a crayfish
　　　　Completely backwards.]

The *rondeau* turns about its own course but reverses itself, at the sign of Cancer (the crab) at the Solstice of June or the middle of the year in the poem's zodiac. It twists the elegant subjunctive mood of the verb *escrire* into the figure of the crustacean. When Marot compares himself to a creature of a submarine order, he heightens his own powers of metamorphosis through analogy that can change a word into a picture or a rebus. The poet's desire is divided between a will to love an infinite number of beings and to bond his faith with one person. The dilemma translates the amphibious qualities of the poetry into a wavering of thought, or a meditation following the path a lobster traces in the sand.

The *escrevice* contains a sign of *vice* in a crevice of writing; the four letters turn back to the *languisse* at the head of the poem, a verb that anticipates the coming of the crayfish by figuring in the pattern of both sound and image the order of crustaceans and fish.[7] "Languisse," a word that recurs with less precision than *clouer*, is commonplace in the idiolect of precious and lyrical poetry. It can be suggested to synthesize sound and sight in the homonym of *langouisse*, that conflates *langue, languir*, and *langouste* (tongue, languish, and lobster). The sideways or backward motion of the discourse runs, as the shape of the noun suggests, contrary to the direction of speech. Writing turns back where speech would move ahead. Inscription of the lobster in *languisse* projects speech toward silence at the very point that speech is uttered *(langue isse)*.[8] The retinal character of words seen in words cancels the effect of the disappearance of discourse which an auditor would expect in hearing or reading the poem aloud.

The elegant visual thrust of the conditional subjunctive draws our eyes to an otherwise commonplace verb in the idiolect of love poetry. *Languir* has the same intensity of inner speech – a speech of silence made manifest by the graphic delicacy of the syntax seen all over the surface of the collection. "En languissant et en grieve tristesse / Vit mon lasse coeur, jadis plein de liesse" (VIII, lines 1–2, 179) [In languishing and in grieved sadness / Lives my tired heart, once full of mirth], utters the young woman married to an old husband, such that *languissant* anticipates *tristesse*, growing out of *lasse* in the verbal shape of the doubled letters. "Voilà comment je languis en malaise, / Sans nulle espoir de liesse plus forte" (XXVII, 4–5) [There is how I languish in pain, / Without hope of stronger joy], sighs the husband with amorous and religious woes, as if some inner ploy of sound and shape brought forth the memory of the *mal mariée* of the lover of *rondeau* X languishing over the thought of having one and many loves. The person without hope signals that he or she lives in the same dilemmas as the figure in "contradictions," for whom "En espérant, espoir me désespère" (XXVIII, line 1, 191). And because the collection draws constant attention to its material form wherever *rondeaux* are mentioned in the *rondeaux*, or where they are set in a network of epistolary exchange, the recurring term both closes off the poems and has them flow over each other. This happens in "Celui qui nouvellement a reçu lettres de s'amie" (XLII, lines 1–4, 200);

> A mon désir, d'un fort singulier être
> Nouveaux écrits on m'a fait apparaître,
> Qui m'ont ravi, tant qu'il faut que par eux
> Aie liesse ou ennui langoureux.
>
> [To my desire, from a very singular being
> New writings have, as I am seeing
> Them, ravished me, so that their order
> brings me joy or tiresome languor.]

Liesse and *languir* form a link in a chain with *languisse*, just as, in the following *rondeau* that sketches an emblem-allegory of the colors gray, brown, and black, *langueur* jumps from an optical center of the poem (XLIII, lines 6–9, 201):

> Car le noir dit la fermeté des cœurs;
> Gris le travail; et tanné, les langueurs;
> Par ainsi c'est, Langueur en Travail ferme,
> Gris, tanné, noir.
>
> [For black means the heart's ardor;
> Gray, the labor; brown, the languor;
> Thus, in Labor Languor locks away
> Gray, brown, black.]

Here *langueur* is colored tan, but wherever it had changed hues in *rondeau* X, here it is marked by the letter. *Langueur* synthesizes the ocular experience of the poem opening and closing its chromatic field. Three colors converge upon the word and emanate from it, its keystone place in the poem setting it adjacent to *tanné*, a term that cannot fail to evoke the *tan-* of the *tenson* or *tanson* of language in dialogue. Objectal properties of the color and surface of the word are quickly remembered three *rondeaux* later, when the lover risking his life to enter into the chamber of his lady fears only "D'être aperçu des *languards* dangereux" (XLVI, line 5, 203) [Being spotted by dangerous tattlers]. These ill-speaking figures survey the imaginary scene (-*guard* recalling *garder*, to see) and engender in the combination of letters the fear that makes the narrative so precarious.

Such are some of the concatenations of the letter in dialogue. Often Marot's discourse traces a circle that its path describes, marking a tension of center and circumference not unlike what we see in the path of the *escrevice*. The crustacean signals how the *Festina lente* common to pictural and emblematic arts tends

26

to expand the *rondeau*. In the twenty-eighth poem (191–92) we discover snakes within writing:

PAR CONTRADICTIONS

En esperant, espoir me desespere
Tant que la mort m'est vie tres prospere;
Me tourmentant de ce qui me contente,
Me contentant de ce qui me tourmente
Pour la douleur du soulas que j'espere.

Amour hayneuse en aigreur me tempere;
Puis temperance aspre comme Vipere
Me refroidist soubz chaleur vehemente
En esperant.

L'enfant aussi, qui surmonte le pere,
Bende ses yeulx pour veoir mon impropere;
De moy s'enfuyt & jamais ne s'absente,
Mais, sans bouger, va en obscure sente
Cacher mon dueil affin que mieulx appere
En esperant.

[In hoping, hope brings me despair
So much that death seems life that will prosper;
Tormenting me with what brings contentment
Contenting me with what brings torment
For the pain of the bliss that I hope for.
Heinous love into venom tempers me,
Then temperance bitter as a viper
Chills me under vehement heat
In hoping.
The child, too, who surmounts the father
Blinds his eyes in order to see how improper
Are my ways, flees me but never takes leave,
Yet, immobile, goes into a darkened lair
To hide my grief so that better I may appear
In hoping.]

Robert Griffin rightly calls the poem an example of a "conventional" use of chiasm: narration is not adequate to its contents; the "reader is immediately involved in building up a language that lacks a corresponding development of thought," where "the imposition of rigid form rules out the subtle and psychologically credible imbalance of feeling and expression."[9] Is the apparent stiffness owed to a borrowing from a sonnet of Chariteo, who had already adapted sources in Petrarch and Catullus for his own ends? Even if the model includes origins in Tebaldeo and Serafino,[10] redundant use of antitheses from the first line to the last exhibits the taste

27

for precious concetti and may indicate one of the sources for Ronsard's sonnet of the *Amours* (12), "J'espere et crains." Critics insist on its "renascent" qualities, its almost human or psychological manner of describing love – subjective evidence which affirms how the attraction for Italian and classical objects dominated the arts in the court of Francis I shortly after his accession in 1516.[11]

Far more crucial than an *idea* of the poem's capacity to describe love à la Petrarch are the letters *drawn* by the chiasms. They test the polarities of the opposition and, hence, tend to make a montage of ambivalence replace the fixed quality of binary comparisons. Sacred and profane love converge and criss-cross. The *rondeau*, as both Pierre Fabri and Thomas Sebillet had theorized in their manuals of rhetoric in 1521 and 1546, was to be executed *discursively*, that is, "roundly."[12] The linear strategy of the cross-over within each line and stanza disavows the refrain that anticipates the speaker's hope of finding love over and again, *en esperant*. As if it were a circle twice bisected by two perpendicular lines, the *rondeau* aims at and turns about the axial *aspre* in the center of its circle. Each stanza of five lines frames a central unit which itself is confined by two lines, one above and the other below. The center of the poem,

Puis temperance, **aspre** comme vipere,

puts *temperance* in view. The term refers to the condensation of opposites,[13] and is apposed to the point that defines the center and circumference. Spatial play now invokes the heraldry of the *Festina lente*. To "make haste slowly" is the idiom of devices that curl dolphins around anchors, twist vipers about Latin crosses, or bend King Francis' Royal Salamanders into a regal form of the S. Latent iconography underscores how the word also identifies a vanishing point in the text. Since the two ends of every line are also in a mobile rapport with their axis, the reader's eyes are free to juggle and turn the form in ways similar to the common practice of the anagram. An anamorphic dimension, that twists meaning into visual figures or letter-emblems, is also at work, summing up and concretizing the entire poem at the axis.

A double chiasmus emerges between lines three and four:

Me *tour* mentant de ce qui me *con* tente
x x
Me *con* tentant de ce qui me *tour* mente.

A twisted contour of linearity that begins and ends at the center, in *ce qui*, grounds the *Festina lente*, the cross, a *chi* or *x*, framed

above and below and to left and right by the two chiastic figures.
Inversion obtained from the visual relation of *tour* and *con* at
either end of the lines arches the eye toward the verbal *x* at the
axis, next to the *qui* which translates *x* into a rebus. Here the
uncanny *de ce*, which offers a glimpse of the view of death —
décè(s), or *d–c*, or *d c'est* — that pervades the thematic layer of
the poem. A more obvious cross is located in the center in *aspre*,
three lines below. The nameless *x* in the *rondeau* becomes the
enigma (or secret) of an impossible metaphysical question that
asks who or what makes the poet and poem live in contradiction.
Alterity is introduced into the poem. But the consequent release
of *con-mentant con-mente* disengages the sight of a series of *tour-
tente-tour-tentant*, or a condition of temptation in a pattern of
inversion and spherical tension. The chiasm signalled by the four
instance of *me*,

Me tour	Me con
x	*x*
Me con	Me tour

establishes a double movement, up and down and left and right,
that draws our eyes to the poem's *contour*. Visibility of the contradictions is caused less by a psychological dilemma than by a graphic
view of the limits of the Christian world. The "circle whose center
is nowhere and whose circumference is everywhere" is felt to be
the perspectival object of the *rondeau*.

Marot was always, literary histories note, proverbially broke.
His poems beg their patron to spare him a dime. Given the global
extension found in the composition of the *rondeau* that "Par
contradictions" summarizes, monetary poverty in the narrative
of the *Adolescence* gains religious wealth in the graphics of its
allegory. The discourse acts out a Pauline morality in which reform
is visibly present in the balance between the poem's shape and
diction. Guilt is scripted into the text through the ambiguous position
that the Father occupies in the twelfth line. In its extension, based
on *-père*, the notion of *espoir* and *espérance* insists on the presence
of the father to guide the adolescent voice through the crisis expressed
in the opening stanza. Hence, with *en espérant, espoir me désespère*,
the poet might be interpreted as crawling toward an area of doubled
negation where, in going "in-and-out-of-the-father" (*es-pèrant*), the
goodness signified by hope makes the rhymster trope the opposite of
dés-es-pérant. He thus denies losing the path that a Biblical tradition
had advised him to take when he follows the tracks of his biological

29

and vocational father, Jean Marot. The roads to poetry and salvation are combined. Already in the second line the bite of death, *la mort*, pushes the poet toward a life leading to a father, in the graphics of *pro(s)>pere*. If *père* comes out of *espère*, we should also recall that *espoir* is associated with the circularity of the world.[14] The psychic inflections of contradiction are found in a precarious coincidence of verbal and physical forms that makes a central point of origin in the *rondeau* impossible to discern. In this sense the hope of going away from the father amounts to returning to him. The œdipal vectors orient the *rondeau* toward a tempering of sacred and profane love.

The same point is underscored in the echo of *-ente* in the fourth, fifth, eighth, eleventh, and twelfth lines. Where *père* dominates the poem, *-ente* opens an area of phonic obscurity. Referring back to the division of *contente* and *tourmente* in lines 3–4, their common term, *-ente*, connotes an area of things unknown. The chiasm disengages *-ente* but reinvests it into *obscure sente* (line 12). The four letters especially refer to a trail leading into a mouth-like cavern, a crypt – or even an abstract feeling inflected with paternal judgment in the tradition of another of Marot's fathers, Villon, who deplores his sins or *lubres sentemens* in the twelfth stanza of the *Grant Testament*.[15] The appeal of the person with whom the poet identifies leads the eye to an uncanny space, a lair, an *-ente or antre* of "betweenness," an *anth-* or *entre-deux* in which the subject of the poem, contradiction, entails irresolution.[16]

Already the status of the poet's adolescence *en espèrant* finds at once an origin and destruction in the ambiguous shape of *le père* first marked at the beginning of the final stanza: *l'enfant aussi, qui surmonte le père*. Since the poem has implicitly announced his coming and going seven times until this moment, *père* does not have immediate impact, except in the vicinity of the *enfant* at the other end of the line. The child who (*qui*) surmounts the father almost personifies the god of Love as if in the shape of a *putto*. But the repetitive *qui*, at the hub, reiterating the chiastic play in lines 4–5, leaves doubt as to its identity. The attenuating "aussi" tends to remove the iconographical connection we might establish between a female goddess of Fate, in *Amour hayneuse* (line 6), whose imposing presence would have identified the child as a poet. In this view of the world upside-down, the child overtakes the father by inverting the terms of subjugation.[17] In *blinding* his eyes (line 13), the child frees himself both to imaginary licentiousness and to the powers figured in the personification of Love.

Memory of allegorical personages calls visibility into question.

In the context of debates about Cupid, *bander* has both physical
and abstract aspects that suggest sight and loss of sight, recovery
and excess that flow into *impropere* (Cotgrave: "an exprobation,
upbraiding, or twitting into the teeth; a reproach, or imputation;
also a nickname, or disgraceful title"). In erecting himself against
an authority, the child commits a necessary symbolic violence which
blinds him to authority at the very instant he overtakes it. In the
graphics of his psychomachia, Marot is never far from the arena of
Totem and Taboo, where blindness and insight are never detached
from the nightmare of erotic loss.[18] Shades of doubt are cast over the
words. *Il appert*, of common usage (Cotgrave: "it appeareth, or
seemeth to be so: also, it is manifest, certainly so"), is attached to
the subject torn up by the stern look of authority cast downward
upon the child. Through the difference of generation and the
ambiguous space that the *moy* (line 11) occupies in relation to the
father and infant (line 9), bound by the axial *qui* (*x*), it appears that
the speaker is both at once. Because the text is ciphered graphically,
we can ask: who speaks, who writes, who reigns? The inner voice of
the speaker's doubt is located in the unknown quantity drawn in
qui, the reiterated locus of the poem.[19]

The paralysis that the last stanza evokes reflects not only that
of the evident criss-crossing of the first quintain but that of the
center of the poem's circle. "Puis temperance, aspre comme vipere"
(line 7) establishes a contradiction by the visual translation of a
word into a figure. The analogy tempers figures and words in a
rebus. *Aspre* recalls the viper (*vipere*, father and devil) by way of
anagram. *Aspre* alludes to the *aspic*, or asp, that is the *vipere*.
Because words and figures conflate in printed letters, no journey
from anguish into salvation beyond language is possible. The lyric
finds its greatest effect of movement in the path of deliberation
traced by its form. Until the last stanza physical displacement
is absent. All of a sudden, action provides false resolution (*surmonte*,
bende, *s'enfuyt*, lines 9, 10, 11) before stasis closes in (*sans bouger*,
cacher, lines 12, 13).

Here study of the letter and the axionometry of the *rondeau*
suggests that some questions of Marot's religion manifest a creative
doubt in the play of voice and writing.[20] The poem translates
amorous and theological anguish into print, but the "contour"
of the text dictates that its cause is not entirely in the poet but
in the constriction of both poetry and history. A cross marking
the meeting of love and theology is drawn everywhere in the poem,
but, for the sake of its secret, it is never quite designated. Perhaps

by casting its doubt in its figural shape, the poem provides a model for the arcane, *mute* poetry that most writers of Humanistic credo would embrace after the Affaire des Placards of October 1534. As Marot and his contemporaries faced persecution, the need to both stay alive and win posterity was bound to finding salvation by entertaining listeners (that is, making money) and writing mutely, in ciphers or arcane codes. The poet had to transgress but remain within traditions of accepted form and conduct. Ambivalence practiced through graphics and speech could yield concealed, visual discourses.

Other *rondeaux* show how and why. Marot, who was castigated for having broken the fast of Lent in 1527, said that he sinned for having *mangé le lard*.[21] His taste for bacon smacks of the same tendency to transgress fixed forms or, as it were, to *entrelarder* what he inherits from his fathers with pieces from others, that reach back to his father's fathers.[22] In "Des nonnes, qui sortirent du couvent pour aller se récréer" (XXXVII, 197–98) the poet finds himself at first not in a *rondeau* but along the hedgerows of the *pastourelle*, an older form that appeals to the memory of fabled meetings of errant knights with nameless maidens. But instead of a blonde beauty he finds a group of nuns:

> Hors du convent lautrehyer soubz la couldrette
> Je rencontray mainte Nonne proprette,
> Suyvant l'Abbesse en grand'devotion:
> Si cours apres, et par affection
> Vins aborder la plus jeune at tendrette.
>   Je l'arraisonne, elle plaint et regrette:
> Dont je congneus (certes) que la povrete
> Eust bien voulu autre vacation
>   Hors du couvent.
>   Toutes avoient soubz vesture secrette
> Un tainct vermeil, une mine safrette,
> Sans point avoir d'amour fruition.
> Ha (dis je lors) quelle perdition
> Se faict icy de ce dont j'ay souffrette
>   Hors du convent![23]

> [Out of the convent lately under the Couldray
> I met many nuns fresh as the day,
> Following their Abbess in grand devotion.
> I run behind, and then by affection
> Happen to meet the ripest and most gay.
> I bargain with her, with regret she sighs nay,
> Whence I know (certainly) on that day

32

She might have wished another vocation
  Out of the convent.
They all had, under their vestments in gray
A rosy tint, a ruddy look, I should say,
Without coming by love to fruition.
Oh! (I could not allay) what perdition
Is done now with my submission
  Out of the convent.]

By virtue of having the sheperdesses veiled in Catholic garb, Marot draws an erotic picture recalling the world of the Troubadours. *Couldrette* and *lautrehier* belong to a tradition that reaches back to the *pastourelle*. In a poem by Marcabru we find the model that Marot appears to be using:

> L'autrier jost'una sebissa
> trobei pastora mestissa,
> de joi e de sen massissa,
> si cum filla de vilana,
> cap'e gone'e pelissa
> vest e camiza treslissa
> sotlars e causas de lana,

wrote the Troubadour, establishing a convention that the *rondeau* now modifies through affinities of print. *Lautrehyer* in Marot's version seems to be inspired by the common term that represents recent time (*L'autrier*). Marot replaces *sebissa* with the *couldrette*, that can indicate a place which resembles the usual locus of the *pastourelle*, now as a grove of nut-trees but also, in the webbing of the collection, the keynote term or hinge, as we have seen in the eighteenth *rondeau*, on which other poems seem to turn. The desire to enter into faith as well as the forbidden body stages a scandal of both sin and poetic craft encountered on the edge of the poem's closed perimeters. The narrator is moved by the sight of "la plus jeune et proprette" but cannot cross the barriers he sees between himself and his erotic object.[24]

The refrain and the visual center describe a circle, the sight of whose closure literally precipitates a desire to transgress. The *rondeau* is the circle itself, but its narrative invites the reader to discover how to cross the barrier. The lyric therefore depends on the beginning to mark a passage that continually keeps the eye at a distance, where it remains *outside* of the convent (and convention) while it lives within the walls of the poem. The inaugural movement ineffably draws attention to the letter as the agent inspiring a scene of desire.

Hors du couvent of the 1532 editions becomes *hors du convent* in 1544. The slight shift in spelling reflects the corporal figure of the poem in light of what it cannot see or touch.[25] The text plays on both forms at once but with innuendo: since in Marot's time a poem, like a map or a letter, carried in itself the reminder of the total shape of a sacred body, the orthogonal difference allows for imaginary movement between the neck and the sex, or between the platonic region of voice and the nether area of the body. Here Eros is extended through the veil of the nuns, forcing the viewer to see the desired zones of the body at once through the vestments and in the play of letters on the surface of the page. And because the text has Neoplatonic inspiration, confusion of different spellings would imply that the writing of the name, *convent* or *couvent*, would be an imperfect approximation of an ideal sanctuary. The visual shift in the montage of words is more effective than the idea of a sacred space.

Play on the printed letter signals how movement turns about an ineffable enigma. The refrain, located at the outer edge of the poem's circle, is anticipated as a point of desire. The shape subverts the very anticipation of which it writes. Thus the inaugural formula, *hors du convent*, depends on the ambiguity that the reader affronts in order to follow the narrative. The refrain both confirms and betrays the first impression we gain in order to vary on its imaginary – and hidden, hence visible – figuration. *Hors* recalls a golden past that differs from the present time of the text. The reflection of *or* (gold) refers to the shape of a medallion; at the same time, because the *rondeau* is *not* the gold of its refrain, it marks an area of exclusion, insinuating into the nuns' bodies the paper currency of a poem representing a highly conventional scene of desire. In a perfect homonymy, the refrain would be the beginning of a speculation, where the topic taken from Marcabru is virtually *or du convent*. And in a monetary sense, the words can be heard as *or dû qu'on vend*, or gold one sells before having received it.[26] The initial refrain anticipates all of these meanings before the narrative is set into place.

Situated at the upper edge of the text, and ordering the dominant rhyme, *couldrette* marks a distance out of doors – *hors* – from the center of the convent and the nuns' bodies. They are scattered but contained in a visible rhyme,

Hors du *con* vent lautrehyer soubz la *cou* ldrette

which stretches the bodily extension of the line in a fashion reminiscent of Villon, whom Marot had recently translated into sixteenth-century language and Roman typography.[27] A double meaning is cast in the

34

shadow of the hazel-nut trees. *Couldrette* has a metaphysical nuance in its field of analogy, where its graphics also imply artisanal work of – once again – sewing and nailing. Reminders of Biblical passion mix with those of poetics, in which the medieval art of *conjointure* is implied.[28] The needle (from *couldre*) and the nail (from *clou*), folded into *couldrette*, were common in contemporary usage (Cotgrave: "'Un clou pour couldre ladicte lucane;' 'Pour troy cens de clou de canyn pour couldre les dictes portes,'"); the trees seen through *couldrette* evoke the center and circumference of a circle as well as a set of Latin crosses, of strongboxes, of locks and picks or other bits of *jargon* and *jobelin*. The axis at the center of the poem is an object of devotion, an emblem or hidden image, in perfect coincidence with the vanishing point marked as the nun's body.

A concealed dimension in "Aucunes nonnains" is glimpsed at its visual axis. At the discursive center of the verse Marot opens a parenthesis in the narrative account, "Je l'arraisonne, elle plainct, et regrette: / Dont je congneus (certes) que la provrete / Eust bien voulu autre vacation / Hors du convent." The gesture is written in a quasi-nautical vocabulary that further underscores the latent theology and politics. The voice came to *aborder* the lady, literally, to board her; it reasons with her, but in the sense of an inspector boarding a ship that may contain hidden merchandise. *Araisonner* conflates a logical process with a virtue of poetry, "rime et raison," and with the ocular activity of ferreting about for contraband. In the absolute center the object of the investigation is almost likened to a vessel, or the shape that opens a cleft in space, such as the sight of a hull of a vessel or the design of a mandorla. The poet, approaching the object, realizes (*certes*), that the girl would have done better to live out of the convent or out of practices that incarcerate all unmarried maidens in religious orders. The instant of certitude simultaneously inscribes doubt about social practices at the point where the parenthesis is visually equivalent to the eye penetrating into space. The arcs are at the exact center of the vertical and horizontal axes,

$$\longleftarrow -------- \text{(certes)} ----------\longrightarrow$$

and in the cartographical disposition of the *rondeau*, yield a perspectival object locating at the axis what is known and unknown, along with what is reasoned and what is seen. Like *aspre* that curls around the axis of "Par contradictions," (*certes*) reflects the poet's eye, like a calligram,[29] that stares at the reader or beholder. It is the useless expression, a *cheville* of sorts, that opens a gap in the text, but that also marks doubt within certitude. The eye is visually struck in the context of the adjacent verb, *cognoistre* (with its portmanteau combination of *connoistre* and *cogner*), that imprints knowledge on the poet by virtually hitting his mind's eye. (*Certes*), then, draws an inner circumference about the *rondeau* within itself and displays graphic proof of the ways that the renascent ideology of the circle and of micro- and macrocosm runs through a poetic tradition when a *pastourelle* is bent into the printed *rondeau*. It is as if the poet elaborated the text according a visual points of stress – edge, center, and spandrel – prior to developing a narrative portrait of the voyeur.[30]

The same apposition underlines and designates the hidden art of the poem, for the obvious *secret* of the text is cast – by dint of anagram – in spatial and discursive terms together, where the greatest expression of certitude is clearly what is indicated through graphic analogy of centers and circumference. This mute side of the configuration displays its closure that opens when the graphemes and vocables are seen in an axionometric relation to each other. They converge toward the center but also disperse into the other characters of the discourse (see opposite). At work in the poet's demonic art is something of a typographical invagination, by which the spatial play of the letters of the poem perform what is forbidden in the narrative. The composition folds upon and in itself all the while it figures, in condensed and scattered letters, something of the object of its own desire.[31]

It might be excessive to think of the poem as a scene mapping in its visual form, in (*certes*), the point of desire, the nipple of an imaginary breast – of what will be the discursive comedy of the "Blason du beau tétin" Marot was soon to send to the Duchess of Ferrara in 1535. Nonetheless, the letter allows us to think of the points where politics, eros, religion, and poetic craft combine. The shape of the *couldrette* shares much with that of the first *rondeau* of the *Adolescence clémentine*, in which the art is explained but concealed in secrecy. The lyric tells the reader, who is given the privilege of being imagined as would-be poet, how to master the genre. Marot's counsel is patently platonic, since the poem (I, 175), as we have noted, answers to an utterance from above that echoes with the vocative refrain, "Maistre Clément, mon bon amy," of another poem:

Hors du convent lautrehyer soubz la Couldrette

Je rencontray mainte Nonne proprette,

Suyvant l'Abbesse en grand'devotion:

Si cours apres, et par affection

Vins aborder la plus jeune et tendrette.

Je l'arraisonne, elle plaint et regrette:

Dont je congneus (**certes**) que la provrete

Eust bien voulu autre vacation

Hors du couvent.

Toutes avoient soubz vesture secrette

Un tainct vermeil, une mine safrette,

Sans point avoir d'amour fruition.

Ha (dis je lors) quelle perdition

Se faict icy de ce dont j'ay souffrette

Hors du couvent!

I

RESPONSE A UNG RONDEAU QUI SE COMMENÇOIT:
MAISTRE CLEMENT, MON BON AMY

En ung rondeau, sur le commencement,
Ung vocatif, comme 'Maistre Clément,'
Ne peut faillir r'entrer par huys ou porte;
Aux plus sçavans poetes m'en rapporte,
Qui d'en user se gardent sagement.
   Bien inventer vous fault premierement,
L'invention deschiffrer proprement,
Si que raison et rime ne soit morte
     En ung rondeau.
   Usez de motz receuz communement,
Rien superflu n'y soit aulcunement,
Et de la fin quelque bon propos sorte,

37

Clouez tout court, rentrez de bonne sorte,
Maistre passé serez certainement
En ung rondeau.

[In a rondeau, at the commencement
A vocative, like "Master Clement"
Can't fail to return through door or port;
The most wise of poets, I must report,
Refrain from using such an element.
 Choose you must, quite firstly
With invention deciphered properly,
So that rhyme and reason won't be bent
 In a rondeau.
Use often many a common word,
Nothing superfluous must be incurred,
Now, at the bottom for wit to explode,
Nail it down, go back to the abode,
A passed master you'll be, in a word,
 In a rondeau.]

The visual center of the poem happens to be *deschiffrer*, or the "narration," the "division into units" that commands the second operation, after *inventio*, in the order of Ciceronian rhetoric. Narration, however, can be a demonic activity. Creating division,[32] it conjures up Marot's own diabolical art that played with sin and damnation at a time when heresy was first becoming a significant issue for Humanists.[33] Marot appears to be acting out strict adherence to orthodoxy as he subverts it from within, with mute secrecy, through the creation of an arcane language of hieroglyphic stamp. The center of the poem marks a code which yields, following the readings of the other poems,

des *x* ffrer,

or the *chi* inserted at the axis of the overall circle.

But *x* is a quasi-anamorphic sign, a verbal death's head or *memento mori*, that sallies forth as it casts a spell on the viewing reader. For Marot proper decipherment depends on our alert apprehension of the force of death or transformation that comes with the mark cast or written on the body. In fact the second half of the *rondeau* moves from life to death or from voice to silence.[34] After the vocative "Maistre Clément ..." is sounded in the second line, the first sign of death emerges from the vision of rhyme and reason dead (*morte*, line 8) before, at its closure – the fateful thirteenth line – the poet becomes a "Maistre passé." We move

38

from a proper, individual noun to an anonymous, dead body: the past master dies and is encrypted in his verse. If scansion of *deschiffrer* unlocks a hidden visual sign of silence at the center, then the poet can, through a montage of serialized space of print, be seen as a figure who will be *very dead*, like the reader, who

Mais tre(s) passé serez certainement.

[But very dead will certainly be.]

The signs of death and exclusion that had informed "Par contradictions" and "D'aucunes nonnains" also prevail here. *Clouez* (line 12) redounds from *couldrette* and *convent* while the *chi* (line 7) figures as a variant of the *aspre* of the viper's tangle of the protopetrarchan *rondeau* seen above. "Raison et rhyme," a code of poetic comportment, signals what is needed if one is not, as befalls the dumb rhymester of "A ung poete ignorant" (the title of another *rondeau* in the same collection), to be taken out to pasture.

But most important, the key to the poem, what allows Marot to enter through the door — for strait is the gate to salvation and the laurels of posterity — is the emblematic *x* of the axis. The key and keyhole are one, and the mute letter, the skeleton key or the *passe-partout* that dots the center and edge of the *rondeau*, where the voice of the poet is confined in solitude or nailed in a coffin. It marks where he is literally *mis à mort*. Marot, an accomplished master of epitaphs, composed a paraph, *la mort n'y mord* ("death nor death" and "death doesn't bite here") coined from his name in anagram (Marot or *à mort*). In this poem it is inscribed anamorphically, like Holbein's death's head in the "Ambassadors," across the characters of the verse.[35] Marot is celebrated and victimized by the letters of his own name as they disseminate in C's and M's of print. He is fixed once written, cast in a social order that he sees convicting him for the heresy at stake in the diabolical operation of writing poetry.[36] The end of the poem indicates that the vocative of the beginning, "Maistre Clément, mon boy amy," is a swansong, a *chant de cygne*, that invokes the graphics of death in the little-*x*, or the petit-*x*, that would become Mallarmé's *ptyx* three and a half centuries later.

It may be that the visual dimension of the *rondeau* displays a counter-writing of mute forms which commits a necessary heresy in face of the sacred nature of Catholic convention in the 1520s. But it orients the eye to an autonomous, highly pictural writing investing perspective and movement into voice and broadening the field of analogy that already, at least in Marot's Christian cosmos, shows where politics and poetry converge. Marot's use of the letter may be part of an idiolect that the Reformation generally embraced. But when, at the time of the heresy trials of 1526 and the frenzy following the *Affaire des Placards* of October 1534, Humanists turned to silence in order to avoid death at the stake, they developed codes of visible and secret writing in other directions. One of the most decisive practitioners was Rabelais, who shares much with Marot's *rondeaux*, and who articulates a broader sense of the letter in the sacred and secular scripture of *Gargantua*. His work promotes a silence inspired in some degree from Marot's secret spaces.

2

THE RABELAISIAN HIEROGLYPH

Gargantua's first instructor might have risen from Marot's graveyard. Brother John of Orléans appears under the name of Master Thubal Holoferne in the fourteenth chapter of *Gargantua*. After listening to his son's ebulliently scholastic account of his discovery of the ideal rumpwiper, and upon recalling how Alexander the Great was put under the tutelage of Aristotle when he showed his father, Philip of Macedonia, how rusefully he could train an obstreperous horse, Grandgousier hires a sophist doctor to instruct Gargantua in the art of letters. Because the "restitution of letters" had not yet come, the poor child, notes the narrator Alcofrybas, "aprenoit à escripre gotticquement et escripvoit tous ses livres, car l'art d'impression n'estoit encores en usaige"[1] [learned to write in the Gothic style and wrote out all of his books by hand, since the art of printing was not yet in use]. Gargantua bore all the trappings of manuscript culture. He read his logical treatises, learned them backwards and forwards, memorized Latin proverbs on his chubby fingers, and digested popular almanachs at the kitchen table before Master Thubal died,

> L'an mil quatre cens et vingt,
> De la verolle qui luy vint.
>
> [In the year fifteen hundred and twenty,
> With pocks of which he had a plenty.]

The line, it is well known, is taken from Marot's epitaphs and cited as if to note an affinity shared with the author of *L'adolescence clémentine*.[2] Both treated of youth and wrote of transitional times. Marot saw his childish past as the growth of a comic bard waiting for conversion to reformed religion, while Rabelais depicted the childhood of the giants Pantagruel and Gargantua. Both used the topic of *institution* to frame the cultural programs they wished to set in place.

The passage from childhood to adult life appears to be bound

41

to the growth of typography. Marot's and Rabelais's innovations entail the advancement of new shapes, designs, and distributions of letters. Even if they were first printed in Gothic letters, their writings herald the coming of Roman font. The novelty of the latter seems to have been less an innovation than a retrieval of an older style. Under new patronage with Francis I, by the 1530s letters were assuming a shape that replaced the Gothic style inherited, on the one hand, from the *flamboyant* in architecture and, on the other, in print culture, from the *lettre bâtarde*. In the typographical workshops since the age of the incunabulum, the Gothic letter had been used to give the familiar appeal of an old manuscript to a new product. Although the first books printed in Paris were set in Roman type, only with the impact of Humanism, after 1530, did most practices actually revert to the classical forms that had had no success in the 1470s.[3] More specifically, it was after the impact of Geoffroy Tory and the imports of Italian books (such as *Le songe de Poliphile*) that letters changed. Marot reedited Villon in the new type in 1533 (Paris: Galiot du Pré). Editions of Rabelais in Roman font would soon follow its initial success in the guise of a mock-chapbook sold at the book fairs of Lyon.[4] New letters promised not just a different style of print but also a new visual perspective of different sensory and aspectual form.

How it functions in Marot's poetics has been an object of study in the last chapter. Rabelais offers a variation that moves from alphabetical to hermetic dimensions and that is inspired by the plastic arts of his milieu. A piece of its marquetry is visible in Gargantua's upbringing and early education, when a sacred secret is revealed through the visual immediacy of printed words. Rabelais's narrator is characterized as a bespectacled scholar who patiently abstracts quintessence from the crannies of the world and its books. He soon tells the reader that Gargantua's institution passed through the ponderous world of allegory – but he does so only after having set forth the ambiguous point that the contents of his tale can be immediately discovered (but also patiently revealed) through lengthy gloss.

Contradiction reigns supreme. At the outset of *Gargantua* the reader faces a paradox of the relation that writing holds to verbal language. On the one hand, mechanical reproduction of writing liberates the world from its chores of copying and invites a collective renewal of education. But on the other, it manifests a renewed nightmare of monsters, of the world at the end of seasonal time when a vision of automation prompts fears of entropy and silence.

The tension of the two forces emerges from the early pages of *Gargantua*, where the plan for a renascence of speech is launched in their architectural, allegorical, and scriptural dimensions of silence. The exuberance of the Rabelaisian mission is legendary, but its doubts and creative fears in the time of growing social and religious tumult, *within* the typographical expression of that mission, need to be studied closely. The first thirteen chapters of *Gargantua* show how they congeal.

The first book, published in 1533, historically follows *Pantagruel*, the second, completed in 1532. Historians generally agree that *Pantagruel*, born of Rabelais's visionary parody of the anonymous *Cronicqs de Gargantua* that had circulated in bookfairs, took hold and, as it was being written, inspired an evangelical mission that embraced a Pauline vision countering growing resistance to Gallican Humanism. As he was taking his first cues from the tales of the giants told in the *Cronicqs* (chapters 2–5), Rabelais discovers how a manifold work can move backward and forward, simultaneously, into popular and arcane worlds, from taverns on the left bank of Paris to the Elysian utopias of fellow Neoplatonist poets. Written the following year, *Gargantua* is said to refine the wondrous beginnings of *Pantagruel*; to work disjunctively and creatively, from the same double origins, to a book that attains a totalizing, complete, but forever unfinished architecture; that strikes ecumenical notes, is overtaken with joy and laughter, and that virtually changes the relation that the modern world holds with language. Yet the exuberance manifest in the beginning gives way to warfare and, once peace is attained, to the silent discourse of the architectural description of the Thelemites' Abbey. Noise and revelry lead to silence of meditation, and the field of festival – the *saulsaie* – of the beginning gives way to an enclosure whose non-walls stave off the threat of conspiracy and *murmure*. Throughout its composition *Gargantua* is fraught with fear over the silent implications of its own program. Or, if it is not, the book's own education grows from a world of folklore into another of contemporary politics.

Doubt about the division of script and voice quite possibly destabilizes the writing and, in turn, invests into its letters uncanny forces of ambiguity. It may be that the consequences of the Rabelaisian vision are folded within its own articulation, or that the expansion of language it announces also brings about a revolution of silence. *Gargantua* sets out to celebrate recovery of the forgotten languages of Egyptian hieroglyphs. They no doubt come to Rabelais through editions of Horapollo and Francis Colonna (noted in

Gargantua, chapter 9 [33]). For both the narrator and reader they signal a virtue of written language that does *not* necessarily translate voice in script. The letters that Rabelais inherits do not necessarily transcribe speech or disappear after being read aloud. Thus the archaic languages he seeks cannot be deemed logocentric or be associated with the relay of information.[5] Their representation includes objects as well as concepts and various stenographies. As in Marot's poetry, the "secret" shape of letters allows a reader – who is also a viewer – to partake of the world as it is seen and touched, and to envisage it without the slightest delay that would come with the gap between sight and understanding. A new relation with things known and unknown is instaured within the perspective that print offers in its own relation to itself, that is, to the physical things it concretizes and to the breath it inspires by its form.[6]

In *Gargantua* a new and totalizing apprehension of the world is called "natural law," by which "un chascun peut soubdain par soy comprendre sans aultrement estre instruict de personne" (34) [any and every one can suddenly understand without otherwise being taught by any one]. The project will change the world in its universal pedagogical efficacity that *relays* ideas quicker than ever before. Yet fear of and pleasure from the unconscious dimensions of writing appear to be born with its design. On one side, the potential infinity of meaning that would call for rediscovery and renewed organization of script figures in a program of restitution concurrent with the view of writing as something quite other, foreign, and irreducibly *unlike* the worlds of birth and renascence being described. Given the divided nature of its letters, the book thus advances and betrays the secrets of its vision and composition.

Allegory, seen as a medieval system that would impede the will to embrace a timeless world of sacred meaning, does not unlock any secrets. Humanists of Rabelaisian credo had called allegory an inadequate mode of interpretation, because it smacked of mysteries concocted only from autonomous form, not the experience of language and life. In the same frame they also saw how writing and reading could become complicitous agents in the closed process of self-containing and self-legitimized revelation. Allegories had thus to be disavowed.[7] Better than allegory, the emblem and hieroglyph offered to the Rabelaisian reader more immediate access to the mysteries of the world. The language of images, notes Michel Jeanneret, purported to contain the essence of things real, or that of presence itself. Discourse or gloss was unnecessary, for in a blink the act of reading could discover a plurality of meanings disseminated within and about letters. A visible writing had to be put forward, but one that would be free of the cumbrous structures of gloss. The books of Humanism had to contain hidden meanings that were everywhere obvious, free of arcana, but paradoxically divine in their hermetic aspect. The book had to become the very objects it described and seal all gaps between characters, words, representations of things, and even the figures of figures of things. The secret of the book would hence be everywhere and nowhere, like Marot's *rondeaux*, centered simultaneously at its ubiquitous center and along its own discursive margins and up and down its spine.

Such appears to be the plan of *Gargantua* at the moment it restores hieroglyphic writing and proposes an instantanteously mysterious language carried back from worlds afar. In "Les couleurs et livrée de Gargantua" (ix), the narrator evokes the art of the readymade, of emblem-puns, or proto-Freudian rebuses that combine one perspective of writing with another of images. On the one hand, they are disavowed as inept – and "typically French" in their simplicity – while on the other (and the text takes care not to underscore the point) they embody the ecumenical immediacy of mystery that the Humanistic enterprise was championing. The site where allusion is made to ancient writing appears no less crucial for the overall plan of Rabelais's book than what it states or belies:

En pareilles ténèbres sont comprins ces glorieux de court et transporteurs de noms, lesquelz, voulens en leurs divises signifier *espoir*, font portraire une *sphère*, des *pennes* d'oiseaulx pour *poines*, de *l'ancholie* pour *mélancholie, la lune bicorne* pour *vivre en croissant*, un *banc rompu* pour *bancque roupte, non* et un *alcret* pour *non durhabit*, un *lict sans ciel* pour un *licentié*, que sont homonymies tant ineptes, tant fades, tant rusticques et barbares, que l'on doibvroit atacher une queue de renard au collet et faire un masque d'une bouze de vache à un chascun d'iceulx qui en vouldroit dorénavant user en France, après la restitution des bonnes lettres. (32)

[In the same shadows are these glorious courtiers and conveyors of words, in their family blazons, who in wanting to signify *hope*, design a *sphere*, put birds' *plumage* for *pains, twisted flowers* for *melancholy*, or a *cockled moon* for *living on the rise*; a *broken bench* for *bankrupt, non* and a *corselet* for *non durhabit*; a *bed without a baldaquin* for a *licentiate*: so inept, tasteless, naïve, and barbarous are the puns that a foxtail ought to be tied to their collars, and for the faces of everyone who would hereafter want to coin them, a mask should be made by plunging them straight into cowshit, now that good letters have been restored.]

The text rejects the childish art of the rebus but, like Freud in *Jokes and their Relation to the Unconscious*, takes delight in extending examples of what it puts under severe criticism. An ambivalent relation is established and extended when the narrator adds,

Par mesmes raisons (si raisons les doibz nommer et non resveries) ferois-je paindre un *penier*, dénotant qu'on me faict *pener*; en un *pot à moustarde*, que c'est mon cueur à qui *moult tarde*; et un *pot à pisser*, c'est un *official*; et le *fond de mes chausses*, c'est un *vaisseau de petz*, et ma *braguette*, c'est le *greffe des arrestz*, et un *estront de chien*, c'est un *tronc de céans*, où gist l'amour de m'amye. (32)

[For the same reasons (if I should call these reasons and not reverie) I could picture a *panier* to denote that it *pains* me; and a *mustard pot* to show that my courage *comes lately*; and a *chamberpot* to indicate a *public servant*; the *bottom of my pants* to be a *bag of farts*, and my *codpiece*, the *signature of a subpoena*, and a *dog turd*, a *stem up tight*, stuck right in the hole of my lady's love.]

These visual jokes he calls *resveries*, a word that Geoffroy Tory had used to define the dream-work (indeed, the *Traumdeutung*) of writing, since the letter, both as part of a word and an element detached from it, can enjoin its beholder to wrestle with infinitely thorny and easy play of analogy. "& cela est appelle ung Resbus, au quel on a resué, & faict on resuer les autres."[8] [& a rebus is called whatever has made one sweat-dream, & that makes others dream and sweat.] For the printer from Bourges, and no less immediately in his intuitions than Freud himself, the dream entailed a rebus because of a typographical identity of **v** and **u**, making "sweating over and again" (*resuer*) the bodily effect of dreaming (*resver*), an analogy with *rebus*, by which the given phonemic resemblance of **b** and **v** and the orthographic resemblance of the initial and medial *s* made into one the art of visual punning, reverie, and the labor of transpiring.[9] Rabelais is almost referring to Tory's praise of ancient language even though he codes "resverie" pejoratively. The jokes he has told all share the mechanisms of more abstruse, higher mysteries that the narrator aligns with hieroglyphs. They are funny enough to be extended − as in a string of conundrums − and hence serve as figures announcing the coming of the letter. *Resverie* highlights the difference between sacred and profane gloss, and likewise underscores the mood of anticipation set with the recent and prodigious birth of Gargantua through his mother's left ear.

The hieroglyph slides into the text, as it were, couched against itself. The narrator decries the invention of silence that comes with heraldic languages that inspire only a mute gaze of admiration. Yet they can be used to partake of a secret, like the unconscious or time, that is everywhere obviously visible but nowhere perceptible:

the reader is invited to wonder if the discourse itself is *already* hieroglyphic in its form or if its explanations display and conceal its own graphic silence. The following chapter (*x*) on colors provides a clue. The printed book can only evoke (or, in its first words, "signify") blue and white livery, it cannot paint them on the page. Colors are indicated but invisible in view of black characters on a white ground. Exposition calls for the reader to see them in and through the words that veil or nuance their presence. They become imaginary, but their meanings are "seen" through natural law. A visual scansion of the text is sought to animate the disposition of colors. When white is glossed, it "extériorement disgrège et espart la veue" (36) [disaggregates and spreads view], as it manifestly "dissolves" the visual (*visifz*) and perspectival (*perspectifz*) minds. It blends in order to establish a limit for vision. Emphasis on inner and outer sight is inserted in the midst of the description of the giant's birth and adolescence and appears to be an excursus having little to do with the design of *Gargantua*. But, like the colors blue and white, the components and the site of the chapter *signify* another and more pervasive obsession with writing.

The tenth chapter is that of an ideal numerical figure. Like Tory's praise of IO in the *Champ fleury*,[10] the goddess of writing embodies the two complementary shapes of the circle and the straight line (I and O) that form the basis of all letters and makes 10 identify the name of Ovid's lady. The opposition gives rise to the *Festina lente*, by which the Arabic numbers of the chapter designate a privileged site just as, to the contrary – at least according to the binary logic that inaugurates the discussion (33−4) – the thirteenth chapter on the invention of the rumpwiper marks a comically unlucky moment in the boy's training. A vaguely motivated relation between numbers, writing, and composition is held in line with some of Tory's elaborate allegories.[11]

In this way an initial plan of *Gargantua* seems to work according to a cyclical rhythm, whose movement is glimpsed through serial repetition or montage of spatial form, by which order and distortion are gained through parataxis of juxtaposed chapter-units.[12] For our purposes, we can observe that the first and the tenth chapters buckle one movement that begins with a hieroglyph in order to leave it and return again. A new perspective is gained by moving forward, backward, and forward again. In "De la généalogie et antiquité de Gargantua" (*i*), the hero's family line is contained in a "goubelet en lettres éthrusques: HIC BIBITUR," placed on top of nine bottles in the midst of which sits a "gros, gras, grand, gris, joly, petit, moisy livret, plus, mais non mieulx sentent que roses" (3) [a big, fat, grand, gray, pretty, little, musty book, smelling more but not better than a rose]. Putting into practice "l'art dont on peut lire lettres non apparentes" (8) [art of which we can read apparent letters], the narrator transcribes the cock-and-bull verse of the "Fanfreluches antidotées, trouvées en un monument antique" (*ii*). Allusion to the Etruscan script anticipates the praise of Egyptian hieroglyphs below. The "fanfreluches" are clearly an emblem-poem which requires sight and sound to be disjoined and realigned. Then follows the story of Gargamelle who carries Gargantua in her womb for eleven months (*iii*). An intermezzo of the musical "propos des bien yvres" (*v*) precedes the birth of the baby through the mother's left ear (*vi*). The next chapter (*vii*) describes how the father, Grandgousier, hastens to impose a name upon him. A description of his clothes (*viii*) ensues before the chapters dedicated to coats of arms and the hieroglyph (*ix* and *x*) close the sequence describing the birth and growth. The chapters appear to be something of a dual unit established through a textual plan borrowed from architectural practice. Each chapter abuts another by providing a contrary view and a support for what precedes and what is being advanced. A scheme of a paradox, a dialectical closure − like the constriction and dilation of Marot's *rondeaux* − becomes apparent. Birth, noise, and naming (*v*−*vi*−*vii*) give way to description and silent gloss (*viii*−*ix*−*x*). Chapters *xi*−*xiv* develop the topic of adolescence − or time wasted in the hero's former age. The same chapters are juxtaposed to a new institution (*xv*),[13] which informs the Parisian sequence (*xvi*−*xix*). These latter chapters take up the problem of old and new education (*xx*−*xxiv*). The dialogue of the two styles also develops by virtue of their cemented oppositions.

The first ten chapters are framed by the hieroglyph. Fashioned according to an allegorical order that is both closed − because it accounts for the past − and open − since it must be able to predict future events[14] − every segment carries the entire shape of the book within the play of its letters, and all the while it engenders movements of figures and sounds along autonomous lines of speech and writing. The sound "track" does not necessarily run parallel to the "image" or "letter" tracks. Their visual form exceeds the thematic material expressed in the semantic register. Chapters nine and ten that assess symbolic writing return, as they should, to the "origins" marked not in Genesis but in the first chapter of ... *Gargantua*. The amiable giant's genealogy goes back to Etruscan titles inscribed about the *goubelet*, and the whole is written "au long de lettres cancelleresques ... en escorce d'ulmeau" (8) [written out in legal letters on the bark of elm trees]. Practicing the art of "reading letters that are not apparent" (8), the narrator alludes to an edifice decorated with writing which is at once both the meaning and the decoration of the whole book.

Italian archeologists had recently discovered lost languages and symbols through the revival of Vitruvius and a reading of Alberti.[15] *Ethrusques* binds architectural and scriptural allusions that suggest how *Gargantua* will be a hermetic edifice of words endlessly dividing and recombining. The regressive moment of the second chapter reveals just how crucial is the visual order for the success of the montage. The "Fanfreluches" take up enigma-poetry and the *coq-à-l'âne*, current genres that resort to macaronic lyric, where obscurities are used to produce sparks of meaning lost in their own illumination.[16] The first and second chapters set the stage for the scene of the birth of a prodigious strangeness recounted in the three chapters to follow. Chapters three, four, and five also mark obscure moments. Gargantua "sees the day." Light refracts into colors sparkling from his clothing and jewelry. Similar to the *abysme* effect evoked in Gargantua's letter to his son in the ninth chapter of *Pantagruel* (206), the chapters can be read in a forward or reverse order. When following both forwards and backwards, in what the text calls a "cancelleresque" fashion, the reader's eyes are aimed toward one of many divided centers. The hieroglyphic frame of the first and tenth chapters surrounds Gargamelle's labor and the description of the infant. At the center is the birth itself that resounds in every cardinal direction, but also returns to its divided origins. In schematic fashion, a trajectory of convergence can be traced through the oppositions:

$$i-ii \text{ } - - - - - - - - - - - - - - - - ix-x$$
$$\text{(hieroglyph)} \qquad\qquad\qquad\qquad \text{(hieroglyph)}$$

$$iii-iv \text{ } - - - - - - - - - - - - vii-viii$$
$$\text{(the mother's labor)} \qquad\qquad \text{(description of the child)}$$

$$v \text{ } - - - \text{ } vi$$
$$\text{(noise)} \quad \text{(birth)}$$

The vanishing point, the spot where worlds known and unknown intersect, or where invisibility and visibility are combined, marks one of the principal *secrets* of the design of the sequence of the "propos des bien yvres."

At this point we can ask how can such an anomalous chapter be forced into the schema. For the mere sake of symmetry? Is the text a simple experiment in fugal transcription of voice? Whatever the answers may be, without any ties to the preceding and following chapters, lacking every sign of continuity that would embed them into a story,[17] the *propos des bien yvres* conflate verbal cause and effect and float bereft of narrative mooring. The remarks resemble somewhat the enigma of chapter *ii*, and in the context of growth and development that is being staged, the loss of viewpoint they effectuate represents another moment of regression. The montage of regress is manifest, for in its return to an earlier stage of genesis, the chapter allows words, figures, sounds and forms to mix. A pre-alphabetical confusion of sensation and legibility is staged.[18] Jacques Boulenger notes that on the one hand, in the first editions, the replies were not separated by any punctuation marks. Everything seemed crowded, compressed, mixed according to no order on the page of the book; and on the other, "c'est pourtant là une conversation où tout s'enchaîne" [it is however a conversation where everything is connected] (16). He locates characters according to jargon revealing their professional affiliations; readers can glimpse through the words a world of clerical figures, lawyers, soldiers, monks, and even a Basque lackey. Once the identities are attributed to the voices, the music within the text would appear to resound, recalling kyrielles, "bransles," madrigals and other rustic motets. In his great opus of Rabelaisian exegesis, M. A. Screech stresses the difficulty that all readers encounter in facing such equivocal exchanges. They are too obscure, he admits, to convey the evangelical ideas that are discernible elsewhere in *Gargantua*. For him, the chapter is a play of pure voice, or a miniature human comedy. "Even an opaque chapter like the *Propos des bien yvres* (which consists of a series of clerkly jokes) can be found amusing with the aid of a few footnotes."[19] Yet, at the potential center of the segment framing the old world and the coming of new letters, the *propos des bien yvres* give the impression of freezing and erasing the signs that would otherwise appear so stable elsewhere; they constitute a *montage* of letters of which the movement depends on the very disappearance of figures as they are glossed. Words become both visible and evanescent, both noisy and uncommonly silent.

The scene occurs on an afternoon of the "iije jour de febvrier" (14–15), although the festive mood of peasants eating tripes and dancing to the tune of "joyeux flageolletz et doulces cornemuses" is reminiscent of the spring that has yet to come in March. The parties in conversation celebrate the beginning of February outdoors, to the contrary of current images of families who would be huddled around the fire in calendars and books of hours. The text is located between the white snow and the first sproutings of Spring. Its music is laden with silence engendered through anagrams that freeze into a scene of silence. The mannequin of the first anagram is the chapter's title,

LES PROPOS DES BIEN YVRES

which releases a graphic echo that contains the scene, when the words are scanned from one end to the other of the title, as

L.........................YVRES

shows how festive noise and clatter are metamorphosed into a bookish, graphic silence resisting seasonal or temporal change. It appears that the medium of letters silences the din that a mimetic dimension would otherwise convey. The text is betrayed by its form.

In the movement between the title and the text, either for reason of retinal suspension or because every reader tries to find the title somehow reiterated, modulated or proven *in* the text,[20] *les propos des bien yvres* appears to command the orthography of the scene and even to dictate how it is staged. The letters of the title are sprinkled into the body of the chapter, in a play of vertical montage and dispersion. Much turns about the question of causality: "qui feut premier, soif ou beuverye?" [what came first, drink or thirst?] (17). Also engaged is the question of title and chapter: which dictates the meaning of the other? In what order? Does one crystallize the other, or does it betray the other? Each of Rabelais's titles takes the issue of allegory that Humanistic thinking had rejected, but in a way that an *either/or* and a *both/and* result from the opposition that the noise of the print seems to be mediating. Critics often note that the "secret structure" of *Gargantua* and *Pantagruel* is owed to a process of nominal rectification, by which a learned name and a serious program supersede carnavalesque ones (such as François Rabelais following Alcofrybas Nasier in the time passed between *Gargantua* and the *Tiers Livre*).[21] But the relation that the name holds with the work also becomes problematic: does "Gargantua" command over and generate the book of his name? Is the allegory developed from an initial, titular order of proper names whose graphic tension can dictate the shape that the narative will take when they are invested in it?[22] The same holds for the rapport of title and text in this chapter, and all the more when its anonymity intercedes in a beginning laden with proper names of every grist.

51

Beuverye is a graphic transcription of *bien yvres*. The **s** of the latter title is mute, while the **n** takes a tumble and turns, in the scene of the world-upside-down, into a **u**. The answers to the initial questions about the origin of drink and thirst (or nature) are scattered everywhere. What was first?

Soif, car qui eust beu sans soif durant le temps de innocence? Beuverye, car *privatio presupponit habitum.* Je suis clerc. *Fœcundi calices quem non fecere disertum?* Nous aultres innocens ne beuvons que trop sans soif. Non, moy pécheur, sans soif, et sinon présente, pour le moins future, la prévenent comme entendez. Je boy pour la soif advenir. Je boy éternelle-ment. Ce m'est éternité de beuverye et beuverye de éternité. Chantons, beuvons, un motet entonnons! Où est mon entonnoir? (17)

[Thirst, for who would have drunk without thirst during the time of innocence? Drink, *because privation presupposes habit.* I am in holy orders. *Whom have full goblets ever not made skilled in speaking?* We innocents drink only too much without being thirsty. No, I, a sinner, thirstless and no less present, at least for the future, foresee it eternally. I drink for thirst to come. I drink eternally. For me it's an eternity of drinking and a drinking of eternity. Let's sing, drink, and funnel a tune! Where's my funnel?]

The montage casts the letters into a pious rapture of words and figures gulped in ecstasy. The toss of the eight graphemes in the title, *bien yvres,* or *beuverye,* in fact clarifies the evangelical promise of the chapter. The participants at the threshold of the new birth are quite (*"bien"*) drunk because *beuverye* is the matter of their ... *breviary. Breviaire* constitutes the secular book (a calendar for shepherds) and a godly one (the Bible), but the book or "livre" stages the scene of livery of *l'hiver. L'ivre,* also the *livre,* spells its bacchic origins through a jumble of letters. Therefore the "hidden" word or secret extending the metaphor is *pressoir,* the machine that produces and is, better than Bacchus, the origin of both wine *and* books. In the system of analogy the Rabelaisian text inherits from Scripture, associations can only multiply. The screw is used to press the wine and to impress the stamp of a hallmark on the register; but its overall shape, as the thirteenth chapter will suggest, is related to the spiral staircases in the new architectural programs of the castles inspired from Archimedes, Vitruvius, and Colonna (see plate 2, page 62).

In this manner the "propos" puts forward a network of characters that all spell the same movement of form. *Gargantua* is projected as a "book-object" or an organic thing endowed with extension, volume, and hidden life, like the Socratian *silène* evoked at the beginning of the prologue, but it resists reduction to abstraction.

Like Joseph Cornell's boxes that contain heteroclite objects inviting and rejecting interpretation, Rabelais's book reminds the reader of its cardinal virtues, its enigma of possible relations holding among letters and forms, and its physical mass. But in the context of seasonal change embedded in the *propos des bien yvres*, the book-object does not change in accord with natural cycles. It represents inertia and can only mime seasonal transformation through whatever symbolical efficacity its reader will invest in it.[23] The writing therefore hints that it is inert in respect to the organic substance it is representing. Only when we animate its letters can the book take part in the movement of living cycles. Poets of the Middle Ages had used verse to mark and to cause change, both to accelerate and modify the violence in play at the cusp of the seasons,[24] and here too the coming of spring is muted by the chill of frozen print whose dialogue with the world will help either to prolong or stop the thaw. The book sings of metamorphosis, but its printed form resists it. By virtue of anagram, paronomasia, or onomastic play, the montage of letters has to precipitate a melting. Frost, winter, ecstasy, "night", or apparent *obscurity*: the text signals its own liquefaction that begins with the transformation of the letters of the title. YVRES evokes the vision of future life coming out of the past, in RESVY. The movement of the chapter is one of reversibility, where *yvres–resvy* also announces the future synthesis of *res* and of a *verbum*, in a dream of a language entirely motivated by its own natural substance. "Bien yvres" provides a set of seven digits that recombine to produce graphic music in fugal patterns that appear to mix verb and thing. The *beuverye* or "beuverye eternelle" is the password that counterpoints *bien yvre*. Between the two a combination of *res* and *verba* emerges:

BIEN YV**RE**

B E   **VRE**

B E U VERYE

It may be that in the title the path leading to the blending of word and thing is indicated digitally, in the bifurcation of the **Y** at the potential axis of the union towards which both words converge when they trace diagonal vectors leading to an *abysme*:[25]

BIEN   VRE

Y

53

The vectors constitute proof of a "dialogic" state of language, in which phonemes and graphemes combine to form a creative counter-discourse that allows its user to venture into the symbolic domain or to build a protective world of nonsense that shields the body from its laws. The latter can only be apprehended slowly, and in this way the dialogical dimension of language is akin to sight, that is, an agency where subjective distance and intimacy are maintained together.[26] These combinations form the "reason" of the poetry that resounds throughout the chapter. The characters' voices seem to be drawn with the letters of the title in order that the echo (that embraces *verba* and *res*) can be inscribed and sealed within the percussive dimension of the words:

CHAPITRE V

en propos de **resieuner** on propre lieu

Brouille

Fouette-moy ce **verre** gualentement

Produiz-moy du clairet, **ver**re pleurant

Trèves de **soif**

Ha, faulse fie**vre**, ne t'en **iras-tu** pas?

Par ma fy, ma commère, **je** ne peuz entrer en bette.

Voire

Ventre Sainct Quenet! Parlons de **boire**.

Je ne boy que à mes **heures**, comme la mulle du pape.

Je ne boy que en mon bré**viaire, comme un beau père **guardian. (16)

A webbing of recombinant letters, the text can be sorted and arranged according to analogy. But word and act are already in coincidence when their convergence is sought on the third day of February. This "causes" them to recur in common nouns and verbs, in *febvrier* at the very beginning, and *beuverye*, and *advenir, la theoricque, la praticque, l'enfuyre, exhiber, boyre, riviere, urine, roigneure, couraige, vuyder, resveille*, ve**oir, *trinque*, and *aureille* – and no less in proper names that fall in the second half of the chapter: Jacques Cueur, Briareus, La Deviniere, A la mode de **Bretaigne**. Other similar sets mark words whose forms are cast between *bien yvres* and *beuverye*. The relation of the title and text extends through other figural words that diffuse letters in myriad directions.

The keynote is *saison*. The changes of tone and temperature are seen in the numbers that date the birth of Gargantua as a latent emblem. In the sentence staging the oncoming of the remarks of the *bien yvres*, the common place-name, *saulsaie*, establishes the site and the tourniquet of causes wound about effects. During the afternoon, "Après disner, tous allèrent pelle-melle à la Saulsaie, et là, sur l'herbe drue, dancèrent au son des joyeux flageolletz et doulces cornemuzes tant baudement que c'estoit passe-temps céleste les veoir ainsi soy rigouller" (16) [After dinner they all went pell-mell to the Saulsaie, and there, on the thick grass, they danced to the sound of the joyous flutes and bagpipes with so much ribald joy that it was a heavenly pastime to see them laugh like that]. Below, at the threshold of the sixth chapter, the place-name returns. When Gargamelle feels the contractions of her belly, Grandgousier gets up to care for her, saying that she "s'estoit là herbée soubz la Saulsaye" (21) [was grassed under the willow grove]. She is "herbed," at one with herself and the world, synthesizing verb and thing, evoking both a plump wench and the green grass she eats. Scatters of letters engender the transformations, each conflating cause and effect in the manner the events are conveyed by the unit of *salé–soif* interwoven through words heralded by the letter *s*: *sauce, saleures, saturnales, beuf sallé, le Sainnais, suillé* (14–18) that precede *soucier, souspire, soubdain, sursaulter* (13–15). As Master Alcofrybas says, "*Si* ne le croyez, je ne m'en *soucie*, mais un homme de bien, un homme de bon *sens*, croit tousjours ce qu'on luy dict et qu'il trouve par *escript*" (23, my italics) [If you don't believe it, I don't care, but a good man, a man of common sense always believes what he is told and finds in writing]. When voice and writing happen to coincide, an effect of truth is established. The page devoted to the *saulsaie*, like Marot's *couldrette*, is a grove of figures planted or sown and sewn together.

The *propos* begin with two sentences that convey the transformation turning death into life. Letters form a montage as soon as objects are infused with verbs. "Puis entrèrent en propos de resieuner on propre lieu. Lors flaccons d'aller, jambons de troter, goubeletz de voler, breusses de tinter" (16) [Then they began to talk about eating on the same spot. Then flagons went, hams trotted, goblets flew, cups clinked]. The scene is one of the *après-disnée*, when speech, laughter, and revelry return, but it remains a paginal site when glimpsed through the moving letters. Not only is the *saulsaie* brought to life, but the convention of the "propos de table" is instaured as well. Animation owes much to a confusion of what is heard with what is written, especially where proper names are dissolved in common nouns, and where toponyms generate the sense of a collective space shared among the social order in the montage of the *bien yvres*.[27] The *saulsaie* is a willow grove but also a reminder

55

of a sausage (*saulcisse*). The tipplers drink near the *pays de Beusse et de Bibaroys*. *Beusse* gives way to clattering *breusses*, while the allusive reminder of winter, a snowflake (*flocon*), becomes a moving flagon (*flaccon*). And the Breugel-like thigh, or *jambon* that seems to walk off the table, is less a piece of ham than a portmanteau combination of the referent and the musical measure of poetry, an *iambe*, that animates the flesh.[28] The figure of the pig, also associated with the months of February and March in popular almanachs and books of hours, brings a memory-image to the cadence of music, and with it seasonal measures syncopate.

In the festive area *voir* is tantamount to *boire*. In fact, in the emblematic dimension of the chapter, when *v* and *b* are suspended together, the Roman numeral *v* becomes a site of visibility that gives graphic substance to the page as the site of the *propos*:

Les **propos** des **bien yvres**

chapitre **v**

The chapter itself begins to see. Or, as one voice exclaims, "Je ne boy que à mes heures, comme la mulle du pape. Je ne boy que en mon bréviaire, comme un beau père guardien ... Voire ... parlons de boire ... Or ça, à boire, à boire çà ..." (16–19) [I only drink (see) at my hours, like the pope's mule. I only drink (see) in my breviary, like a good guardian father. Indeed (see/drink), let's speak of drinking (seeing). Now then, drink (see), drink (see)] And, more arcanely, "pour néant boyt qui ne s'en sent" (17) [He who can't feel it drinks (or limps)/sees for nothing]. In this light, where transubstantiation is part of revelry, so is the role of writing, whose form changes into scriptures other than the vernacular. Some of the tipplers speak in Greek letters. Given the polylingual context, the words in French can be seen transmuted into other shapes of the same inextinguishable substance, such as that in "pour néant boyt qui ne s'en sent." "Qui ne s'en sent" transliterates into s *ne s'en* (t), *sen*(t), or x *naît* (t) *s'en* (t) (qui naît s'ente, x n'est sans *t*, santé, etc.), where the alterations of the meaning are guided according to tabular as well as discursive vectors of the text:

sen: ne s'en sent

— — — — — — — — — — →

← → →

nes: ne s'en sent

← → →

The product is a multiple birth, a *nascence* or *naissance* out of *senescence*, that originates from ciphers placed in "cancelleresque" directions. The vocables acquire a subliminally sacred dimension of Scripture if *qui* is seen as a devout Christian sign, and the mute **t** of *sent* is an ineffable crucifix casting a shadow over the revelry. Again, the hieroglyph offers both a sacred and a profane version of its characters.

The moment between winter and spring floats in a confusion of script and voice. It is a respite, or a "trêve de soif," but also a time when the world is eaten and drunk in ecstasy. Throughout the letters rebirth is staged over and again, where dreams are imbibed or, following the mode of Tory's program of hieroglyphics, where a rebus is a *res*, a thing in an oblique case but also a conflation of a *rêve bu*. The rebus constitutes the utopian dream of a living writing, where figure and referent would be no less unified than breath, voice, and body. The sommeliers of the text (17) bring the words out of their sleep only because *sommeil* is written into them, just as all the implications of imbibing and pissing ("perannité de arrousement ... la pissotière n'y aura rien" (17) [perennial sprinkling ... the pisspot will get nothing] bring the words back to origins where things and verbs flow together in a renewal of the rebus, that is, the syntax of the gods' languages. The chapter ends on this note, with multiple figures, but on the very grass that had grounded the scene:

> Net, net, à ce pyot!
> Avallez, ce sont herbes! (21)
>
> [Swig, swig, to this wine!
> Swallow, these are herbes!]

The revelers gulp down the common properties of the place, *herbes*, as a verbal potion (*herbes* being synonymous with *verbes*), but their clarity (*net, net*) recalls a Socratic moment of poetic furor and drunken lucidity.[29] The clear vision foresees the very birth that its own graphics engender (*naît* equalling *net*). The ecstasy is no less Christian when one of the voices declares, "J'ai la parolle de Dieu en bouche: *Sitio*" (20) [I have the word of God in my mouth: *I thirst*]. Taken from the Gospels, the exclamation makes the thirst of vision something of an eternal instant that another voice calls "asbestos," the miraculous stone that is as unquenchable as the thirst of "Paternité" (20).

Because Christian and Socratic visions are joined, it may be that *sitio* reflects the secret dimension, the unconscious, of a highly obvious language. The moment where the Evangelical and popular registers combine is of course the first sentence of *Gargantua*, no doubt written after the first chapters had been sketched out. For the sake of giving praise to the public, the text characterizes its readers as *bien yvres*. The famous figure of the *Silènes* − boxes having something of the appearance of asbestos − is entertained, but in ways that the graphic complexities of the fifth chapter help to elucidate. The narrator of the prologue begins,

Beuveurs très illustres, et vous, véroléz tres précieux (car à vous, non à aultres, sont dédiéz mes escriptz), Alcibiades, au dialoge de Platon intitulé *Le Bancquet*, louant son précepteur Socrates, sans controverse prince des philosophes, entre aultres parolles le dict estre sembable ès *Silènes*. *Silènes* estoient jadis petites boites, telles que voyons de présent ès bouticques des apothecaires, pinctes au-dessus de figures joyeuses et frivoles, comme de harpies, satyres, oysons bridéz, lièvres cornuz, canes bastées, boucqs volans, cerfz limonniers et aultres telles pinctures contrefaictes à plaisir pour exciter le monde à rire (quel fut *Silène*, maistre du bon Bacchus); mais au dedans l'on réservoit les fines drogues comme baulme, ambre gris, amomon, musc, zivette, pierreries et aultres choses précieuses. (3, my italics)

[You illustrious drinkers, and my dear pocked friends (for these writings are dedicated to you, and not others), Alcibiades, in Plato's dialogue entitled the *Symposium*, praising his teacher Socrates, beyond the shadow of a doubt the prince of philosophers, among other words, called him comparable to *Silènes*. *Silènes* were once little boxes such as nowadays we see in apothecaries' windows, painted on the outside with joyous and frivolous figures, like harpies, satyrs, yoked geese, horned hares, ducks in harness, flying goats, deer in rein, and other such pictures drawn with pleasure to bring the world to laughter (as was Silenus, Bacchus' good master); but inside were hidden rare drugs like balm, ambergris, cardamom, musk, civet, jewels and other fineries.]

The prologue, a text of resolute ambiguity in respect to what it heralds and practices, a guide, a buffer, and a transitional object for the whole book,[30] also announces, in the silence of a secret, the elements and the politics of its hieroglyphic style.

The ambiguity is historically clear. The publication of *Gargantua* became quickly embroiled in the heresy trials that the *Affaire des Placards* had suscitated in October of 1534, at the time the book went to press. Francis I, who had favored the cause of the Humanists, changed his point of view that had earlier espoused the programs of Humanists of Rabelais's circles. Persecutions accelerated, and soon the Reformers of letters went into exile and silence. Marot took refuge in Ferrara, and Rabelais soon found sanctuary in Italy under the protection of Jean Du Bellay. At first glance the hieroglyphic dimension of the preface, written *after* the major body of the work, would appear to be the figure of the grotesques or strange creatures Rabelais lifts from the *Silènes*. They are no doubt cribbed not only from the *Symposium* but also from the forms discovered in Italian excavations that were decorating domestic architecture in the "new style" that the king had launched, after the Milanese campaigns, to replace the flamboyant decor he had patronized up to the 1520s. The opening of *Gargantua* would hence be a writing, like a new architecture, that shared the taste of things Italian and the practice of the *Festina Lente* that came with the king's blazon of the Royal Salamander.

Yet, no sooner than the new style and the new ideology were launched than repression followed. In the vision of "simultaneity" that the Humanists advocated, when a Humanistic text reveals its secrets in instantaneous illumination, it follows that the "new" allegories could explain the occurrence of events in times both past and future. The arcane hieroglyph of the first sentences of the prologue can only be embodied by the grotesques that festoon the *Silènes*. On another level, however, the figural part of the text appears to account for the historical resistance it encounters. If the Humanists were forced into silence after 1534, would it not be possible to read in *Silènes* a cryptogram that combines silence as an appeal both to Reformers of the author's persuasion and to Francis himself? The emblematic look of the letters suggests a positive answer: Alcibiades is said to say that Socrates is

semblable ès Silènes. Silènes estoient

in former time little boxes. ... The repetition of the bizarre proper noun − that requires explanation on the part of the "master abstractor" or bookhawker where other, more recondite words do not − engages a reversible scripture and happens upon a figural shape that embodies in print exactly what is conveyed in voice. It is a mirrored writing,[31] one which betrays both mystical and childish elements, and frames the first visual stoppage of the book, its first *period*:

ès Silènes. Silènes es

At the caesura of the line of words, at the center lacking any sign, the sibilant shape determines the alliteration of a silence. The soft slippage of -es, S−s−S−s, scripted four times, in a handsome mannerist fashion in the style of Primaticcio's and Il Rosso's women and geese, turns speech into a silent play of serpentine letters.

Does the allusion to the Silenus and its sibilance make a veiled appeal to *silence*? Or to a program, a "réforme de mots," of Humanists put to silence by the advent of recent history in the *Réforme de Meaux*? Can it refer to its minuscule, the "petit-s" that might be the shape of the emblem of Claude de France, the king's spouse, and to the Royal Salamander that had become his virtual signature? When, for Humanists of Rabelais's conviction, change is so slow – *si lent ce* – it may be that the shape of the majuscule **S** rhymes with the mute, unchanging aspect of a book, like the *propos des bien yvres*, whose montage and, no less, whose politics can only be animated through the reader's visual faculties. It is a world where "restitution" or Humanistic "rectification" must take place in silence, and where only the *promise* of seasonal or ideological change can be projected. *Silènes* and Socrates become ineffable shapes but also voices of silence, or a

silent-s.

They are the Humanists' signs of goodness, of the **S** that Tory had advised all good readers to inscribe over the portals thresholding their libraries, where meditative silence could reign supreme in the most difficult moments of historical turmoil.[32]

In this light the lusty drinkers of the fifth chapter disavow the fears that underpin the prologue. Two styles converge. One, of the *bien yvres'* popular wisdom, what Bakhtin calls the "lower body," is at odds with the other, that of exegesis and Neoplatonic wisdom taken from Socrates. Like Pantagruel and Panurge who are each other's alter ego, so too is the stamp of writing that conflates different orders of speech and action. On the one hand, the printed page aspires to translate itself into voice and music while on the other, it tends to be figural, if not even animistic and creatural, in design. Its extraordinary range of virtual meaning is of course concretized in ways that the grotesques of the prologue turn into other figures in the body of *Gargantua*. The *oysons bridés* carved on the apothe-caries' boxes are something reminiscent of an arrested or bridled sound heard only in the silence of print (as *oy-son bridé*). But it also prefigures a twisted allegory – shaped like an **S** – that informs the notorious thirteenth chapter on the marvelous invention of the rumpwiper.

Often called the "propos torcheculatifs," the dialogue between father and son over the experience leading to the invention combines language with matter. Not that Rabelais associates, as will Montaigne, the printed letter with fecal waste.[33] The chapter blends the plastic art of the emblem and hieroglyph with the dialogues at work in contemporary architectural and pictural practices.[34] The first and most obvious connection it shares with the structure of *Gargantua* links the prologue, with its panegyric of the *Silènes*, to the outhouse – the *sanctum sanctorum* of graffiti-jokes – to chapbooks, and also to the Renaissance design of the Abbey of Thélème which ends the book. Its edifice hence carries both a medieval and an Italian design somewhere between secular flamboyant decor and the centralized order of the châteaux of Rabelais's homeland along the Loire.

The synthesis of letter and architecture in the thirteenth chapter may have a more precise origin in allusion to the Francis I wing of the castle of Blois that was remodeled in 1526. On a cursory glance the bird with which Gargantua wipes his bottom can be likened to a swan framed in the escutcheon of Claude de France, the Queen of France hailing from Savoie. It seemingly combines the noble device with a likely architectural form, an encorbelment or the *cul-de-lampe* – one of which in fact can be seen in the Louis XII wing at Blois – on which beams were placed. The design is often comic and self-signifying. The *cul-de-lampe* at Blois depicts a woman wiping a baby's buttocks, and here the scene is literalized in the narrative. Also found on *miséricorde* sculptures decorating late-fifteenth century pews, vignettes of toilet training are a common icon of the period. The thirteenth chapter fits in the current iconography. The five-year-old giant recounts his experience with about sixty-eight rumpwipers before he reveals the magic and majestic essence of the neck of a downy goose, of the *oyzon bien dumeté* (46) [well-plumed goose]. Prior to the discovery of his "invention," Gargantua had begun to find his wit in obscene ripostes with the Lords Francrepas, Painensac, and Mouillevent (Freemeal, Breadbag and Wetwind), three pompous visitors in Grandgousier's castle who could not find stables large enough for their steeds. Rather than taking them to an adjacent wing, the boy leads them up the great stairwell, "passant par la seconde salle, en une grande *gualerie* par laquelle entrèrent en une grosse tour" (40, my italics) [passing by the second room, in a great gallery through which they went into a stout tower]. They went up other stairs and asked the steward if the child were leading them, if not awry, perhaps in a direction diametrically away from the stables. The tower and the double set of stairs appear to allude to Leonardo's helical plan at the center of Chambord or, better, to the exterior spiral staircase adjoining the Francis I Wing of Blois.[35]

61

Plate 2. Detail of twisted core of the exposed spiral staircase (1525) on the François Premier wing at the Blois château (photograph by the author). The torsion shares analogy with Rabelais's verbal composition. Bosses on the crossings of the ribs contain emblems of Francis I and Claude de Savoie, while the shafting is decorated with cockleshells and grotesques that inspire Rabelais's figure of the *silènes*.

The Rabelaisian hieroglyph

The architecture of *Gargantua* and the thirteenth chapter are announced when the youth displays his wooden *phryzon* (41), the wooden miniature of the great workhorse of Frise that, along with the *cronicqs* of Gargantua, had been sold at the Lyon fairs. *Phryzon* is a hobby-horse but also, because of its orthography, becomes a horse, a bird, a goose, and a book-in-a-tower. Because of the hieroglyphic discourse, *phryzon* refers to a comic variation of the wooden horse, or the shiver it produces in its *frisson*; but especially, because of *-yzon*, it alludes to *oyzon* of the prologue (3) and to the volatile of the next chapter (46). After having mocked the lords with his obscene riddles, Gargantua remarks that his guests are inept equestrians. In a parting shot he asks, "Se il vous falloit aller d'icy à Cahusac, que aymeriez-vous mieulx, ou chevaulcher un *oyson*, ou mener une truye en laisse?" (42, my italics) [What would you prefer, gallop on a goose or lead a sow by the reins?]. *Chevaulcher un oyson* forecasts the end of the next chapter, where the boy will tell of drawing the neck of the downy goose through his legs, which becomes a grotesque analogy to the figure of Alexander the Great taming the unruly horse in chapter *xiv* that follows (47).

But in the hobby-horse sequence the answer to Gargantua's riddle is, "J'aymerois mieulx boyre" (42) [I'd prefer to drink], a remark uttered not just to end the string of jokes, but through the design of the letters to align *oyson* with the orthography of *boyre*. An emblem is fashioned by letters in contiguity:

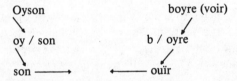

In the analogy, *boire*, which the passage of the *bien yvres* had associated with sight, in *voir*, now entails sound and hearing, in *ouïr*. The goose makes visible the sound of *ouïr*, in *oy-son*, but the torsion of its emblematic figure, of the curve of a *Festina Lente*, animates the figure of the letter **S**. The orthographic form combines with the serpentine thrust of the bird's neck, yielding a hieroglyph that contains, like Tory's IO, the tension of difference and division of speech and writing.

The *oyzon bien dumeté* (46) that Gargantua pulls between his legs to generate the "mirific rapture" from the downy softness and the warmth of the goose is taken from emblems and devices, but only through the medium of printed writing does its graphic dimension

63

alloy with architecture. *Torcher* verbalizes the scene. "Je me torchay une foys d'un cachelet ... me torchay ... puis me torchay aux linceux ... puis me torchay d'une poulle ... mais, concluent, je dys ..." (43–46) [I once wiped myself with a handkerchief ... then wiped myself with linen ... then wiped myself with a hen ..., but in concluding, I say...]. "Je me torchay" recurs in comic litany, and reverses verbal direction when cause and effect, like drink and thirst, invert. Gargantua syllogizes, "Il n'est poinct besoing *torcher cul*, sinon qu'il y ayt ordure; ordure n'y peut estre si on n'a chié; chier doncques nous fault devant que le *cul torcher*" (46, my italics). [There is no reason to wipe one's ass unless there is shit; there can be no shit unless we have shitted; we must therefore shit before our ass is wiped.] The word is twisted and turned as if to exceed the simple act of wiping. Repetition suggests that *torcher* implies torsion and torque. When the pleasure of the *torchecul* is "communicated" (46) from the bumgut up through the body's vertebral spiral staircase to the head, the shape of the sounds and letters has the sensation spin upward "jusques à venir à la région du *c*ueur et du *c*erveau. Et ne pen*s*ez que la béatitude de*s* heroe*s* et *s*emi-dieux, qui *s*ont par les Champ*s* Ely*s*iens, *s*oit en leur a*s*phodèle, ou ambro*s*ie, ou nectar, comme di*s*ent ce*s* vieille*s* y*c*y. Elle e*s*t (*s*celon mon opinion) en ce qu'il*z s*e torchent le cul d'un oy*z*on, et telle e*s*t l'opinion de Mai*s*tre Jehan d'E*s*co*ss*e" (46, my italics). [Don't think that the beatitude of heroes and half-gods, who are in the Elysian Fields, is due to their asphodel, ambrosia or nectar, as old ladies say down here. It is (in my view) because they wipe their ass with a goose, and such is the view of Master John Duns Scotus.] The visual assonance of the closing lines summarizes the allegorical and scriptural configuration of the chapter. The heraldic *s* emerges as a both dominant and median form, as a shape binding language, body, myth, sculpture, and architecture.

The S traces the spiral course of the central screw which literally emblematizes the printing press, a machine historically fashioned from the technology of oenology, the cause of which the book is the clearest effect. But perhaps too the letter internalizes the ideological and printed form of the chapter. It begins, in historiated fashion,

Sus la fin de la quinte année (42)

[Upon the end of the fifth year], and is placed in a majuscule that hints at the analogies at work in the text. On only one other occasion in fifty-eight chapters [*xxiv*: "S'il advenoit que l'air feust pluvieux

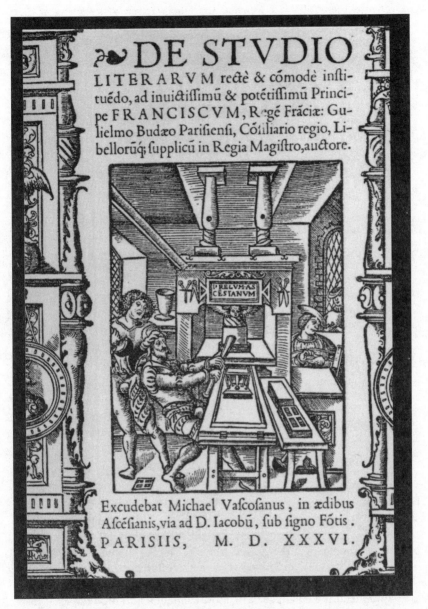

Plate 3. Title page of Guillaume Budé, *De studio literarum*... (Paris: Jodocus Badius, 1536), decorated by Oronce Finé. Lines converge toward the screw of the printing press, the perspectival object, located at the center. As in *Gargantua*, the image plays on the tension of the rectangular frame and the twisted form of a vanishing point.

et intempéré" [If it happened that the weather was inclement or raining]) does **S** herald a unit of prose to follow. Most often, the incipit is discursive ("Quand...," "Atant...," "En ces premiers jours..."), but in the hieroglyphic moments the text begins with a letter heralding (or "historiating") the shape of the chapter. The prologue announcing the *Silènes* begins with the **B** whose upper and lower curves resemble human lips when seen in profile, whence coming the vowels and consonants of their name: "Beuveurs très illustres..." (3). The first chapter on genealogies begins with Tory's originary **I**: "Ie vous remectz..." (7). The "fanfreluches antidotées" are hidden words, hence all minuscule: "ai? enu le grand dompteur..." (9). Chapter eight, on Gargantua's jeweled clothing and abundant codpiece ("Je advoue Dieu s'il ne la faisoit bon veoir!") (28) [I swear to God if it weren't the prettiest sight!], begins with *Luy*, or an emblem of the young giant [*lui*] and his illumination (*luit, luyct*, etc.). Most compelling, the *bien yvres* begin with a portmanteau figure combining discourse with the well of infinite drink whose windlass they turn to draw their life and wit: "*Puis* entrèrent..." (16) [Then they began... (or entered the well of wine)]. The initial *Sus* of the thirteenth chapter is no less suggestive in its range.

In anticipation of the figure-poems that lend architectural and calligraphic dimensions to the book, the doublet on the outhouse, the graffito,

> Tousjours laisse aux couillons esmorche
> Qui son hord cul de papier torche (44)

> [Always he who with paper wipes his dirty ass
> Leaves on his balls mucous crass]

and a line of rhymes punctuates the text and, further, suggests that it has a spiral form, because the title of the poem printed immediately below, *rondeau*, written in the style of Marot, endows the text with previously unseen torsion (see opposite). Even though the poem rewrites one of Marot's occasional pieces or is taken from the *Rhétoriqueurs*,[36] in the context of the thirteenth chapter the recurring letter twists the configuration, like a printer's lever and the shape of the spiral staircase, round and about. It forces the reader to apprehend the language in its most elemental and productive – indeed, economic – articulation. The configuration of the alphabetical shapes is that of the things from which they originate.

When the sight and form of the letter allow the discourse to merge with other plastic arts, the visionary "secret" of the Rabelaisian

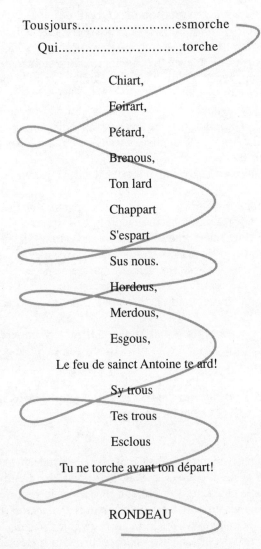

Tousjours.........................esmorche

Qui..............................torche

Chiart,

Foirart,

Pétard,

Brenous,

Ton lard

Chappart

S'espart

Sus nous.

Hordous,

Merdous,

Esgous,

Le feu de sainct Antoine te ard!

Sy trous

Tes trous

Esclous

Tu ne torche avant ton départ!

RONDEAU

program becomes an illumination. In the thirteenth chapter Gargantua is praised, as he was in terms of his livery, as a clean and clear-headed lad. "En tout le pays n'estoit *guarson* plus nect que luy" (43, my italics) [In the whole country there was no cleaner a boy than he]. Orthography reveals that *guarson* makes Gargantua a synthesis of a pervasive rupture between sight and sound, between *guar* (from *garder*, to watch over) and *son*. Grandgousier, returning from the Canaries, "visita son filz Gargantua" (42).[37] He visited or "saw" (from *visitare* and *visere*) sound emblazoned in the name-of-the-son. Whence the lesson of the "petit guarsonnet" (46) – the good little boy or even the anticipation of a sonnet seen – telling readers that every member of the family shares a beatific and generous vision. In addition to their buccal virtues ("Gar," "Grand," "Panta..."), the names of the giants embody a sense of sight: **Gar**gan**tua**, **Gra**ndgousier, Pant**agru**el and, later, P**anu**rge. G-U-A-R becomes the common ensemble of traits that makes them the lettered visionaries they are.

The names of the good giants make them extensions of the faculty of sight. But, as they eat and see together, convincing us that "eating is believing" in human and religious registers alike, the letter is responsible for combining the faculties of taste and vision. What, after all, gives these characters their genealogy? It is not either natural nor pregiven in the narrative because the narrator Alcofrybas tells us so, but because the names have the same origin in a rebus of Roman typography. Tory invented (or inherited) the famous rebus, that Voltaire would later employ, that has a **G** eat an **a** (see Plate 4). The big *G* – *G grand* – ingests the small *a* – *a petit*. The device translates "J'ai grand appétit" [I'm very hungry]; in other words, according to the play of lettrism, Big *G*, little *a*. Hunger is assuaged in the very form of the device, since the mouth of **G** is about to mandicate the **a**. The rebus solves the riddle of thirst and drink of the *propos des bien yvres* at the same time as it codes the shape and will of the great heroes of

G ... argantu ... a.[38]

The ostensively "other" side of their character, their traits as conveyors of great ciphers, makes the Rabelaisian family members of majuscule character. Verbal and physical athletes and acrobats, they are the world and the printed figures that name them. They celebrate their own synthesis in hieroglyphics; ramify its hidden language into revolutionary evangelical programs; launch a popular and erudite writing that both names and figures its meanings and also reflects its own ambivalence and doubt. Their politics embraces a silence that came after the *Affaire des Placards*. After that moment the work begun in *Gargantua* attenuated through the ensuing books of 1546 and 1552 when revelry led to hangover. But nonetheless a program had been set in place. Its endless will to form became the unconscious dimension of later literature, which would only apparently be of a higher calling under the patronage of Henry II

Plate 4. G-a rebus by Geoffroy Tory, in his *Champ flevry, Au quel est contenu Lart & Science de la deue & vraye Proportion des Lettres Attiques...* (Paris: Geofroy Tory & Gilles Gourmont, 1529), f. xlii. v°. The gridded design confirms Tory's doubts about ambiguities of voice and writing. To the left of the rebus: "En telles sottes choses la bonne Orthographe & vraye pronunciation sont perverties bien souvant, & causent ung abus qui souvant empesche les bons esperits en deue escripture." [In such silly things good orthography and true pronunciation are often perverted, and cause abuse that often impedes good minds in correct writing.] The solemn words extend the very puns advanced in the context (*abus* invoking *rebus*, and *pervertie* a green P approaching a T, etc.).

and Charles IX. Study of Ronsard in the following chapter will determine how some of the elements of Marot's poetics and the Rabelaisian hieroglyph work in the industry of sonnet-writing.

3

RONSARD'S SONNET-PICTURES

In the first chapter we saw how axionometric designs of the *rondeau* pushed language into space, and how the printed letter became a hinge on which visibility and discourse appeared to be turning. In the second chapter, we observed that the Rabelaisian program signaled the creation of a silent hieroglyph binding writing to the dynamics of a world in rebirth and political change. Both Rabelais and Marot worked in turmoil and found destiny in the mediated fortunes of Humanism in the reign of Francis I.[1] The visual design of their work reveals an ideology of poetry running against the grain of dogma and, because of its demonic qualities, along the margins of censure. Vanguard writers in the print-culture of the 1530s, Marot and Rabelais changed the shape of the forms they inherited through a medium in flux. Elsewhere, in artistic programs underwriting the nascently central state, in which authority used writers and artists to glorify its image, Rabelais and Marot would appear to have exerted less influence. In the years of the ascending Valois monarchy, at least from the middle period of the reign of Francis I, the "signature-effect" of the king would appear to have depended increasingly on the styles of architecture and painting associated with him.[2] Ambivalence engendered by the protean dimension of the letter, and the seemingly unconscious areas that loosen the hold of a text's meaning, were not what patrons asked of their poets and historiographers: if the king was to be eternalized, the literary aura he contracted from his valets had to be written to insure his glory. According to this view, in the context of the monarchy and its esthetic programs, the arts would be conceived as highly mediated and subject to narrow channels of control. They would serve incumbent power and leave no doubt as to what they did, whom they advocated, or the extensiveness of their association with the king.

Such is the view we might apply to the Renaissance through the filter of the classical age that followed the Renaissance. Experimentation and the suppleness of the relations the artist held with

70

his Maecenas may have been greater and more complex in an era of increased religious conflict following the mid 1530s. Ronsard, the renowned poet of the French court for over thirty years, seems to underwrite his king all the while he used the world of print to change the status of poetry and politics. Contrary to Rabelais and Marot, Ronsard writes more from the center than the margins of France. He embodies wit and literacy that enable him to display to his monarchs the ideals of language they could never attain. Yet, paradoxically, the ambiguities of his poetry share much with the visual innovations we have seen in earlier or marginal literatures. Ronsard is often received as a poet who imports "Southern" or Italian traditions into the rose gardens of Touraine. He also owes much to the "Northern" practices of the letter that reach back to a common inspiration in Villon and his contemporaries. In this section I would like to see if the *Amours* (1552−53) extend the innovations of print developed among Humanists of the 1530s, and if the context and the tactics Ronsard uses confirm and betray an official literature that desires to be impervious to change over passage of time.

Despite holding the status of an institution carving its lines into the memory of every French school-child, his writing develops effects of the letter that fashion an unconscious rhetoric. Its graphic and textual nature allows meaning to move in ways that speech cannot control, and simultaneously to transform verbal expression into pictural movement. The sonnet becomes a medium in which visual properties of the print are essayed in terms of center and circumference, of vanishing points and verbal anamorphosis. Montages and transformations of style are staged in the sonnets by virtue of the serial disposition of typography. The letter constantly shifts between pictographic, ornamental, and discursive roles, becoming a figure literalizing its referent in its own form, thus acquiring plasticities that call in question its verbal or "phonocentric" functions of relay. Ronsard's lyrics are so graphic that they can appear to fit in a renewed "reform" of writing − that is aligned with Louis Meigret − but their poetic license grants transgression of its principles.[3] The poet gains greater glory when he breaks the laws of his own constitution.

Marot and Rabelais use the pun to foster expansion and revolution of poetry. Equivocation unsettles speech, it divides and multiplies meaning wherever letters can break unilateral movements of reason. Ronsard seems to abandon the *équivoque* in favor of the oxymoron. But when he folds the anagram into the oxymoron, the visibility

71

of the letter is used as it had been with writers of the earlier years of Evangelism. The delicate rapport of equivocation and oxymoron can serve as our mode of entry into Ronsard's sonnets. Now since by 1552 the sonnet had replaced the *rondeau* as a preferred form of lyrical verse, we have to wonder how spatiality also changed. Marot had played upon center and circumference and opening and closure. The narratives within the textual space of his *rondeaux* appeared to be a function of the figure of the circle. By contrast, the sonnet seems to disavow a central point of origin and to extend a horizontal axis that aligns its aspect with a pictural frame. The supple flow of lines within its perimeters might provide for an errant, wandering narration that need not "return" to fixed points as it had in the case of the *rondeau*. Thus, even if the sonnet is a "short" poetic form that lends itself to lyrical tones, its also provides space enough for the creation of verbal landscapes and narratives within its cadre, and also of a simultaneous play of "mimetic" and "diegetic" roles of language.

When seen together, the tension of landscape and of narrative shows how the writing of the sonnet mixes pictural and discursive elements. The play of description, fabulation, and allegory engenders a pictographic world determined by the letter's visibility. The latter figures as an agent in a network of greater serial configurations that supplant voice or speech, and that make rhythm a graphic condition of verse. Each sonnet becomes thus an allegory of its own production. Words do not always work as single vocables, units of meaning, or the mosaic bits of a greater representation.[4] At the same time as Ronsard was drafting the *Amours*, the Italian artists residing at Fontainebleau were finding extraordinarily complicated ways of collapsing representation through multifarious allegories that crossed boundaries of poetry and painting.[5] They distorted scenes taken from classical literature by combining the original descriptions with arcana, grotesques, and ornamental designs from print-culture. Ronsard elaborated his poetics both through the world of their imagination and the tradition of Latin and Greek poets his "brigade" had been studying under the tutelage of Jean Dorat in the 1530s.

In this context the sheen of *description* that appears to take hold in allegory masks and reveals a more forceful display of words having rapport with their own contours. They are in dialogue, as in Marot or Rabelais, with seasonal and erotic drives. Description takes part in rhythmic compositions of letters that are cast as pictural and serial units. Once again, typography displaces the notion of either seasonality (presence of change or difference itself) and Eros (an originary force motivating language and engendering new and future forms) into self-reflective and self-authenticating worlds.[6] At these points the letter conflates *pictura* and *poesis*: writing makes a picture of what it describes, and pictures become the writing they had originally foregrounded as either images or referents. Ronsard appears to cultivate inversions and confusions of the two registers.

Doubling and bending mark Ronsard's most famous sonnets, in which displacement of narrative takes place at points where meaning and graphic forms become visibly redundant. The same redundancies overlie one another, they multiply and, as it were, congeal the meanings of referents in their own graphic shape. The sixtieth sonnet of the *Amours* was printed thus in 1553:

LX

Comme un chevreuil, quand le printemps destruit
L'oyseux crystal de la morne gelée,
Pour mieulx brouster l'herbette emmielée
Hors de son boys avec l'Aube s'en fuit,
    Et seul, & seur, loing de chiens & de bruit,
Or sur un mont, or dans une vallée,
Or pres d'une onde à l'escart recelée,
Libre follastre où son pied le conduit:
    De retz ne d'arc sa liberté n'a crainte,
Sinon alors que sa vie est attainte,
D'un trait meurtrier empourpré de son sang:
    Ainsi j'alloy sans espoyr de dommage,
Le jour qu'un oeil sur l'avril de mon age
Tira d'un coup mille traitz dans mon flanc.[7]

[Like a shammy, when the Spring smashes
Lazy crystals of the jellied dew of morn,
To better browse the honeyed grasses,
Out of his wood at Dawn will flee
    Alone, and sure, far from dogs and scorn,
Over a golden hill, or down in a valley,
Or even on a wave traced apart and afar,
Free to follow his foot that will lead him a way:
    Of net or arrow his freedom has no fear,
Unless, then when his life is at bay
From the blow of a shaft blazoned with his blood:
    I wandered, never with fear of fray,
When an eye gazing on my April's youth one day
In my breast shot a thousand shafts with a thud.]

On a cursory glance, the poem imbues a Petrarchan model with an immediacy and sensuality the Italian verse had never known.[8] The sonnet draws its figures from Bembo and Scève[9] and stock expression from themes of melancholy, the black spring of depression. Yet the effects of melancholy are undone by wit of graphics. The type and letter of the poem open the verse on to a field of arcane and comic play. None of the *Amours* would appear to illustrate better how a pictural sense of oxymoron extends the condensed points, puns and patently equivocal epithets first glimpsed in Marot.[10] Few of Ronsard's poems display so obviously syntactic combinations that meld opposites, such as in the first and second lines, where scansion shows that spring, generally a personification of birth and life, *murders* its subject when the eye reaches the end of the first line,

... quand le printemps *destruit*,

or in the chemical compounding of ooze and crystal that immediately follows, in

... *l'oyseux crystal* ...

Increased sensation of movement comes with distension of analogy, leaving the impression of errant words breaking the symmetries of Marot's heritage of "fixed forms." The visibility of two separate forms in one figure, unlike equivocation, that tends to be more comic than descriptive, is able to convey complexities of doubt, fear, and the indecision of love. In this way *l'oyseux crystal* represents dew between two seasons, melting and freezing, just as *la morne gelée* equates a melancholic condition with dawn, when the sad gel of winter, shown in the previous oxymoron of the same line, makes ready either to congeal or to warm the sap of love. Heavy presence of oxymoron invests a new sense of desire into the lyric, in which unrequitedness or unfulfilled wishes ground a greater will to write. The allure of a condition of nauseous desire (that we know best from the experience of Sartre) is merely staged to make the sonnet fulfill itself in its own compositional scheme: sadness generates depressive life needed, according to a scheme of creation known in our world of existentialism, to yield good poetry.[11] In this light Ronsard might be seen partaking of the tradition of the vanguard that writes great verse to mock the sad movements of emotion said to inspire writing.[12] The honeydewed grass of *l'herbette emmielée* would reflect the tearful melancholy of the poet who sees himself as a chamois (shammy), roebuck or goat-like deer lost in a landscape in springtime.

But sadness only underscores the poet's comic mendacity. Somehow the "lazy crystal" and "sad jelly" seem either too evident, obtuse or even redundant to herald a poem comparing a cervine to a writer. After having broken the ice of the inaugural line with the metaphor of the poet as shammy, the beast roams about until the tenth line, after its premonition of an arrow brings the beast and writer to their bloody demise. Enmeshed in a sonnet treating of desire, the poet and deer are found in a crossfire of cause and effect. Through the extended comparison of the poet to a deer emerges the system of distortion that heightens the pictorial dimension of the sonnet.

Here and in other sonnets the poet is typified as a prisoner of love. His melancholy tells of sadness that the graphic wit immediately betrays. A webbing of letters translates the mood into technical issues of rhythm and space. In fact, the striking movement of waves ("Or sur un mont, or dans une vallée ...") appears to be an enchantment whose melody almost forces us to disavow the closure of the pictorial composition. A description of the objects includes all the necessary information to stage the narrative. The time is April Fool's day, the temperature is about thirty-two or thirty-three degrees Fahrenheit; we are at the edge of a field and a forest, where deer hunters stalk their prey at dawn, when the animals are prone to forage before settling down after mid-morning. The light is golden, with the "rosy-fingered" dawn casting shafts of light through the trees under which the hunter sits in silence.

But all of a sudden, ice melts into glue. With *l'oyseux crystal* the dull edges of crystallized dew turn the tactile sensation, anticipated in the figure of ice and ooze, to the hidden vocabulary of fowling (*oiselerie*) that includes nets used to trap *both* roebucks and little birds (*oiselets*) — which the text confirms with *retz* or "net" seven lines below. The prey, or *oiseau*, is already contained in the "inganno" or stratagem used to capture the bird, in the honied stickum or birdlime, that is, the glue mixed from manure and honey that fowlers apply to branches and rocks on which birds are wont to perch. *Oyseux crystal* is thus not a simple oxymoron, but an allusion to the craft of catching small birds that is mixed with figures used in the lexicon of the hunt for bigger game. One register flows into another. The feathered animal is congealed or sticks to letters that describe venery in general. In, for example, *De retz ne d'arc sa liberté n'a crainte* (line 8), *retz* denotes a fowler's net and, by extension, what hunters in the Touraine use to catch small deer. But *retz* pertains to the prison of love that had been central to metaphors of hunting ever since the *XV joies de mariage* early in the fifteenth century. At first we thought we were chasing deer, but now we are fooled enough to see that Ronsard is confusing mammals with fowl. The poem appears to contain a taxonomy of available techniques of venery.

The figure thresholds a series of questions: will the deer be hounded by a pack of dogs? Like a bird, will the *chevreuil* be trapped in a net? Or will it fall prey to some kind of an arrow? or all of them at once? All outcomes are possible, since evidence in the verbal texture indicates the presence of yet another instrument that kills both bird and cervine. With *l'oyseux crystal, la morne gelée* underscores the presence of a common term, the half-named *arbaleste à gelais*, a "stone-bow" used to shoot all types of prey. Cotgrave registers it among an array of names that Ronsard knew well: "Arbaleste: f. *A crosse-bow; also, a Bow-net; also, the sinewie Crosse-Bow, wherewith a man shoots, not deere, but his deerest.* Arbaleste à boulet. *A Stone-bow.* Arbaleste à gelais. *The Same.*" The instrument seems to be a hidden form in the field of letters opened between one figure and the other:

l oyseux crystal

l arbaleste à gelais

l amorne gelée

The instrument mediates the net, the glue, and the bow all the while it negates all causality that would move from the hunter and weapon to the shooting of the prey. *Arc* of the eighth line swings back to the deadening effects of the shaft already literally – graphically – frozen in the second line. The honey-like fields where the roebuck loves to graze, rendered in *l'herbette emmielée*, appear to draw upon a commonplace of poetic description, but only enough in the montage to outline the silhouette of the stone-bow between *herbette* and *gelée. Herbette emmielée* abbreviates the more common poetic diminutive, *herbelette*, that had been stock and stuff of descriptive poetry of the early years of the century.[13] Through the mask of *herbette* cast over *herbelette* emerges *arbaleste*. But *herbette* can be read alternately with *herbelette*, because, on the one hand, it mediates the homonym, *erre beste*, which spells out in silence the figure of the wandering roebuck, the "errant beast" of prey or the *chevreuil* itself; and on the other, because *herbelette* alludes obliquely to the weapon already signaled in *morne gelée*. Its name is twisted anamorphically in the descriptive plan of

76

the text to confound an order that leads from origin to finality. Though never mentioned, *arbaleste à gelais* acquires a pervasively fantasmatic, unmarked presence through the disposition of the letters that comprise the same figures. Visual analogy is prompted through half-hidden terms that emerge from the configurations of words and characters that flow in and about each other.[14]

The time of the poem, we have noted, is morning. Nature is dull, indistinct, hence in dreamy confusion that, in the world of language, would resemble amphiboly. The moment has to be animated or awakened from its topical slumber in order to explode into life. With *morne gelée*, morning gives way to *morne*, a precondition to the ideology of creation or, in Cotgrave's words, a saturnine feeling: "sad, heavie, lumpish, low; pensive, agreeved, in a melancholic mood, all in dumps; also, dull, stupide, sottish, senceless, blockish." *Morne* "describes" the effect of *oyseux* in its most visible reading, but it reverses itself in turning the reference to venery back to an iconic rapport with spears and arrows. *Morner* ("to dull or blunt the point of a weapon") was close to the adjective *morne* that was attached to lances, designating blunt heads used to strike birds of prey.

The series is quadruply redundant; the decasyllable sticks in the glue of letters since *crystal* concludes, before the fact, what *gelée* announces. And in terms of the iconography of melancholy, *oyseux* is already *morne*. The doubling has undone what the spring of the first line "destroys," so that *oyseux* conceals the calm of a nauseous silence, it seems, of a lettered or eternally bookish condition that music cannot bring to life. The melancholic figures of each oxymoron have the impact of blunting creation through their congealment in the typography. The poem betrays the allure of seasonal and other differences located in the first four figures of the three opening lines (the poet as a roebuck, spring on the edge of winter, birds caught in the glue of ice, and the morning crystallized in dew).

Literal and metaphorical characters "freeze" the poet's love; they marry incompatible terms that are already joined over and again throughout the rest of the poem. *L'oyseux crystal*, the queasy symptom of melancholy, redounds in the barks of hounds heard through *oy* (line 4): from the aural dimension of barking in the first instance of the second line (**oy**seux) is echoed the *boys* (line 4) of the *aboys* before the dogs are designated in the following verse. Their effect precedes their presence, just as the foot (or hoof) leads the body of the deer in the image of errancy first connoted in *herbette* that leads to the formula, *libre follastre où son pied le* *conduit* (line 8). The figure and its echo meet only afterwards, when the twelfth line retraces the second half of the analogy of dogs and barking begun with *Comme* ... in the first verse: "ainsi j'alloy sans espoyr de dommage" (line 12).

These are only the first of many ricochets defining the spatial frame of the sonnet, and also the abyssal graphics in its central zone. Implied is that Ronsard's perimeters of description, like those of any poet exploiting the genre to its limit, are written to mark infinitely receding planes of figures in visual perspective. This is indeed a variant of anamorphosis, and of mirror-writing[15] that displays a number of vanishing "points" which are indicated by the individual letters of the sonnet. An initial and crucial point is found at the axis of the poem; it can be detected by a converging trajectory that is marked in the graphics. The poem appears to have a narrative that follows the path of the chamois. Yet the overall form leads us not only from beginning to end, but also from the periphery toward the center. The sonnet uses its visual structure to mime the hunt, when hunters close in upon the quarry from the four corners of the forest where it roams. In this respect, *or* reflects one of the limits and axes of the tableau. Hovering near the virtual center in a volley of anaphora that appears to evoke the visible undulations of water and sound,

> *Or* sur un mont, *or* dans une vallée
> *Or* pres d'une onde à l'escart recelée,

or seems to be an instance of a litanic repetition that does *not* equivocate on "then" and "gold," as the *Grand Rhétoriqueurs* had done so often.[16] The two letters convey a logic of spacing, of movement, but also of allegory. Allusion is made to the landscape of a Golden Age, where shimmering surfaces of amber hue – of sun and the money of poetry – convey the effects of glorious eternity. Because the aural echo rebounds across the entire sonnet from the flurry of anaphora in the middle[17] (see opposite) to the upper and lower edges, all the attributes of reality are found gilded, glazed and polished in the yellow haze of a closed diorama. Golden hoarfrost, a golden pasture, a rolling golden hillside, and golden eyes are suggested in the mimetic layer of the sonnet. In its graphic configuration that engenders the movement, *or* is nonetheless a sign of amphiboly in the letters *o-r*. They figure as gold in a monetary sense, since by way of *or* the silent music or uncommon beauty of what Ronsard has written is signified to bear exchange-value. The curvilinearity of the poem likens it to a sign of money. Because of

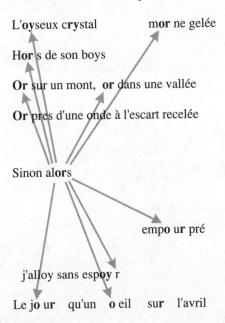

L'oyseux crystal

Hor s de son boys

Or sur un mont, or dans une vallée

Or près d'une onde à l'escart recelée

Sinon alors

mor ne gelée

empo ur pré

j'alloy sans espoy r

Le jo ur qu'un o eil sur l'avril

their central position in the picture, the two letters draw attention to the conditions in which the poem is written. It is a polished, esthetic creation that implicitly carries its price tag in its form,[18] and in this way is not that far from the monetary shape of the *rondeau* that Marot had associated with a coin. Like his predecessor, Ronsard appears to be composing poems in view of the returns he will gain from their beauty, with the difference that the sonneteer, having less investment in spiritual salvation than his predecessor, pays more heed to the working relations he keeps with his patrons and readers.[19]

The ricochet of *or* throughout the sonnet implicitly identifies economic with spatial freedom. The liberty of the poem turns into a strictly defined closure that tells of an implicit pact: if a poem is successful, it will shine with the reflection of what it will bring to the author. Thus the anagrams that have the letters *o-r* reverberate freely through the space imply an associative infinity but are really set within a pattern of constrictive redundancies set at either end of the lines and the top and bottom of the poem. A term at one end is mirrored in letters or in meaning by a similar term at the other. Constriction of movement results, and so does an effect of visible claustrophobia. Schematically, if the consonance of figures and letters is mapped, closure operates vertically and horizontally at once:

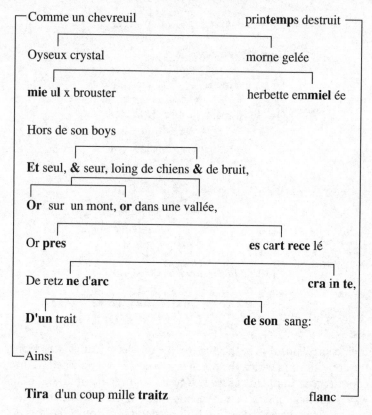

Freedom of verbal metamorphosis in both the shifting patterns of words and their plural combinations is arrested in linear duplications and mirrorings recurring visually in the cadre of the sonnet, in the structure of the decasyllable, and even in the coextension of the same units of letters at either end of each line. The landscape is charted according to a logic that places letters in spatial tension. From the outset, the narrative is already self-reflective when *comme* announces the coming of an extended metaphor framing both the roebuck and the greater portion of the poem. The figure unwinds from the first to the twelfth line and closes with the arrival of *ainsi*. On the one hand, echoes are doubled over the letters so that when reading is begun, the telling of the buck's tale has *already* been done. The pattern of simultaneity disperses from the first line to the others and races through its networks: we note, instantaneously, that many words are reflecting each other through sets of recurring vocables. *Res* and its variants can be mapped thus:

Comme un chevreuil, quand le printemps destruit

L'oyseux crystal de la morne gelée,

Pour mieulx brouster l'herbette emmielée

Hors de son boys avec l'Aube s'en fuit,

Et seul, & seur, loing de chiens & de bruit,

Or sur un mont, or dans une vallée,

Or pres d'une onde à l'escart recelée,

Libre follastre où son pied le conduit;

De retz ne d'arc sa liberté n'a crainte,

Sinon alors que sa vie est atteinte,

D' un trait meurtrier empourpré de son sang:

Ainsi j'alloy sans espoyr de dommage,

Le jour qu'un oeil sur l'avril de mon age

Tira d'un coup mille traitz dans mon flanc.

A net-effect is produced such that the graphic picture of the poem embodies the figure of the *retz* in which both birds and *chevreuil* are caught unawares. In this respect the silent rhythms of the poem depend on serial placement and recurrences of the term *res* or *retz*. It appears that the letters of the poem are "mapping," gridding, or furnishing coordinates for a spatial reading. The serial disposition, recurrence, and distortion of groups of vocables emerge to form a basis for the harmonics of the text. If they do, then it could be said that the enthralling music of the verse has visual inspiration.

The play of letters depends on a skein of figures within enclosing borders. It appears that the *chevreuil*, so akin to the poet, contains in anagram what might be the *levrier* or hound that barks after him. Pursuit leads to the *livre*, suggested in *libre*, which encrypts the poet's desire. The signs of the beginning are marked in *œil* at the conclusion. Sheen of "un *œil sur l'avril* de mon age" (line 14) masks an echo of the *chevreuil* heralded as the first figure of the poem, as in the chimera of a *chevre-œil*. The craziness of the moment

81

("follastre") or of madness under a saturnine sign of the zodiac (*fol-astre*, or mad star) is called forth at the opening of the fourth month when the liberty proclaimed in the lyric is simultaneously foreclosed. April becomes an omnipresently graphic souvenir of winter, or *iver*. *Avril* (line 13) arches back to the suspended warmth announced in *quand le printemps destruit...*, the moment when spring offers destruction in the place of rebirth.

Everywhere eyes stare out of the poem. The *chevreuil* is a sort of errant pupil. Then l'*oyseux* crystal is the mannequin that discloses the presence of the same eye. We can remark that the poem uses language in a manner that resembles a spherical or lenticular aberration that draws the words back to two points of origin in the middle of the sonnet. Center and circumference are discerned as axes of a contour and border of the middle (lines 6–8) turned along the creases of a statement echoing at once the end of seasons, of language and of the illusion of space:

> Or pres d'une *onde* à l'escart recelée
> *Libre* follastre *où* son pied le conduit:
> De retz ne d'arc sa *liberté* n'a crainte.

In the shift from April to the icy liberty in the center, the buck's hoof and the poet's foot are found frozen in their visual meter. In an emblematic turn that again recalls anamorphosis, the sign of death is creased into *c-r-â-n-e* that slips along the sharp edge of the feared arrow, in the sight of an oneiric death's head in the point of a fearful arrow (*crane* embedded in *ne d'arc...crainte*, in which we see what the roebuck fails to discern, but in the words that the beast cannot decipher). The bones of the skeleton are obvious in *oyseux* above or even in the flow of a wave rolling from a watery referent to a figural enigma in the *onde* of the text over the redundant *où*, the enigmatic "where" that marks the secret space of the poem and the poet.

In the relation of economy, writing, typography, and simulation of death that has been suggested up to this point, Ronsard appears to be a poet signing his name under the aegis of destiny. The demise planned for the roebuck is undone by the sheer brilliance of the graphic play of letters within and beyond the narrative.[20] The poet *arrests* death in the graphic strata of the song, most obviously in the double-edged opening – and closing – of the clearing by the trees, in what, if we follow Yves Bonnefoy's terminology, might be the *vrai-lieu* of the poem, the optical center, in:

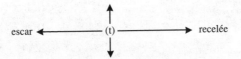

At the vanishing point we happen upon a figure that half-traces and squares or quarters itself, *escartelée*, along four sides at once as trace and trees, tendril and fret on the border and groove already frayed before the poem has reached its outer or lower edges. The *t* traces the voiceless rhythm of another *memento mori*: in *escart recelée*, it literalizes a sign of silence; but also, of a trace that moves, or of a tress that waves; it suggests that the *t* can elide into *retz* to make a *trace*, the very palinym of *escart*, or the square disposition of the poem. *Trez* and *Retz* recur elsewhere in the graphics, in such protean form that they tend to arrest the movement of the letters at the same time as their meaning pushes them backwards and forwards:

printemps de**str**uit	l'oyseux crys**tal**
brou**ster**	l'**escart** recelée
folla**stre**	
retz ne d'arc	**crainte**
tira d'un coup	**traitz**

A variety of echoed retracings, redundancies and verbal antici-pations races over what has already occurred in the descriptive layer of the sonnet. They are allusively drawn along simple repetitions of words. *Trait* engenders *traitz*; *et* leads to *et*, *&* is doubled by *&*. Semantic bends go along with those of the landscape, with *mont* leading to *vallée*, or the serpentine *onde* softening the angular con-notations of *escart*. Specular shapes multiply, when *un trait* is both one and many in the expression of *d'un coup mille traitz*. *Boys* becomes an equivocation, the word heralding the bark or *aboys* of the *chiens* just as the hoof announces the deer that follows. Para-grammatical or unconscious orders become evident: *son* shifts from a possessive pronoun modifying *boys* to the graphic echo of sound (*son*). The noisy bark of dogs is transmuted into a silent fantasm of lust. A rebus-shape of accumulated letter-targets seems to emerge as bulls' eyes in the shape of **O** in *or, ou, oeil, coup*, etc. Plastic aberrations of the same shapes run over each other through parono-masia (*dommage* is half-visible in *de mon age* that resembles *dans mon flanc*, and so forth).[21] The text races through its labyrinth of lines.

Plate 5. Chimerical letter "O" in a French edition of Plutarch
(Paris: Abel Angelier, 1584). The silvan figures who grasp the
outer arc of the letter belong to the tradition of grotesque
developed in the School of Fontainebleau. Their shape and
movement appear at odds with the fixity of the letter in the
ornate frame. The name of the engraver is unknown.

At the same time the allure of a melancholic deer leads to a ribald
farce of force, or to laughter. What, we can ask, is it to be "like"
a roebuck or a chimerical *chevreuil*? To "brouste" or browse the
honey-sweetened grass? To be both on a hill and in a vale? To be
free where a member leads the body? Ronsard alludes to a number
of half-clichés, or proverbs of folkloric stamp which put the image
of the forlorn chamois on the hillside against a comic backdrop.
The underside of the text must have been obvious to Ronsard's alert
readers. Current verbal emblems are recalled, such as "Où la chevre
est liée faut qu'elle brouste," "A la chandelle la chevre semble
belle" or "Chevauchons la chevre en la vallée," whose flavor
Cotgrave retains in Elizabethan English: "The goat must brouse
where she is bound," "He that chuses a wife by candle-light, or

84

by other eyes than his own, may perhaps be foully deceived," and "Let us undertake a dangerous taske." Things goatish are always horny – endless, desirous, cornucopian and erotic. The roebuck is a wild goat in rut, but only partially in garb of a love-stricken animal of desire. When the echo of the proverbs is heard from the imprint of the words, laughter dismantles the framework of the source and the original effect of unrequited desire.[22]

In later editions of the *Amours* Ronsard prunes the text and cuts away much of its proverbial force. The heritage of the sonnet shows how it accedes, via its own censure, to a more stable condition of metaphor in final form in the 1587 edition. In general, the system of description remains closed and unchanged if the axial ensemble of *comme– chevreuil– printemps* and *ainsi– un œil sur l'avril– mille traitz* is treated as a set of oppositions pivoting about *Libre– livre* at the nexus. But since the substructure is articulated by the doubled closure of graphic terms at every point along four cardinal directions (both up and down and left and right) that traces multiple binds and a collapse of cause and effect, the later variants indicate that seemingly conscious confusions of confinement and venery (for example, the identity of the themes of containment and hunting, in *chas* and *chasse*) are excised. The unconscious that mixes and elides words and letters is written out or, in other words, rectified in a style signalling a square measure of the classical style that was to characterize the art and poetry of the following century:

LX

> Comme un chevreuil, quand le printemps détruit
> Du froid hyver la poignante gelée,
> Pour mieus brouter la feuille emmielée,
> Hors de son bois avec l'Aube s'enfuit:
> Et seul, & seur, loin de chiens & de bruit,
> Or' sur un mont, or' dans une vallée,
> Or' pres d'une onde à l'escart recelée,
> Libre s'egaye ou son pied le conduit:
> De retz ne d'arc sa liberté n'a crainte
> Sinon alors que sa vie est attainte
> D'un trait sanglant qui le tient en langueur.
> Ainsi j'alloys sans espoir de dommage,
> Le jour qu'un oeil sur l'Avril de mon age
> Tira d'un coup mille traits en mon coeur.[23]

> [Like a shammy, when the spring will smash
> The cold winter of the bite of morn
> To better browse about the honeyed leaves,

85

Out of his wood at dawn he flees,
  Alone, and sure, far from dogs and scorn,
On a golden hill, or down in the valley,
Or even a wave swelling over and afar,
Free to dip where his foot will lead him away:
  Of either net or bow his freedom has no fear,
Unless, then, when his life is at bay,
From a languid arrow blazoned with his blood:
  Thus I erred, with neither fear nor fray,
When an eye gazing on my April's age, one day,
In my heart shot a thousand shafts with a thud.]

In breaking the ice of the former *l'oyseux crystal de la morne gelée*, in order to glide from winter to spring without coagulation of two oxymorons, the second line gains meaning by underscoring the seasonal change announced in the first line. Spring replaces winter with less conflict, triumphing immediately in the undisturbed break from the first to the second line; thanks to the shift of the genitive in the second line, which had established so much mobility in the two redundant figures of 1553, in the later version the reader's eyes flow with a syntax marching forward along the line of scansion. Louis Terreaux notes that modification of "L'oyseux crystal de la morne gelée" through *froid hyver* and *poignante gelée* is difficult to interpret. The change, he notes, is "expressive" since "la gelée n'est poignante que dans un hiver froid" [the frost bites only in a cold winter].[24] The critic seems to be looking to life in search of poetic truth. A cold winter cannot tell us why Ronsard rewrote the line. Since the poem stages a pictural and graphic complex of issues, the line appears to be less "expressive" simply because it represses earlier ambivalence and redundancy that had been gained through the use of oxymoron and verbal anamorphosis. It motivates the melting of ice phonically. As if the poet were victim of his own illusion of oral plenitude, Ronsard rewrites the second line to project the same feel of flow as in the fifth, sixth and seventh lines. The errant beast that runs in every direction, in the amphiboly of *herbette/erre beste* of 1552, is now turned far more correctly − and bookishly − as a *paginal* leaf. As if, too, he were expunging all the fears engendered by the mixed jargon of archery and fowling in the latent text of the first writing, Ronsard looks to the aura of poet-roebuck browsing through the gilded pages of his past, redressing and correcting himself, *pour mieux brouter la feuille emmielée*. In other words, the confident poet writes of the act of his own rewriting. Orthographic change all but erases the equivalence of honey of *mieu(l)x* with its inscription *emmielée* in 1553. In glossing the rewriting of the sonnet, we see Ronsard seeing himself in his own past and revising it according to the needs of the present. The changes that are applied amount to a screen-writing, or the lamination of one surface over another that makes a past form disappear and come into view in the same flicker of montage.[25]

If Ronsard was capitalizing on innovations that had marked the anagram and equivocation in the 1530s and 1540s, his extended metaphor of errancy, so present in the text of 1553, now follows a fairly orthogonal trajectory. Pieces of words traduce the writing of a subject – an author with a signature – whose body is compressed into pages and incised with characters. The poem is now the living evidence of the writer whose presence is in the ink, paper, and embossed contours of the book. Through the poem Ronsard has become a *li(v)re follastre* or a "foliated body," a *corps folié.*[26] In this way *Libre s'egaye où son pied le conduit* tightens the rapport of the process of metaphor to the description. *Follastre* of 1553 had verbalized madness and traced the astrological forces determining love; its grammatical sign was supple enough to function first adjectively in rapport to *libre* so as to project the epithet into a *livre*, since *folastrer* (Huguet: "répandre capricieusement," to display capriciously) appeared to be a form less common than *follastre* (adj.) or even *folastrie*. The inflection of browsing, confirming the statement of the third line, was turned into chimeras produced by dismantled syntax – a view on to a scene of language disrupting the order of an implied contract between the poet and the reader being addressed. In effect, after *Libre follastre*, a foot is immobilized, it has nowhere to go. But with *s'egaye*, the trajectories of arrow, career and writing are straightened. In 1587, not only does the anagrammar betray the contract of communication with the sign of *s-a-g* – ostensively, the sagittal trait of December in Ronsard's zodiac of wit – but also its meaning of stretching, amplifying, spreading forward, dispersing or following a line projects a more orthogonal condition of language. *S'egaye* undoes the ambiguity of *libre* and forces its meanings to follow the path of the advancing foot and the broader analogy of the poem in the rhythm of the comparison with *comme*. Obviously the verb shares euphony with *de retz* in the next line and allows anticipation to replace the doubly specular and self-erasive movement of unsettled discourse in the 1553 version.

But we may be forcing a reading of the 1587 text to adduce how Ronsard loses sight of the potential of the letter. True, the later

editions lack the graphic ambiguities of the work of 1553, but nonetheless Ronsard moves ambivalently, sometimes forward, but also
backward, faithful to much of the indeterminacy that typography
had generated in the earlier *Amours*. *Libre s'egaye* does concur with
the image of castration in *Hors de son boys*, since *egayer*, or the
homonym *aiguayer*, means "to cleanse a horse or dog before the
hunt" so that its odor will not cause the prey to flee. The revision
follows the anamorphic twist initiated in the 1553. In *aiguayer*, it is
clear that where a hunted animal washes itself in a pool of water,
it does so to avoid letting its captors sniff its musky aroma. The
beast pursued is seen using the ruses of its hunters. Ronsard evokes
again the morning dew from *aigue* and *aiguail* (Larousse du XIXe
siècle: "rosée du matin qui demeure par petites gouttes sur les
feuilles et les brins d'herbe," morning dew that remains on leaves
and shoots of grass in droplets) within the verb and alludes now
both to the venery and horticulture implied by *égayer* (to sprinkle
or, in *s'égayer*, to plunge all of sudden in water) and to cut, pare
and prune in the fashion of figures printed on calendars for the
months of March and April. Again, the poem absorbs in its vocables
the figures of the seasons as depicted in contemporary iconography.
But with the change from

> D'un trait meurtrier empourpré de son sang
> Ainsi j'alloy sans espoyr de dommage
> Le jour qu'un oeil sur l'avril de mon age
> Tira d'un coup mille traitz dans mon flanc

into

> D'un trait *sanglant* qui le tient en *langueur*
> (...)
> Tira d'un coup mille traits en mon *cœur*

neglect of the visual aspects of love promotes greater mimesis.
Hence the sight of language disappears once its meaning is grasped.
The doubled unit of self-reflective difference of *"trait meurtrier"*
is restricted to specularity in the adjective – *sanglant* – in the ribs.
In 1587, the bloody shaft tends not to penetrate but to accompany
the beast. Replacement of *flanc* by *cœur* turns the poem into a
Valentine card conventionalizing the vocabulary and wiping away
the blood clotted on the roebuck's dark winter fur of 1552. The
rewriting seems to indicate that Ronsard is afraid of the force of
his own text, of an earlier, unconscious stage that he watches over,
sometimes censures, veils, but also reveals through a mania to retouch
and revise.

Now we can advance some summary remarks prior to taking up
the relation of the letter as enigma in the frame of the *Amours*.
Obviously the allure of a referential plenitude of a natural landscape
and a scene of venery are summoned only to be twirled in graphic
anamorphosis through distortion of sound and figure. A verbal
picture and a grid of letters is produced. The poem is a silent scene,
in which the threat of the lover's gaze is mirrored by the pleasure
of the reader looking upon the characters that turn the hunt into
a serial rhythm of letters. Silence and din of dawn are mirrored;
the hunt takes place in the noise of a glass house, in miniature,
where all effect is a form of baiting, or the recounting of origins
within themselves.[27] In a fashion not at all dissimilar to Baudelaire's
and Sartre's insistence on the incapacity of letters to reflect anything
except our mania to copy them, the text of "Comme un chevreuil..."
and its rewriting turns its mimetic world in an act of *tracing*. The
roebuck follows the path of the text but is arrested in typographical
silence. Since the acts of writing and hunting are suggested to be the
same, the sonnet opens on to its economic dimension as a graphic
performance made to gain *or*, the aura of gold that will perpetuate
the author's body and name. The *retz* happens to be its net effect,
but also a race or a pursuit for capital gains. The poem is a sign of
itself as a lettered object, a *res*, a thing, of entirely material form
that tells us how its effects are obtained and in what conditions it
is written. Above all, the vocables and letters appear to be mapped
according to spatial and serial codes that have a visual grammar
independent of, and at play with, the verbal dimension. The sonnet
internalizes modes of pictural and emblematic composition, and
through the process the unconscious of the text emerges, especially
in retinal suspension where their differences are conflated. Typographic form produces an effect of camouflage that hides and reveals
the art of its dissimulation, that is, its venery.[28] No less, in "Comme
un chevreuil," the temporal frame is placed between the end of
March and the beginning of April, but also on the border of a verbal
mirror, between *l'iver* and *avril*. The sonnet articulates a montage
of conventional figures from other poems all the while its form
reproduces common images in emblem-books.[29] From the melange
emerges a moving, almost cinematic writing of shapes that appear,
dissolve, and recur through variation.

We can now wonder if Ronsard's poetry in general entertains a
similar relation with the unconscious. Is there a paragrammar that
works in conjunction with a pictural sensibility? Or is it confined
to only a few sonnets? Does Ronsard really control all the innuendo

of movement in the ingenuity of his designs? To continue dialogue with these questions, we must look to other sonnets that span the years of his career and then inquire about the politics of his innovations.

4

THE TURN OF THE LETTER: FROM CASSANDRE TO HÉLÈNE

In the third chapter we saw that Ronsard's sonnet is printed as both discourse and picture, and how, from their coextension, fantasmatic languages are born in silence. The *Amours* display a cardinal disposition of space and tend to engender subliminal, arcane figures within and about their printed letters. The sonnet is conceived as a latent grid on which characters move and recombine. Points of stress, connecting links, and perspectival objects are located through shifts of letters in serial rhythms that do not always follow a logic of description or narration. In this chapter we must ask further why the sonnet is crafted in such a manner. We will do well, now, to expand the field of inquiry, and see if it figures in a general transformation of discourse.

Associated with a cultural project that touched on orthographic reform, Ronsard defended the dominant church in the name of the laws of analogy that Catholic doctrine offered to its believers as proof of the divinity of the natural world. Yet, since his poems treat of poetry and its origins, they turn about themselves and their own conditions of being. As we have seen, they camouflage their modes of dissimulation, and stage imaginary regress to their beginnings within the scope of their completion. If the sonnet is born of the tension of its composition as both picture and a text, it must also tell of its birth while offering a vision of its eternity. The fantasy of the origin of creation that the poem projects would align Ronsard's name with myth and serve to mask the economic relations of patronage and politics that determine the writing.

We can begin with the notion of the letter as an agency of regress that Ronsard's sonnets proudly display in their mythography. In both a typographical and psychogenetic sense, as one critic has noted, "the letter gives way to an imagery vast as cosmography; on the one hand, it signifies extreme censure (O letter, how many crimes are committed in your name!), while on the other, extreme bliss (all poetry and the unconscious are a return to the letter)."[1] The letter in the *Amours* disrupts the continuity of its effects, but it also takes us back to the genesis of its composition. In a very general way such returns also stage a subject's initial and ever-repeated entry into the symbolic domain of language and its social laws. Imaginary regress to origins varies on the intertwined theme of autobiography and "adolescence."

In the middle years of the French Renaissance, when Ronsard published the first edition of the *Amours* of 1552–53, France saw itself in economic downslide, in increased civil strife, and facing unforeseen growth of its lettered classes. In these developments came debate over educational reform, the expansion of the middle class, and a general calming of orthographic experiment. Rhetorical orders were shifting toward visual schemes that could be taught more immediately than by Ciceronian models based on memory. Creeping into graphic sketches of daily life were scenes depicting the travails of the schoolmaster. With the dissemination of Alciatti's *Emblems*, pedagogical reform embraced the ways that images could teach official and vernacular tongues and imprint codes of moral conduct.[2] In ways that bear comparison with these general social trends, Ronsard's poetry "institutes" his readers through graphic ploys and transitional means that confuse letters with pictures, and pictures with writing. The work becomes so arcane in these areas that explication or "commentary"[3] on the poems sustains their secret and hermetic dimensions and enhances their overall worth.

Ronsard "returns" to the letter in order to fashion the drama of an originary glimpse of language and the birth of the reader as subject. Feigned regress depends on a studied conflation of legible and visible orders of discourse. A dialogical sensibility is entertained in the visual disposition of the sonnet, one that has Freudian connotations if dialogism can be understood to mean a liminary area between "primary" and "secondary" processes. In this respect the letter serves as a point of transition – if contemporary terminologies are used – between the "arbitrary" and "motivated" status of language, or "semiotic" and "symbolic" orders. If the trends of the sixteenth century are held in view, the letter would appear to mediate a subject's use of vernacular and classical language or, perhaps, serve as a material object that institutes a child who gains sudden access to print-culture and national education. The letter brings one to the threshold of languages, but also to worlds of ambivalent and manifold sensation. If a Freudian view can be recalled, it is an element of pictogrammar, a language of figure-sounds or portmanteau creations – fantasms and verbal chimeras fashioned from hidden, private languages — that analysts discover in their patients' words in the course of clinical therapy.[4] The same holds for a reader: because they share the gift of making from any form of writing a surface of contours and lines, letters dissociate writing from meaning, and thus become points of vanishment that can occlude meaning or direct language toward visual inscription. As we have seen, the typographic mark can serve as an *objet de perspective*[5] when it is grasped independently of its verbal relation in discourse. Since Tory, the square has defined and framed the bed of the letter and is integral to its overall signifying virtue.

Within this tradition the *Amours* appear to be one of the more effective experiments in the play of visibility, the letter, psychogenesis, and literary art. The 1552–53 editions celebrate the surface of letters in a universe of plastic tension. As a form both fixed and supple in its disposition, quite unlike the *rondeau* of Marot, the sonnet allows the poet to exploit and even speculate on its potential variety. When Ronsard first mastered it, he did so akin to a potter with clay or an artist with a brush,[6] using at once the verbal and visual arts to produce word-pictures that betray evidence of lettered "strokes" or traits. The sonnet appears to be something of a sketch of words and letters or lines, as we have seen, drawing up the net or "retz" of words. In the drift between the words *figured* as language and *seen* as lines is staged a calculated return to "repressed" dimensions in which letters and pictures are identical. Language and image move as an undifferentiated flow of energies that congeal, disperse, scatter, and flow, at some moments in recognizable patterns, at others in ways that produce configurations of grotesque, hidden languages that twist and turn with particular stress laid on movement.

Yet the concealed discourse in the dialogic areas of language being born can only be seen as fake. Ronsard appears to reach back to beginnings for the sake of putting his autograph at the origin of the world. Near the center of the first edition of the *Amours* we find a sonnet (XC) that uses Petrarchan form to refashion the *blason*, a genre of recent vintage in French circles of the 1540s. On the one hand, the *blason* uses detail or realistic "touches" to give marvel or erotic splendor to a part of the female body that is singled out for encomium. Attention to the grain and texture of flesh had been the stuff of Villon's *Testament*, recently unearthed by Marot, translated into Roman font, and exploited in the "Blason du beau tétin." For Marot, Villon's "Regrets de la belle Heaulmière" accumulate unsavory details that make up the aging woman's body and a source for his *contre-blason* of the "laid tétin." The old lady's thighs, spotted like sausages (*cuisses grivelées comme saucisses*), figure as elements from which the aspect of the whole of her person can be deduced. In the famous ballad of hate that is to be carried by the scribe's valet, Perrenet de la Barre, to his loathsome beloved, Villon spells his own name in acrostic but ends each line in *r*, the letter that incarnates his own rage and chagrin.[7] Ronsard transplants the themes and movement of Villon's poems throughout the *Amours* through the intermediary of Marot and others. But on the other hand, the *blason du corps féminin* had been an explosive genre of short but intense duration in the 1540s that had run its course. It self-destructed by mocking the circumstantial rhetoric at the very basis of its form and could not be sustained without some modification from without. Ronsard could make use of the genre's taste for fragment and detail to invoke Neoplatonic schemes from which every reader might deduce the greater cycles of life and spirit that were said to order the universe. At the same time, he could transpose the genre into the sonnet in order to animate a process of psychogenesis, or an instantaneous staging of the birth of subjectivity.[8] In the most minuscule shapes a path from object to ideal is drawn, and all the while the poem can move, as it had in the blason, to and from material and platonic registers.

Ronsard varies on the models taken from Villon, Marot, and poets of the 1540s. The words of the ninetieth sonnet curl and unfold; they caress the waves of hair they describe and retrace. Ostensively a blazon of his Cassandre's *chevelure*, the poem also stages a cliché taken from Aristophanes's fable of sexual origins told in the *Symposium* (xiii), in which the scission of indistinct matter into male and female components marks the beginning of the world. The sonnet sets the moment in place but enacts movement vacillating between primary and secondary mass in the play of letters and figures. As in other sonnets, visual tensions are established along the edges and center of the whole:

XC

Soit que son or se crespe lentement
   Ou soit qu'il vague en deux glissantes ondes,
   Qui çà qui là par le sein vagabondes,
   Et sur le col, nagent follastrement:
Ou soit qu'un noud diapré tortement
   De maintz rubiz, & maintes perles rondes,
   Serre les flotz de ses deux tresses blondes,
   Je me contente en mon contentement.
Quel plaisir est ce, ainçoys quelle merveille

Quand ses cheveux troussez dessus l'oreille
D'une Venus imitent la façon?
Quand d'un bonet son chef elle adonize,
Et qu'on ne sçait (tant bien elle desguise
Son chef doubteux) s'elle est fille ou garçon?

[Whether its silken gold is twisted slowly
Or whether it flows in two sliding waves
Swimming down along a bosom that cleaves,
And by the neck turns playfully:
Or if a knot that diapered twistingly
Of many a ruby and many rounded pearls
Squeezes the flow of these two blonde curls,
I fill myself with pleasure fulfillingly.
What a joy it is, rather, what ever sheer
Delight when her hair, lifted over her ear,
Can be the smile of Venus' great renown?
When with a cap she adonizes her crown
Can one know (so her disguise, so coy
Her face's frown) whether she is a girl or a boy?]

The lines of the sonnet follow the flow of his lady's flaxen hair. But the *chevelure* also embodies a verbal movement, a montage of graphic shapes that resemble not hair but their own act of being traced and molded into print. Curling down Cassandre's shoulders, swimming over her alabaster breasts, twisting, protean, the words follow the meanders of tresses "adonizing" her face and flow toward the fleece of her sex. Following a Neoplatonic mode, the poem "imitates the fashion" (line 11) of an idea seen through the approximation left in the movement of reading and writing.[9] Because of its proximity to that tradition, especially in the light of the ways Marot had played with its secrets, it is clear that a graphic mark is located at the virtual axis of the sonnet, but so that the quadrature of the whole can be reflected in miniature, in the shape of perspectival object visible *within* the vocables at the center. More exactly, at the middle of the second quatrain, the letter c is transformed into a pronoun in a hermetically plural possessive:

De maintz rubiz, & maintes perles rondes,
Se rre les flotz de **ses** deux tresses blond **es**,
Je me contente en mon contentement.

In this quatrain a graphic redundancy, like those seen in "Comme un chevreuil," establishes a relation of inner duplication between the center and edge of the median line. The initial **S** of *serre* recurs

95

doubled in the central figure, *ses*, so that its serpentine contour appears to mime the descriptive movement that depicts Cassandre as a reincarnation of Botticelli's Venus. The duplicated s of *ses* sets an imaginary mirror at the center, a mirror reflecting the lateral movement of *Se* and *es*:

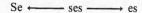

Hardly by chance, so it seems, the vowel **e** appears mute before the visual splendor of the sibilant – and sibylline – consonant it modifies. The possessive *ses* tends to give allegorical weight to Cassandre's hair in terms peculiar to painting and typography. Because of the shape and the site of *ses* in the central line, and in accord with mannerist practice in the School of Fontainebleau, the female is transformed into an androgynous body. *Ses* can be either masculine or feminine, and it can be a neutral letter, a *c*, that prefigures scission into male and female nominations.

In one mold are cast two different forms. The open *e* of *ses* tends to divide the letters that compose the pronoun, but also make the line murmur to itself (as in line 8) and, in doing so, to incarnate the very myth of androgyne from an ineffable idea into a visible and organic form. At the center of the sonnet the two serpentine parallels, **ss**, become halved into a **c**: *ses*, or *s-e-s* in the vocal dimension of the lyric, agglutinate into **c**, a palatal consonant, like a living swan of the same shape and demeanor, deprived of voice. The androgynous figure is thus at once *ses* and *c*, **s** doubling and mirroring **c**. The first initial and double letters of **C**assandre's name are muted in typographical script mirrored along the vertical axis, by which a reverse *c*, set over a *c*, makes an *s*. Placed together and twisted in the graphics and the vocal work of the sonnet, the two identical consonants sketch a stenography that can be read in the form of the question, *est-ce?* (or: *S...?*) as a point of interrogation that will pose the question or enigma at the basis of the narrative. The same enigma is at the center, but it scatters everywhere and engenders a play of sexual and graphic ambiguity. Broken, framed, and reconstituted, the figures at the vanishing point of the sonnet denote the two consonants inscribing, in minuscule, the detailed signature of Cassandre. Invoked before they are named (and in a fashion that resembles the ways Mallarmé dissolves proper names in his sonnets, so as not to fall victim to nomination), the seven characters of Cassandre are caressed but never spelled out in the tortuous folds of the letters.

Verbal scansion requires that *serres* be seen transformed into tresses as if, thanks to the arts of anamorphosis, the unit **rr,** a double sign of the so-called "canine" letter, were transmuted into figures of silence. Witnessing the twisting movement of a beloved body of letters, the poet arrests the reverie at the end of the second quatrain by staging a scene of the voice whispering to the reader (or to itself), "Je me contente en mon contentement." Would this be a narcissistic pleasure in which the "I" becomes enveloped in the redundancy of his or her (or even its) desire – where the poem becomes the poet's temptation? In a new version of the myth of Pygmalion, the poet seems to delight in the thought of being indistinguishable from the body he contemplates. Would the eighth line convey a moment of jubilatory and illusory pleasure that marks the poet's travail of un-requited love told through the whole of the *Amours*? No matter what the answer, the line displays an identity of body and letters. It can be seen as supreme evidence of feigned or "secondary" nar-cisssism, in which the subject uses a mobile visual order both to attract its desired object and keep it at a keen distance from itself.[10] The "contentment' (or *con-tente-ment*) in which the voice bathes anticipates a desire to resolve any ultimate difference of gender invested in an opposition of **s** and **c.** The line owes its effect of move-ment to the recurrences of the mute *e,* the letter at the center of the poem, which is now set in a weave suggested by the twists between the consonants **m** and **n**:

At the same time as it forges its illusion of narcissistic plenitude, visual symmetries of the line betray the figure of the poet counting on the revenue gained from writing about a scene of desire or temptation. By scripting such a handsome line, by the temptation that the "je" produces in extending these metaphors, he *counts* (so it is suggested) on his contentment. He tells and takes account (*compte*) of the illusion he is writing. Like an artist who lives by his or her commissions, Ronsard makes clear the cost-effectiveness of the verbal picture he is crafting.

In the two tercets the poet's voice modulates the same tensions of voice and figure. Again, **s** – a rebus of *est-ce, c,* and *?* and as an almost identical rebus of *c'est* – is scattered almost everywhere. Letters allow us to see the whisper that refuses to identify the am-biguous body that is being described. The two tercets can be read

Plate 6. Historiated letter "P" from a French edition of Plutarch (Paris: Abel Angelier, 1584). Like Ronsard, the artist has the look of a poet. He ascends skyward, his right foot on a globe. He wears a bard's laurel and appears to be both writing and drawing on the V-like easel.

as a movement that goes to and from an identity of **s** and **c** insofar as each is alternately voiced and scripted throughout the text:

(S) S (C) S (C)
Quel plaisir est ce, ainçoys quelle merveille

C (S) (C) C (S) S (S)
Quand **ses c**heveux troussez de**ss**us l'oreille

(S) S (C)
D'une Venus imitent la façon?

(S) (C)
Quand d'un bonet son chef elle adonize,

98

The turn of the letter: from Cassandre to Hélène

C (S) (C)   (S) (S)
Et qu'on ne sçait (tant bien elle desguise

(S) (C)   (S)   S(C)
Son chef doubteux) s'elle est fille ou garçon?

Once seen and heard in their patterns of evidence and latency, the alphabetical figures vary on the letters s and c vocalized as whispered marks. Right from the beginning of the last tercets the s generates a rhythm of twisted figures. The two questions are established by means of the matricial s that is systematically twisted, contorted and ultimately stretched into a question mark. Seen and read at once, the sonnet appears to seal all difference – be it sexual or grammatical; what demarcates vowels and consonants; or even what distinguishes reading from seeing – in the ambivalence of a curved letter. Divided between writing and voice, and always rebounding between its graphic form and its sound, c follows the tortuous contour of the s common to any *Festina lente* in the fashion of the Royal Salamander in the heritage of Francis I's totem. The play of letters alludes to Cassandre without ever spelling her name. She is glimpsed fleetingly through the interlace of the first character of her Christian name. Seen from another angle, the torsion of the s, unfolding from a c (as c is in intimate rapport with the *ss* of Cassandre), radiates from the center of the poem and hence inflects the entire configuration (see following page). In the relation that the poem holds between the axis and the border of its tabular form, the lines follow both a Christian and Neoplatonic cosmology of a world of center and circumference.

The heritage of this vision inflects the letter in various ways. The body of the character is unveiled through an enumeration of reflections which advance toward an ideal form. Following Tory's allegories of the letter (such as the I inscribing Pico's ladder in its body or the *L*, casting the shadow of the I of an Idea by the man reclining against it), the letters at once reflect, indicate, and concretize a multitude of "ideas." [11] Hence the sonnet follows a narrative line which enumerates details that imply the presence of a protean whole, not only behind the shadow it casts, but especially in its own physical form that *exceeds* its idea. Gold, water, breast, neck, navel, hair, pubis and skull: in sum is it (*est-ce?*) a girl or a boy? The question at the terminus of the poem is begged by the literal, graphic figure of *sound* or possessive and noun, the *son*, of the initial line. *Son* what? The vocable is located approximately at each of the four

Soit que son or se crespe lentement

Ou soit qu'il vague en deux glissantes ondes,

Qui çà qui là par le sein vagabondes,

Et sur le col, nagent follastrement.

Ou soit qu'un noud diaprè tortement

De maintz rubiz, & maintes perles rondes,

Serre les flotz de ses deux tresses blondes,

Je me contente en mon contentement.

Quel plaisir est ce, ainçoys quelle merveille

Quand ses cheveux troussez dessus l'oreille

D'une Venus imitent la façon?

Quand d' un bonet son chef elle adonize,

Et qu'on ne sçait (tant bien elle desguise

Son chef doubteux) s'elle est fille ou garçon?

cardinal corners of the sonnet and establishes the coordinates of a frame or cartouche: "Soit que *son* or" and "deux glissantes *on*des" define the upper edge of the tableau while "*Son* chef" and "garçon" mark the lower border. The most successful twist of *son* is woven through the undulation of the curious formulation, "d'un bonet son chef elle adonize ..." (line 12) in which torsions applied to the linear order of speech reveal the movement and visibility of the poem. Its unconscious is seen in its plasticity. Yet in the drive to write and to master the world — that is, to produce in the name of one's own creation a map of its entirety — the poet inscribes the sign of an exchange-value, of a "good sonnet" (*un bon sonnet*). Hidden and twisted in the vocables, self-legitimizing figures of worth emerge from the site of an enigma. In "un bonet son" we discover *un bon sonnet*. The same duplicity of figure, value, and visibility of montage marks the next line, in "qu'on ne sçait," in which the whole form of a sonnet and female sex (a sonnet and its unnameable organ of generation, its "origin of the world") are engendered in the bend of an accolade reminiscent of the ogee curve from flamboyant architecture. In the hidden rebuses are located reverse bends tipped into the graphics to resemble the flow of Cassandre's hair:

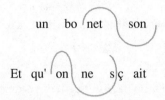

As soon as the sight of the word *sonnet* is apprehended anamorphically, in the twists of the letter and the white space around them, silence dominates the scene of description. Lines and the white forms between them become part of the poem's signifying matrix. The *deux glissantes ondes* of the second line project a graphic alliteration of **s** in order to make manifest a verbal montage. In the suggestive movement of letters, *son* orients the text in directions which lead to our apperception of an unconscious figuration along the margins of meaning. *Son* is between *glissantes* and *ondes* such that our fantasm of *sound* is *seen* between the letters.[12]

As we have seen, **s** is a monogram of torsion. Its form casts the poem into a sort of verbal lap-dissolve[13] that reveals the narcissistic relation that the poem keeps with its typography. The reader or beholder is allowed to glimpse a dialogical, even androgynous, language which precedes the imprint of sexual or symbolic difference. A common pronoun that draws the reader into the text stands at an umbilical nexus − or "noud" (line 5) − of the poem and of the woman.[14] Paragrammatically, the knot of hair is also the shifter that comprises the writer, *he* (the voice) and his field of readers, or *we* (*nous*). But *noud* also remains what the poem is not, for it figures a nudity covered by the letter of the word itself and of the sonnet in its sum. In the first tercet, emblazoning Cassandre, the poet invokes one of any possible serial numbers of "Venus," it appears, in order to convey the absolute beauty of the name he has chosen to fall in love with.[15] Venus is one of any number of ideal forms which come to the poet's mind. Allusion to Botticelli is patently obvious, but since the letter **V** concretizes and arrests all metaphorical movement, Venus becomes the site of the origins of visibility and responds to the *Voeu* at the frontispiece of the *Amours*. As Erwin Panofsky has shown, the goddess had been the topic of debates over Cupid blinded, over divine and mortal love, and over things both visible and invisible.[16] Here, Cassandre, seen in travesty of Venus, is a self-sustaining, ever-doubled image. "D'une Venus elle imite la façon" produces a mirrored syntax where, in the visible field, the decasyllable incorporates the idea of a nude and total Idea, that is, of a *V nu* (or *V-nous*) which would be framed and reflected by the mercurial play of writing. The poem projects

$$\text{d'une} \quad \overset{\longleftarrow \;\; | \;\; \longrightarrow}{V} \quad \text{enu s}$$

in a palindrome, a miniature palinode, a specular − hence narcissizing − configuration in which the letter is *both* double and indivisible. V, the stylus and phallus of the sonnet, also heralds the form of the goddess' pubis, and denotes sexual difference within the two opposed identities contained within its converging lines. *Written* as V, the latter is male, but *seen* as V, it is female.[17] V inscribes the trace of the primitive being recalled from Aristophanes' tale in the *Symposium*, but now the myth is translated into concrete evidence.

In "Soit que son or ..." the question mark, the parenthetical marks, and the cedilla share force that binds typography and metaphor. These three non-semantic forms embody traits that *neutralize* the scopic drama of the Cassandre-Venus figure being unveiled. They indicate that the birth of visual desire comes with the sign of writing as an erotic veil. In the fourteenth line, the cedilla and the question mark become pictograms that stage a regress of desire. Elements that are used to fabricate an effect of the body, they jump forward as forms that both double and supplant the subject of the poem.

The only pronoun that determines Cassandre's identity, a pronoun held in check until near the end of the sonnet, is *elle* (line 12). Up to the last tercet, the eyes follow the tracks of the hair that is transformed into *or* in filigree. When the figure begins to "adonize son chef d'un bonet," his or her visual aspect becomes equivocal, confirming why no grammatical sign had yet cast any sexual distinction. Paradoxically, the shape of the question mark *answers* the doubt or enigma raised by the serpentine figures that dominate the poem and ultimately beg its question. An *S* above a period, a sign that responds at the circumference to the *ses* of the center, the question mark buckles and ends the poem all the while it is embodying and summarizing it. Who knows what she (*elle* ... or perhaps, L) is? On the one hand, contraction of *si elle* into *s'elle* underscores the theme of the originary womb of the primitive being. But, on the other, insofar as the word also spells a nominative *selle* (line 14) that brings forth other meanings in the paragrammar, the portmanteau combination can designate the "maistresse forme" of Nature as it might have existed before division from elementary matter into distinctions of male and female. *S'elle* can be seen as a matrix that produces human forms of either gender. At the same time, the reminder of a coprophilic state (in which *selle* would refer to a stool or a saddle) turns ideal matter into generative residue at the literal and corporal bottom of the text. Here "Soit que son or..." opens upon a scene where an indifferent matter, which remains below and beyond all metaphor, is seen as a raw material for creation that endures.

The context of the last line suggests that the figure of the androgyne will inspire the reader to follow a line of regress that accompanies the description of Cassandre's hair: a remainder before all sexual differentiation, the matter of *s'elle* will fertilize the flowers of metaphor and bring us back to the imaginary beginnings of creation. As an effect of loss (at least connoted by the absence of the vowel *i*), the word seals parenthetical sexual difference and turns male and female into a single substance.[18] The word annuls all difference when the poem elaborates the fantasm of a return to a stage of sexual development preceding a genital phase. By suggesting the presence of an anal condition, the bottom of the poem evokes the figure of an androgyne in the lower, bodily world of the sonnet, but it has not obviated passage through a sadistic character that resides in all narcissistic description.[19] *S'elle* refers to the ideal matrix that assumes the form of a saddle placed, as it were, on the back of Pegasus. In this way the polysemic dimension of the word cannot fail to encourage a quasi-Freudian reading, according to which the perpetual transformation of letters and figures in the word-rebus opens the fourteenth line upon a horizon of infinite ambiguity. From this point the typographical marks no longer belong to the semantic layer of the sonnet but determine the play of ambivalence that has been making the poem disseminate itself within its own form.

In the fabric of "Soit que son or...," *s'elle*, located as it is at the lower edge, responds to the genetive *ses* situated in the center. But in the logic of the statement, *s'elle* has to equivocate with *fille*, since the word spells *elle* after the gap opened by the apostrophe following the initial *s*. According to the same process of analogy, *fille* contains *il*. A chiasm inverts the distinction between boy and girl in the dream of an indifferently sexual *and* grammatical congress of the poet and the spectre of the beloved. At the lower right corner of the sonnet, *garçon*, the key to its architectural vault, happens to be no less ambiguous. Spelling its sonorous effect, *gar-son* corresponds to the incipit, *Soit que son or* .... Thanks to the fixing of speech by the cedilla, *garçon* acquires an added erotic fold. From the standpoint of its visibility, the cedilla becomes another question mark in minuscule and placed in focal inversion and at a clear visual distance from its upside-down analogue at the end of the last line. The mark is attached to the lower part of the body of the letter *ç*. Deprived of a supplementary coda − like Venus without an acute accent over her *e* − *garcon* would be another regressive figure in tandem with *s'elle*, or *gar-con*. Once again the cedilla refers to the *s* − and to the *est-ce?* − embodied in the pervasively visual tenor of the sonnet. In the fashion of mannerist painting, the *ç* appears to be an s projected on a horizontal plane and toward a vanishing point. The final question mark at the end of the fourteenth line baits us into seeing in the graphic configuration our own desire for a collapse of sexual difference.

The two tercets end in the form of an interrogation. We still wonder whence originates the voice of the sonnet. Is it an interior dialogue, or a mere *effect* of dialogue in which the diction mimes the sight of ourselves at an imaginary threshold of language, when our eyes seize upon a fragment in order to obtain a sense of distance and perspective in the symbolic world of objects and other discourses? In the context of the tortuous movement of the *Amours*, the parenthesis of the two final lines stages the same regressive phase. A *cheville*, the aside fills out the poem by offering a concrete manifestation of the poet's inner, graphic voice. But speech plays no less decisively on the ambiguity of *doubteux* within its form. The parenthetical division, a moment of creative doubt, marks the hemistich (of a measure of four and six syllables), right where it closes in the following line. But the character also bends from one line to the next and, according to a tabular design, almost *follastrement*. In

on ne sçait ⎛ (tant bien.....

doubteux) ⎞ s'elle est

we follow the parentheses of a montage of lines that trace at once the path of the hair and the contour of the medial *s*.

Clearly the play of the left and right parenthetical marks above one another suggests analogy with the shape of the cedilla or the ogee curve. Historical evidence confirms that the fantasms generated by the typographical marks are not a product of chance or Ronsard's own poetic license. In 1552 the cedilla was still a fairly new character in the printer's world. The French *cédille* owed its origins to Spain where, in exile and incarcerated between June 1525 and February 1526, Francis I had the fortune of reading the popular *Amadis de Gaule*.[20] Herberay des Essars retained Spanish orthography in his French translation that the king ordered upon his return to France in the following year, in 1527. Here the role of the letter in Ronsard's poetic vision melds esthetics, politics, and institution: might Ronsard have read S. Silvius' translation of Ficino, the *Commentaire sur le Banquet d'Amour*, that appeared in 1546, in which the ç, following the precepts of the grammatcal reform set forth by Meigret, is used before *e* and *i*? According to the visual reading of the ninetieth sonnet of the *Amours* of 1552, the poet transforms a problem of desire and of philosophical convention into a shape of poetic and graphic inspiration.[21]

From this angle "Soit que son or …" appears to be significant as a document in debates staged over the state of printed language in the middle years of the French Renaissance. The *blason* of the hairpiece, the description of Cassandre's figure, and the dream of a narcissistic plenitude are only pretexts for a more vast speculation on the analogy of letters and meaning and the both arbitrary and motivated status of the printed sign. In the *Amours* the logic of the letter is double and diverse. Seen from one point of view, the poem seeks its mythic figures (the scar in Aristophanes' tale in the *Symposium*, the Neoplatonism of gods made flesh, or the tale of the loves of Venus and Adonis in Ovid's *Metamorphoses*) in a printer's workshop and a painter's studio. A line which unwinds and unravels, the *grotesque* configuration of the typographical character complements the platonic themes of love; the sonnet appears to be anchored in the coded campaign that in the second quarter of the sixteenth century engaged another "restitution of letters" figuring in a general politics of art that sought to decorate the attributes of French royal power with effects imagined, perhaps, as exotic linguistic treasures from foreign shores.

The ultimate proof of the graphic, sexual, and poetic travail of the ninetieth sonnet might be found in the art of the cipher. In the princeps edition the text is crowned with the Roman numerals **XC**. Why not see, in an almost anamorphic inscription, the vocable "Qui (**X**) c'est (**C**)?" or … "Qui sçait?" "Qui sçait … s'elle est fille ou garçon?'' An enigma which floats over the poem, concretizing the very metamorphosis that is its essence, the cipher slides into the same play of the dominant visual forms. The sonnet becomes transformed into the illusion of a movement among words, letters and figures, and remains a supreme rebus that responds in its figural shape to the question it is asking. X is the spot of C(assandre) that marks and eternizes narcissism of writing.

For the sake of perspective and a view of Ronsard in the greater span of his career, our reading of "Soit que son or..." can be tested through comparison with one of the most celebrated sonnets of the later *Amours*. If, in the industry of his lyrical writing, Ronsard interprets the sonnet as a place melding sense and form, we should have reason to seek other graphic instances — if they exist — of the same wit where it would not seem so evident. Does the contradiction between forces of "logocentrism" (that Meigret's reform advocates and with which Ronsard identifies) and graphic license (which is reserved for poets) hold toward the end of his career? By 1578 has Ronsard's adolescence matured enough to demonstrate that his verse obeys the canon of more restrained taste? He has begun to work with his sonnets in a schematic logic more appropriate to the innovations of Ramism? Sifted and filtered by the violence of the 1560s with shifts in political power and the advent of the civil wars, the new and more heroic or elegiac sonnet would appear to repress, as we have seen to some extent in the third chapter, the younger Ronsard's excess. The self-censure would seem to reflect greater epistemic transformation surfacing during the turmoil of the Wars of Religion.

The letter appears to be a fragment of the body, a remainder of the poet transformed into a corpse of ossified signs in "Quand vous serez bien vieille, au soir à la chandelle," of the *Second Livre des sonets pour Helene* (1578). Spatial disposition of the bodily pieces offers a contrast to the graphic dimension of anamorphosis in the works of 1552–53. The sonnet is inspired by emblems, classical themes and, again, Villon, now in the "Regrets de la belle heaulmière." But the verbal ambiguities and daring montages of characters of the young Ronsard seem to have matured. When seen as a picture, in terms of mobile centers and circumferences, the poem displays Ronsard's signature at the end of the first hemistich in the line marking the poem's vanishing point:

The turn of the letter: from Cassandre to Hélène

XXIV

Quand vous serez bien vieille, au soir à la chandelle,
Assise aupres du feu, devidant & filant,
Direz, chantant mes vers, en vous esmerveillant,
Ronsard me celebroit du temps que j'estois belle.

Lors vous n'aurez servante oyant telle nouvelle,
Desja sous le labeur à demy sommeillant,
Qui au bruit de *Ronsard* ne s'aille resveillant,
Benissant vostre nom de louange immortelle.

Je seray sous la terre, & fantaume sans os:
Par les ombres Myrtheux je prendray mon repos.
Vous serez au fouyer une vieille accroupie,

Regrettant mon amour, & vostre fier desdain.
Vivez, si m'en croyez, n'attendez à demain:
Cueillez dés aujourd'huy les roses de la vie.

[When you'll be old in the evening, at the candle,
Seated by the fire, sewing and weaving,
You'll say, singing my lines, in marvel sighing,
Ronsard sang of me when my beauty was immortal.

When you'll not have a single servant, hearing this word
Already half-sleeping over her work, laboring
Who, at the sound of "Ronsard" can fail to awaken,
Blessing your name with praise eternally heard.

I will be under the earth, & a phantom without bone:
Under Myrthy shades in my repose I will be one.
While on your hearth you'll be an old hag

Regretting my love, and your haughty disdain, in sorrow:
Live, believe me, but don't wait for tomorrow:
Gather now the roses of life but please don't lag.]

The poem varies on the anagram, a medieval mode of creation that Du Bellay advised his listeners to use in the *Deffence et illustration de la langue francoyse* (1549), and that Ronsard exploited frequently (especially in 1555, in the seventh poem of the *Continuation des amours*: "Marie, qui voudroit vostre beau nom tourner, / Il trouveroit Aimer: aimez-moi donq, Marie..." [Marie, whoever might wish to turn your pretty name would find *love*: therefore, Marie, love me]). Here the "bruit" or renown of Ronsard resonates when death jumps forth from the graphic configuration of Ronsard's words. *Bruit* is not interference, but graphic music. In the multiple allusions to hearing, the proper name of the poet, set in the center of the kingdom of the sonnet, radiates outward through the visual meter of anagram. Ronsard's echo throughout the poem or over its pictural extension lures us into celebrating the poet's eternity through the trope of antonomasia. In moving to and from a proper and a common form, the seven digits throw out sound and shape in particles infused with the glory of the poet's name:

Quand vous serez bien vieille, au soir à la chandelle,

Assise auprès du feu, devidant & filant,

Direz, chantant mes vers, en vous esmerveillant,

Ronsard me celebroit du temps que j'estois belle.

Lors vous n'aurez servante oyant telle nouvelle,

Desja sous le labeur à demy sommeillant,

Qui au bruit de Ronsard ne s'aille resveillant,

Benissant vostre nom de louange immortelle.

Je seray sous la terre, & fantaume sans os:

Par les ombres Myrtheux je prendray mon repos.

Vous serez au foüyer une vieille accroupie,

Regrettant mon amour, & vostre fier desdain.

Vivez, si m'en croyez, n'attendez à demain:

Cueillez dés aujourd'huy les roses de la vie.

A composition of echoes strung and scattered in anagrams through the verse, the sonnet fixes the glory of the poet at the vanishing point of his verbal icon. The placement of the name and its radiation surpass the contingency of his love for Hélène de Surgères. The array of letters both circumscribes and extends meaning according the same modes that articulate "Soit que son or..." and "Comme un chevreuil..." Here, however, the order appears to be centralizing in its design, and closer to a logic that associates glory and vanishment with a hidden signature in the center.

The turn of the letter: from Cassandre to Hélène

In the poem to Hélène the descriptive realism that we recall from Villon forms a series of graphic elements that silence the oral rhetoric of the poem. The rhythm of its warning, couched in the topos of the *carpe diem*, is established by means of diverse spacings, recurrences and redundancies *within* given words, and even through interstices between the letters. The poet implores us to learn well the lesson of the *ubi sunt* topos. The figure of the old lady at the "fouyer" inspires the memorably solemn sentence crowning the sonnet,

> Cueillez dés aujourd'huy les roses de la vie.

The line resembles an epigram, incised at the bottom of the poem but over the poet's imaginary tombstone above his coffin in the center. Without any typographical juncture, though implying a break at the end of the sixth syllable, the *alexandrin* gathers at either side of the hemistich two objects – a day and roses – in the weave of the fairly stereotypical maxim. Does the poet beg his mistress to gather, *dès aujourd'huy*, as of today, the "roses of life?" Or rather, is he asking himself to gather *des aujourd'hui*, "some todays," a plural synonym of units of time for writing that equivocates on the roses of life? The acute accent is in fact so nascent in character that it does not favor either one of the two inflections. It appears to be an opaque mark that assures a coextension of the two meanings in the same line.

Because the stereotypical vocabulary of the *carpe diem* requires that dawn be colored in a rosy tint, *aujourd'huy* of the last line would, in the natural movement of metaphor, be the "morning" inverting the "evening" of life (of the old lady, or of the old life) that had been set forward in the opening lines. The time of youth in the poem (the beginning, in the first quatrain) takes up senescence, while its lower body, its tomb (under the earth in the last tercet), invokes a commonplace of the opposite. Just as the seven letters that spell R-o-n-s-a-r-d in the center are scattered around its periphery, *aujourd'huy* figures at the bottom but is echoed redundantly everywhere above. A word clearly inscribed in a favored site at the bottom of the picture, *aujourd'huy* modulates two identical substantives. Redundancy of the formula, "le jour du jour" (in "au *jour* d'*hui*") indicates that the substantive is varying on vowels that are mirrored throughout the lines above. **Ou** and **huy** generate uncanny tensions that blend acts of sight (*voir*) and hearing (*ouïr*), in the sense that the echoes seen in the word *voir* indicate that a vanishing point is marked in *o−u*, a word-knot of sight and sound together, an imaginary crypt of emptiness, or perhaps a concealed emblem of death, that the eyes discern as a perspectival object on a grid of graphic tensions:

XXIV

Quand **vous** serez bien vieille, au soir à la chandelle,

Assise aupres du feu, devidant & filant,

Direz, chantant mes vers, en **vous** esmerveillant,

Ronsard me celebroit du temps que j'estois belle.

Lors vous n'**aurez** servante **oyant** telle nouvelle,

Desja **sous** le labeur à demy sommeillant,

Qui au **bruit** de Ronsard ne s'aille resveillant,

Benissant vostre nom de louange immortelle.

Je seray **sous** la terre, & fantaume sans os:

Par les ombres Myrtheux je prendray mon repos.

Vous serez au **fouyer** une vieille ac**crou**pie,

Regrettant mon amour, & vostre fier desdain.

Vivez, si m'en c**roye**z, n'attendez à demain:

Cueillez dés au**jour**d'**huy** les roses de la vie.

The sonnet appears to imply that an alluvial pattern of figures of hearing is fanning out in the overall composition. Yet other, contrary sets of figures are set in dialogue with this pattern. *Vieille*, the complement to *aujourd'huy*, comes as an antonym in symmetrically inverse relation to the bottom of the poem. Through the agonistic rapport of *vieille* and *aujourd'huy* at either end of the poem, Ronsard seems to be staging a verbal and pictural psychomachia. *Vieille* appears to be a word-pivot focalizing the movement of transference taking place in the narrative: Ronsard is old; he would like to regain his youth; his paramour is far younger than he; therefore, for the sake of balance, he must, in a patently Freudian gesture, pass his old age on to Hélène through the writing of the sonnet. Thus he might equilibrate an overly great temporal and biological difference between himself and his erotic object. Without the mediation of writing, the difference cannot be assailed. By depicting Hélène as a shrivelled hag, he can buy himself − at least for a fugacious moment consumed in the writing and reading of the sonnet − a glorious instant of youth and immortality.

The poem thus stages a typically perverse symbolic exchange that is matched by its dialogism in the graphics of the text.

In this way *fouyer* (line 11) becomes not only a visible site by dint of its evocative force, where the fire in the chimney figures the flaming love as extinguished and void in the hollow space that death occupies in the empty fireplace. *Fouyer* also refers to a *memento mori* common to emblems, that reaches back to Scève, Holbein and others. The analogical force of language, however, requires that the visibility of the word, like a picture, be evident in the extension of other objects evoked throughout the poem. Orthography encourages us to see in *fouyer* the scopic presence of *foyer*. The *fouyer* would be the spot where visible and invisible realms converge, and where linguistic and psychic projections of old age and vigor meet before being inverted or separated. The "foyer" seems to be the lenticular focus of the poem, the axis of condensation where an image on one side will be inverted on the other. The word mediates energies whose origins are reversed in the course that leads from the beginning to the imprecation of the final line. If the immemorial line of *aujourd'huy* at the end is connoted before its final and late inscription in the line crowning the end of the tomb-sonnet, *vieillesse* figures as its counterpart in a second visual scansion:

XXIV

Quand vous serez bien **vieille**, au soir à la chandelle,

Assise aupres du feu, devidant & filant,

Direz, chantant mes vers, en vous esmer**veill**ant,

Ronsard me celebroit du temps que j'estois belle.

Lors vous n'aurez servante oyant telle nouvelle,

Desja sous le labeur à demy som**meill**ant,

Qui au bruit de Ronsard ne s'**aille** res**veill**ant,

Benissant vostre nom de louange immortelle.

Je seray sous la terre, & fantaume sans os:

Par les ombres Myrtheux je prendray mon repos.

Vous serez au fouyer une **vieille** accroupie,

Regrettant mon amour, & vostre fier desdain.

Vivez, si m'en croyez, n'attendez à demain:

Cueillez dés aujourd'huy les roses de **la vie**.

By virtue of the scatter of the letters, the poem enjoins the reader to see the echoes of age in the field defined by *vieille* and *aujourd'huy*. Since the sonnet treats of the limits of life and love while establishing a symbolic exchange in its relation to Hélène and ourselves, the text also essays those areas where language and visibility overlap. The letters appear to anticipate Montaigne's famous statement, "Si vous le voyez, vous l'oyez; si vous l'oyez, vous le voyez" [If you see it you hear it, and if you hear it, you see it].[22] In the fashion of recall from concealed regions of the unconscious, *ou* and *oy*, folded into the topos of the *ubi sunt*, uproot the sterotypical meaning by tracing a pattern of obsessive figures – each being a sort of death's head or *memento mori* – of destiny.

The pattern becomes clear when the voice declares in the ninth line,

Je seray sous la terre, & fantaume sans os,

in order to allude to the spell it would like to cast upon the haughty mistress. Just as we have observed in "Soit que son or ...," the poem's orthography suggests that grammar and Eros are almost identical. Ronsard will be a fantom bereft of his own skeleton, that is, of his *o* and *s*. Soon he will be transformed into a ghost through a new "reformation" or enlightenment of language. All the recurrences of *ou* in the poem are, because of contiguity, garnished with *s*, which suggests that the recall of voice is tracing each printed character in the form of a bone, or of an element in the picture of a *memento mori*. Thus, the most innocuous-looking pronoun, *vous*, connotes that the integument of a skeleton is visible in its form (v**o**u**s**). Such, too, is the case for "rep**o**s" and the "r**o**se**s** *de la vie*." A mark of *os*, the couple *o*–*s* (lines 1–10, line 12, line 14) inflects the poem in general.

Furthermore, the ninth line plays a role in a historical context of typographic programs in which Ronsard figures in his reflections on poetry. In the chapter entitled "Des personnes des verbes François et de l'ortographie" at the end of his *Abrégé de l'art poétique françois* (published in 1565, thirteen years after the princeps edition of the *Amours*, and also thirteen years before the publication of the *Sonets pour Hélène*), Ronsard announces how an economy of writing is required for print to reproduce voiced meaning. Poetry will be of a brief, dense order, and written without any typographical excess. Poetry will reproduce voice as good language should – except in matters of poetry. Ronsard appears to follow Meigret's logocentric views when he avows,

Tu eviteras toute ortographie superflue et ne mettras aucunes lettres en tels mots si tu ne les prononces en les lisant.

[You'll avoid all superfluous orthography and not place letters in such words that you don't pronounce in reading them.]

His argument appears to be convincing, but only until the next sentence, when he states:

Tu pourras avecq licence user de la seconde personne pour la premiere... tu pourras aussi adjouster par licence une *s* à la premiere personne.

[With license you can use the second person for the first ... through license you can also add an *s* to the first person.]

The contradiction holds until we realize that it is not voice but *sight* of the word that becomes a criterion of poetic virtue. Creative orthography must then be at the basis of lyrical language. Spelling and its effects are independent of the meanings that words reveal simply because orthographic variety can multiply meaning within any given verbal form. Where as theorist Ronsard would like to insist on the privilege of voice in poetry, he slips away from his plan by appealing to metaphors of painting. These guarantee the material virtue of his craft at the expense of the spirit of voice that would transcend printed writing. Like poets of print-culture, painters are those who use necessarily superfluous forms when they fashion a work of art:

Tu diras, selon la contraincte de ton vers, *or, ore, ores; adoncq, adonques, adoncques; avecq, avecque, avecques*, et mille autres, que sans crainte tu trancheras et alongeras ainsi qu'il te plaira, gardant tousjours une certaine mesure consultée par ton oreille, laquelle est certain juge de la structure du vers, comme l'oeil de la peincture des tableaux.[23]

[You'll say, according to the constraints of your line, *or, ore, ores, doncq, adoncques, adonque, avecq, avecque, avecques*, and a thousand others that without fear you'll transform and lengthen as you please, all the while you keep a certain measure advised by your ear, which is the true judge of the structure of verse, just as is the eye for the painting of pictures.]

The orthography of the twenty-fourth sonnet of the *Sonets pour Hélène* apparently follows the remarks in the *Abrégé* of 1565. Ronsard's *fantaume* in the eighth line is a dessicated, shrivelled "fantosme" bereft of its flesh and bone, that is, its *o–s* that alternate orthography can offer. In the folds of the sonnet partially cast as a *memento mori* Ronsard displaces the pathos of the seductive words whispered into Helen's ear, for in the paragrammar historical and

contingent issues about orthography suddenly emerge in the place
of musings about the poet's immortality. A poetic technology
concretizes a discourse in dialogue with space, in the ploy of the
anagram and the careful scatter of letters. In posterity, Ronsard's
body is subject to the same logic of analogy and orthography
passed from 1552 to 1587. Here and elsewhere, according to the
analogical imagination that he historicizes in his *Discours*:

> Si tu es divin, tout sainct, tout glorieux,
> Tu peux communiquer ton corps en divers lieux.[24]
>
> [If you are divine, entirely saintly and glorious,
> You can pass your body into many places.]

One of these *divers lieux* is the site of the typographical mark.
Ronsard projects the letter as a shape identical to the body but
in perpetual metamorphosis and dialogue within and outside of
it. Under the "Myrthy" shadows of death he remains faithful
to the silence that had initiated the graphic play of the *Amours*
in 1552.[25] The poet's voice may disappear, but his body will remain
as a complex code of characters in serial and digital variation.
These will be his being, his essence, his music and, above all,
his signature. The letters are immortal but have to be animated
and revived by others in the passage of time. The letter of the
sonnet assures transubstantiation of matter. Print contains spirit,
but spirit never entirely evaporates from the ink congealed on
paper. Because he has crafted letters in a unique design of spatial
rhythms, he will be immortal and infused in all material forms.

One path of study that leads from Ronsard's adolescence to
his crypt might also consider the ways that practices of the 1550s
are retooled in the later poetry; another would have to determine
exactly how the obsession with sight, so dominant in the lyrics,
evolved in a context that became increasingly charged with ideological and historical issues taken up in civil war; or, perhaps,
how the topic of the "world in degeneration" took hold in Ronsard's
career as it waned along with national fortunes. By the 1580s
increased emphasis on visibility was tending to stabilize typography. The oral tenor of language does not appear to have
held a relation of the same productive ambiguity that had been
current in the years of Humanism or the Pléiade. To see if this
is the case, we can now study Montaigne to contrast the graphic
effects of *Les Amours*. If Ronsard extended the analogical range
of French through his bold experiments with the sonnet, the author
of the *Essais* may have been no less innovative in his relation

with memory, allegory and autobiography. Like Ronsard's, his body was marked by the strife of contemporary times. And Montaigne, too, may also have been one who found in the material of writing a politics that projected a consciousness of the subject and subjectivity.

5

MONTAIGNE'S TEST OF STYLE: *DE L'EXERCITATION*

Blaise Pascal calls Montaigne the "incomparable" author of "De l'art de conférer" (III, ix) [Of the Art of Conversation]. In that remarkable essay Montaigne spells out the ways he has fashioned the *Essais* as a work of style. We are, he says, "sur la maniere et non sur la matiere du dire" (928) [on the manner and not the matter of expression]. The remark signals how he has woven a handiwork of figures that display wit by means of a style that underscores the grace of touch and tactility of writing. Despite its carefully wrought or refined manner, the essay counts among his more garrulous dialogues with the imaginary interlocutor who reads him. Montaigne tells us that he would rather have his son learn the art of speech in "taverns rather than schools of speakery" (*escholes de parlerie*), and that for all his good intentions, even a classic like Tacitus reads clumsily because he lacks the touch of "tacit" language that speaks within and by itself. In immediate contrast to the Latin historian's, on the page before our eyes, Montaigne's does. And it does so with graphic ploys so simple that they can change thought into movement by inserting an *n* in the place of a *t*, transmuting matter into manner, and raw material into a living, writing form. Montaigne's style often looks to the literal *characters* of writing for its best invention.

The essays can be read as an endless experiment of form and expression. They raise questions about verbal movement that is born of montage and displacement of printed letters. Since the essays evolve into a self-portrait, we must ask exactly when and where Montaigne's idea of self-study coincides with the birth of his graphic wit. If, as Pierre Villey argued, Montaigne moves from a skeptical view of his life and times through a fideistic crisis before discovering a mature, Epicurean Humanism, how does he revise, stage, or even mask that evolution in the textures of writing? And if the *Essais* are composed, as Michel Butor and others have argued,[1] according to a pictural and allegorical model of elliptical centers

116

and circumferences, how exactly do they bend the lines of the frame that encloses them? The author gives the impression of discovering his elements of style as he continues to write the *Essais*: but when and how does he simultaneously happen upon *and* articulate a style that is as material and protean as evidenced in "De l'art de conférer"?[2]

Such are questions that even casual readings of the *Essais* bring forward. The first section of this panel of two chapters will approach the essays in view of what Montaigne appears to develop in the feigned discovery of his own style, fashion and self-portrait through the art of the printed letter. Insofar as the essay partakes of the conventions of emblematic writing, its apparently increasing appeal to visibility needs to be studied.[3] An allusively pictural and verbal style comes forth especially in 1588 and beyond, but, on close view, also pervades the work of the first two volumes published in 1580. The verbal manoeuvers are perhaps best glimpsed in the self-reflective shards offered to the reader, particularly when Montaigne recounts the time he stole himself from death. In that instant, developed in the tale of an accidental fall from his horse in "De l'exercitation" (II, vi), an arcanely graphic style emerges. Its play of letters becomes crucial for the oblique and concealed articulations of both an autobiographical and a political hieroglyph.

The *Essais* can be qualified according to a view of writing which, as I have tried to show in the world of Rabelais, is "hieroglyphic," not simply because a secret language of former gods or dead souls is invoked, but because the mode of composition develops along divided axes of figure and text. A force of meaning sallies from a simultaneity of difference and identity of graphic inscription, visual form, and meaning.[4] Such appears to be an articulation, in Montaigne's writing, that works between different cognitive registers or "tracks."[5] The style of the *Essais* is crafted to some degree from combinations that subvert voice or speech claimed to be united to writing. They also use montages to make letters twist into foreign shapes and project a changing visual design throughout the three volumes.[6]

"Le parler que j'ayme, c'est un parler simple et naif, tel sur le papier qu'à la bouche" (171) [the speech that I love is a simple and naive speech, such on paper as in the mouth]. Speech is heard through this remark (in I, xxvi) about his writing but it is congealed in characters on the printed page. Willed confusion of paper and body directs our eyes toward identities forged from sight and sound. Much of the proverbial force of the style appears to originate in condensed figures, but they are so mercurial that networks of letters body forth, appear to move and then shift position or emphasis within a fixed semantic field. Throughout the first two volumes (published in 1580) the author tests – he essays, sifts, balances, or "tries"[7] – his topics in a balance of analogies treated by means of resemblance and dissemblance. Words weave skeins of figures both hidden and revealed through recurring visible marks set in and along the edges of their discourse. The meaning of the grammatical dimension is sometimes secondary to other, unconscious, at once alphabetical and pictographic designs. Unsolicited shapes surge up when visual traits flash through the ostensive meaning and illuminate the work in unpredictable ways.

In, for example, "De la ressemblance des enfans aux peres" [Of the Resemblance of Children to Fathers, II, xxxvii], Montaigne meditates on genealogy or resemblance passed genetically from father to son. But the mark of the title, an irreducible number, 37, is odd, or *impair*, unlike what is *pair* (even) or fatherly (owed to the *père*). *Impère*, "De la ressemblance des enfans aux peres" is set not only against odds and evens, but is self-perpetuating in its singularity in respect to the difference of prime and reproducible figures. *Aux pères* is also a verb: the resemblance of father to children *opère*, or "operates," thus performing an intellectual, a physical, and even a surgical operation in language seemingly independent of the author's control. Likewise, "De trois commerces" [Of Three Kinds of Association] crowns an essay that falls under the number of the volume (III) and chapter (iii) that matches the triad of its ciphers. The title is quartered – twice divided – in respect to the first sentence that turns about the tension of letter and figure. "Il ne faut pas se clouër si fort à ses humeurs et complexions" (818) [We mustn't nail ouselves too firmly to our moods or complexions]. *Four* complexions or humors offset the *three* of the title, just as the *fort* encodes (4) so as to produce an operative dissymmetry between cipher and text and items odd and even. In the same chapter, when he notes where he lives and writes, the author states that in winter, when cold wind prevails, he spends time in his tower "moins continuellement; car ma maison est juchée sur un tertre, comme dict son nom" (828) [less continually; for my house is perched on a hillock, as its name indicates]. He is between three and four, *car*, either *for* or 4 (*quart*, even in the visual form of *écart* or square), because the name to which he apparently alludes is "Montaigne" or "mountain," but also *tertre*, a triad in a triad that divides into *tt/ee/rr*. And in "Des boyteux"

[Of cripples] Montaigne chooses III, xi to classify the chapter on sorcery. It happens that eleven is the digit of the devil because the integer *1* is doubled into *11*; but when the author remarks that *10* days have been added to the Gregorian calendar in October 1582, the numerical count can be as much as *10* or *11* days, the number matching the "bissextile" tension of the chapter. When he pleads for peace in "De la phisionomie" [Of Physiognomy, III, xii], the number twelve (*douze*) of the chapter has been chosen to provide a rebus of "*douce*ur," calm, or respite. For certain faces, especially his own, "il y a des beautez non fieres seulement mais aygres; il y en d'autres *douces*, et encores au delà fades ..." (1059, my italics) [there are some beauties not only proud but acrid; others are soft, and beyond that, wan]. Other ciphers of sound, letter, or number abound, each hinting that the style depends on tensions generated in the heterogeneous space of print.[8] Expression seems to move between inscription, letters, numbers, and discourse. Poetic fragments of a "primary" process of association break the finished look of a prose into arcane figures, or miniature "testes," letters that jumble and move indiscriminately or atomistically about the essays. An unconscious is glimpsed through the gaps and crannies opened by the visible art of writing.[9]

Where the unconscious is apprehended in its graphic evidence, there are, upon his brush with death, the first strokes of Montaigne's self-portrait. The exemplary tale that dominates "De l'exercitation" [Of practice] recounts Montaigne's fall from his horse. He leaves his home one day and ventures out, "à une lieue de chez moy, qui suis assis dans le moiau de tout le trouble des guerres civiles de France" (373) [about a mile or so from my place which is set right at the hub of all the stir of the French civil wars]. Upon returning, riding an untrained horse, Montaigne is passed by a steed that tosses the author from his mount and knocks them to the ground. Thrown a good twelve feet from his saddle, he remains unconscious. His servant sights his limp body, assumes him to be dead, and carries him back to his domain. After several days the author arises from the soft slumber of his coma and returns to the excruciating pains of life. Floating in a beatitude between death and birth – an almost imaginary, umbilical condition – he is suddenly racked with pain. Return to life and language mimes the fictive memory of the origins of birth into language, for alive, but paralyzed and immobilized, shackled in a dream, the author cannot make the slightest sign to alert his attendants around him.

The crisis literally *astonishes* him. Its parabolic account leads

119

the essayist to pass from reverie to speculation. Throughout the chapter the verbal texture implies – between, we always note, the register of the representation offered of both a zombie and an author fabulating his condition of paralysis – that something ought to be made of the accident: it must be put to good use; have a dense, emblematic or numismatic shape; be wrested from its conventional look of a deliberation on death. It must be forged or coined in order to bring his readers to a capital awareness of themselves and also to produce royalties for its author. Here the graphic dimension of the essay discloses how it stages the beginnings of its self-portrait. What comes to life is a possessive individual's drive to produce a discourse of his own signature; to mediate the relations between confession, "secondary revision," and political realities in view of the posterity and glory he seeks; to feign psychogenesis in a self-styled, proto-Freudian "writing-cure" that engages regress to a pictographic language at the origins of consciousness; not least, to self-fashion his image to make the spectacle of himself writing the characters we see in print become tantamount to his essence.[10]

"De l'exercitation" takes as its task to stylize what amounts to a dearth of lived experience, that is, life that is not marked or "tested" by the figure of death, in other words, printed writing. A flow of sensations that passes outside of language constitutes the timeless and ineffable register of life that the essays bring back into the scatter of letters. The author's task entails creation of a tautological "style of inscription" portraying events that are both originary (treading a path for the first time) and secondary or highly recognizable (that is, already there, pregiven and visibly drawn from familiar sources). The text must revive what is "lived" or lacking the symbolic propping of language through its skein of ineffable ciphers.

The essay picks up strands of "Que philosopher c'est apprendre à mourir" (I, xx), but now edits the scholastic pose of that essay and inverts its topical composition that had aligned the *ars moriendi* with the *memento mori*. The rewriting suggests now that "To 'die' between inverted commas is to learn how to 'philosophize'." Stylization of an approach to death constitutes sportive "exercitation," or a sort of military exercise that entails measure, rhythm, and tempo of writing. Expiring in style carries the bonus of allowing the author to go back and forth from life and death. By borrowing or mortgaging events taken from life, the essayist can invest and shelter them in his book for future benefits. His accident can be moneyed when articulated between allegory and nascent self-portraiture.

Death is figured as an immobile mark, or a literal letter that replaces life, that the essay animates by means of its art of montage. Terence Cave has shown that death pervades the *Essais* as "a kind of arch-topic" that "both provides a measure" for the scope and value of other topics, "and levels or empties them by means of its own total neutrality," or an "absence in view of which the language of life attempts to organize itself."[11] Gisèle Mathieu-Castellani specifies that death, a preferred topic for both emblematists and Montaigne, engages the meeting of the visible and the invisible or whatever refuses reduction to representation.[12] The same opacity or absence of figurative virtue seems, in "De l'exercitation," to be invested in typographical marks. Letters are inert, dead matter that must be animated by traits of graphic wit. The latter brings life into the letter by articulating movement and recombination at the level of the signifier.

The signifier is carefully embedded, however, in a narrative picture. Upon cursory view, the essay has five sequences that devolve from Montaigne's initial inquiry about the worth of studying death: (1) Belief and instruction lead us to action with great resistance on our part. Philosophers have often taken a "path" that leads to the threshold of death, but not one of them has gone into the "myrthy" world of shadows and come back again to make honest reports about it. Nonetheless, real philosophers abandon themselves or let their reins fall before the ultimate issues that haunt them. But (2) philosophy can scarcely be an adequate example of human or meditative activity before the inevitable fact of death. Words are fugacious and even meaningless where death marks their ultimate origin and finality. All the same, Montaigne confesses, he (3) has occasion to essay death more directly than philosophers because of the utter novelty of his exercise, since, it is implied, he has a written style that their discipline sorely lacks. Accounts of sleep and dreams provide him with the leisure to undertake the task. (4) For during the recent civil wars, an exemplary accident happened. A recent encounter with death now allows him to estimate directly the worth of life. The (5) self-portrayal that has emerged from the tale of the event becomes part of a *une espineuse entreprinse* (378) [a thorny enterprise] yielding more than the initial fruits of its experience. No one, he states proudly, has fashioned himself so boldly or with such overtly useless zeal.

That is what the narrative seems to say. But the essay betrays an obverse composition, in which vocables and letters disperse from the moment the author falls from his horse. Following a self-reflective design, the "head" of the essay – its title and number, volume two, chapter six or "sis" – sits on top of its graphic mass which it concretizes in miniature. The essay therefore begins to disaggregate the letters of the title no less strikingly than the accident does the body of the essayist who writes of its traumatic effects and infers from their impact its political causes. We are never quite told why Montaigne ventures out of his house; but we are led to believe that the journey might be occasioned by religious strife. From the outset the substantive of the title, *exercitation*, is juxtaposed to its analogous verb, *essayer*: "Mais à mourir, qui est la plus grande besoigne que nous ayons à faire, l'*exercitation* ne nous y peut ayder. On se peut, par usage and par *experience*, fortifier contre les douleurs, la honte, l'indigence et tels autres accidents; mais, quant à la mort, nous ne la pouvons *essayer* qu'une fois" (350, my italics). [But to die, which is the greatest task we have to undertake, exercise is of no help. One can, by use and practice, be fortified against pain, shame, indigence and other such accidents; but as for death we can essay it only once.] The words are balanced, poised, sifted, tried and tested: they – and their characters – will ultimately be the proof of experience and death, whereas the empirical world will be seen in its dialogue with their movement.

The essay devalues the veracity of its empirical dimension by feigning not to remember exactly how much time has passed since the accident,[13] nor how many people carried the author back to the warmer confines of his home. When he is oblivious to facts, a sense of truth comes only when print fixes the matter of his memory. In those moments he nascently "tries" death through the minuscule characters of style:

Pendant nos troisiesmes troubles ou deuxiesmes (il ne me souvient pas bien de cela), m'estant allé un jour promener à une lieue de chez moy, qui suis assis dans le moiau de tout le trouble des guerres civiles de France, estimant estre en toute seureté et si voisin de ma retraicte que je n'avoy point besoin de meilleur equipage, j'avoy pris un cheval bien aisé, mais non guiere ferme. A mon retour, une occasion soudaine s'estant presentée de m'aider de ce cheval à un service qui n'estoit pas bien de son usage, un de mes gens, grand et fort, monté sur un puissant roussin qui avoit une bouche desesperée, frais au demeurant et vigoureux, pour faire le hardy et devancer ses compaignons vint à le pousser à toute bride droict dans ma route, et fondre comme un colosse sur le petit homme et petit cheval, et le foudroyer de sa roideur et de sa pesanteur, nous envoyant l'un et l'autre les pieds contre-mont: si que voilà le cheval abbatu et couché tout estourdy, moy dix ou douze pas au delà, mort, estendu à la renverse, le visage tout meurtry et tout escorché, mon espée que j'avoy à la main, à plus de dix pas au-delà, ma ceinture en pieces, n'ayant ny mouvement ny sentiment, non plus qu'une souche. C'est le seul esvanouissement que j'aye senty jusques à cette heure. Ceux qui estoient avec moy, après avoir essayé par tous les moyens qu'ils peurent, de me faire revenir, me tenans pour mort, me prindrent entre leurs bras, et m'emportoient avec beaucoup de difficulté en ma maison, qui estoit loing de là environ une demy lieuë Françoise. (373)

[During our third or second conflict (which one really doesn't come right to mind), going for a ride about a mile or so from my place which is set right at the hub of all the stir of the French civil wars, sensing myself safe and sure with the best men around me, I took an easy-going but scarcely firm horse. On returning, a sudden occasion allowing me to use the horse to make an unfamiliar move, one of my men, who was big and strong, mounted on a powerful steed that had a very hard mouth and was fresh and vigorous, to show his force and pass his companions, happened to loosen the reins and go at full bridle in my path and knock over the little man and the little horse like a colossus, and strike him like a thunderclap with his force and mass, sending both of us topsy-turvey: there we were, the horse beaten down and in a daze, myself, ten or twelve feet away, dead, stretched out upside-down, my face bruised and lacerated, the sword I was carrying in my hand more than ten feet beyond, my belt in pieces, and with no more movement or sensation than a log. That is the only swoon I have ever felt up to now. Those who were with me, after having tried by every means they could to bring me back, took me for dead, took me in their arms and carried me with great difficulty back to my home about a half a mile away.]

As he went further and further away from his domain Montaigne approached the center that he had just left, that is, his "seat" at the hub (*moiau*) of the civil wars. The backward motion of his memory is determined by an exact serial repetition, by which the *troisiesmes* (3) and *deuxiesmes* (2) of the wars lead to *une lieuë* (1), a privileged site of Montaigne's body, a locus of calm in the center of the turmoil. Allegorically, *moyau* encircles the hub through allusion at once to: a middle; a means, that is, the *moyen*, or the going and coming; the modes or money of the characters tracing the tale; the displacement of the self from itself to somewhere else (*moy-au* or *moi … au … delà*). Montaigne's nightmare of death appears to be a fantasm where, lacking his means of writing or of style – his horse, his sword, his saddle, his accoutrements or "effects" – he is left hapless. When immobilized and in a coma casting him in a condition where he felt sensations but was unable to convey them through language, he remarks, "Je n'imagine aucun estat pour moy si insupportable et horrible, que d'avoir l'ame vifve et affligée, sans moyen de se déclarer" (375) [I can imagine no state either so impossible or horrible than having the spirit alive and afflicted, but without means of making itself known]. His exercise will depend on the style that spurs movement enough to declare those impressions where, in the silence of writing, they cannot be declared. Here the letter allows him to go beyond experience, but within the words that mark the perimeters of sensation. In terms of visible characters that establish the geographical axes of the parable, *moy* is moved outward, toward the circumference or outer limits of the chapter, both beyond and not-beyond, free but arrested in the tourniquet of a *pas au-delà*, a step-not-beyond. The centrifugal movement (which complements the centripetal spiral toward the center of the *moi* in *émoi*) is marked in visible cadences of *là* ("voi*là* ... douze pas au de*là* ... à *la* renverse ... à *la* main ... à plus de dix pas au-de*là*") and the cipher heralding the letter of death ("*m*oy ... *m*ort ... *m*eurtry ... la *m*ain ... *m*a ceinture ... n'ayant ny *m*ouve*m*ent ni senti*m*ent").[14] Ten or twelve steps further and further away from his demise, cast on the ground like letters on a page, his armament scattered, Montaigne is almost dead. Only the rhythm of the *pas-au-delà*, printed writing within and beyond the event itself, holds the eye at the center of the essay where the author is safely placed.

That Montaigne's *moi* is at once the means (**moy**en) and the axle (**moy**eu or **moy**au) of the essay seems clear. That the combinations of graphemes and vocables produce the evidence may be less so. Few of Montaigne's essays appear to turn about a single word with so much persistence. The recurrences of the mark of *moy* are so frequent that three inscriptions resurface in other constellations of fragmented signs. Sleep, or *sommeil*, the figure that engages the exercise of death, dominates the essay, but also contains the *moi* in its spell (som*m*eil). "Ce n'est pas sans raison qu'on nous fait regarder à nostre *sommeil* mesme, pour la ressemblance qu'il a de la mort" (372). [Hardly without reason do we have to look at our very sleep, even for its resemblance to death.] He adds, "A l'adventure pourroit sembler inutile et contre nature la faculté du *sommeil* qui nous prive de toute action et de tout sentiment, n'estoit que, par iceluy, nature nous instruit qu'elle nous a pareillement faicts pour mourir que pour vivre" (372). [Occasionally it appears that the faculty of sleep that deprives us of all action and affect would be useless and contrary to nature, were it not that through her means nature tells us that she has designed us equally for living and dying.]

Felt across the sight of his body spattered with the blood he has
vomited, the first impression of his fall from the horse was "meslée
à cette douceur que sentent ceux qui se laissent glisser au *sommeil*"
(374) [mixed with the sweetness felt by those who let themselves
slip into sleepiness].

Montaigne slides into oblivion through discourse and diction. He
asserts that life "ne me tenoit plus qu'au bout des lèvres" (374)
[held me only at the edge of my lips]. He no longer vomits; he closes
his eyes to protect himself from the pain of life. The approaches
of death were like "le beguayement du sommeil" (375) [the stuttering
of sleep]. The essay "comes to its senses" when Montaigne, his soul
"comme lechée seulement et arrosée par la molle impression des
sens (376) [as if only licked and sprinkled by the soft impression of
the senses], evoked the return to a symbolic order, that is, to the
history of his rebirth. In the same fashion, *sommeil* rises out of its
inertia by virtue of the reader, miming Montaigne's style, uncovering
other words in *sommeil*. *Mol*, an adjective recurring often in the
essay, appears to be linked to the sight of *mort*, or death.[15] To
adduce the truthfulness of his reverie he offers the exemplum of
those stoic souls who have had their eyes put out or their virile
organs ripped away, "de peur que leur service, trop plaisant et trop
mol, ne relaschast et n'attendrist la fermeté de leur ame" (371)
[for fear that their service, too pleasant and too soft, might loosen
and soften the firmness of their soul]. Softness, or *mollesse*, generates
the sleep (*sommeil*) of death through the striking figure of its contrary, that in the letters of the words is visually likened to it. As in
Ronsard's poetry, the words describe one thing, but their form figures
in another design across the mirror reversing them. Most people,
Montaigne notes from apparent experience on the battlefields of civil
strife, that "nous voyons ainsi renversez et assopis aux approches
de leur fin ... ou blessez en la teste, que nous oyons **rommeller** et
rendre par fois des souspirs trenchans" (374) [we see thus turned
over and sleepy at the approach of their demise, or wounded in
the head, whom we hear groaning and sometimes rendering trenchant
sighs], fascinate our eyes. Sound and sight are aligned, but then
broken when the more conventional **grommeler** (Cotgrave: "To
grumble, repine, murmure, mutter betweene the teeth") is replaced
by **rommeler** ("To rumble, grumble, grunt"). Sleep is elided into
the whisper of what slips into sleep, going from drowsiness to softness, or to *mollesse* (**glisser** au **sommeil**), and folds, mutely, into
a visible whisper. When the author notes that he felt the pain of
his body signalling his return to life, it was thanks to the sight of

his "membres tous moulus et froissez de ma cheute" (375) [limbs ground and shaken from my fall], but also to the resemblance of *mollesse* to *sommeil* by means of the slippage of anagram.

The writer succeeds in making an essay of death by which he exceeds life through passage in and about printed letters, in the way he sows and gathers figures through their orthographic configurations. The visual style of the characters – the digits – of meditation builds linkages and ruptures of sight and sound, and these in turn produce the essay or "effect" of death.[16] Announced thus is the birth of an unconscious. In this respect several groups of letters appear to chart the essay's overall design. One, knotted around *sommeil* and *mollesse*, arches toward those connoting death. Its effects come softly to Montaigne, as if in sleep, for the good reason that these groups are formed through graphic resemblance and not syntax. A loose but visible order of connections, a syntax of dreams, is put forward. Each set of letters becomes a vanishing point of sorts, or a center of tension that provides a surrounding context whence others can come forth and recede as well. The points are everywhere and can multiply according to the disposition of the reading. But here, in moving from the tale of his fall to its moral consequence, Montaigne praises the enterprise that will parade his dead body in public. "Je m'estalle entier: c'est un *skeletos* où, d'une veuë", les veines, les muscles, les tendons paroissent, chaque piece en son siege" (379). [I display myself entirely: it is a *skeleton* where, in one view, veins, muscles, tendons appear, each piece in its place.] The printed writing, seen on the page of the book, is both his living body, taken from the past, and a sign of its biological posterity in the future.[17] In this context, according to the biological tradition inherited from medieval science, his body functions by virtue of a process of analogy that can be likened to hydraulics, where pressures are exerted and released; or, of dynamic correspondences, by degrees of resemblances which correct imperfections through comparison of the corpus with the effects of the world, through endless equilibrations of signs and movements.[18] The body puts into circulation letters that it exchanges through the work of the organism that ingests and digests them. In respect to *mollesse, sommeil*, and *skeletos*, the scriptural body of Montaigne acts no differently: ciphers circulate from one word or piece of a sentence to another, but all following the dynamic internal coherence of the body that the sum of words and figures produces and serves to reconfigure according to changing contexts.

Involuntary and unconscious movements dart through the overall skein of characters before the reader's eyes. *Skeletos* projects the figure of the author's body with more graphic immediacy than *squelette*. The echo of the Greek in *skeletos* does more than merely invoke an official or medical term. The foreign word is attached to Montaigne's own language by means of the presence of bone and flesh, *chair et os*, in the printed writing. *Skeletos* is sifted, tried, and essayed. Transliteration from the Greek into the French alphabet fits his overall design better than either the original (or the French translation, in *squelette*) because of the visual presence of *-os* that marks the suffix. Hence, by means of the bone, **os**, hidden in **sommeil** that now slides into **mollesse**, Montaigne's nightmare surges up from dreams and comes forward over time. Montaigne's *skeletos* seems to recall the emblematic tradition of the *memento mori*, the *danse macabre* of Holbein's anamorphic illustrations in the *Simulachres de la mort* (1538), or the same artist's historiated alphabets whose letters are props for the play of skeletons about them. Montaigne continues to revive Death by the sight of its signature and ciphers traced in *rommellement*, the soldier's last gasp coming from a space beyond life but congealed in the montage of characters translating it. The words mime and parody common pictural forms of death.

As everywhere in the *Essais*, the thought of the "approach" of finality is far more painful than its fact or fixed form. At the time of his accident, Montaigne "dies" before he has time to think (or, he feigns, to write) about it. There was never time enough to be afraid. Thus, erasing the gap between apprehension and event, the constellation of letters that conveys this thought also winds the *effect* of death within the *causes* anticipating what has already been spelled out.

Other patterns of simultaneity spin from the core of *os, sommeil, skeletos*, and *mollesse*. The verb *estonner* establishes contiguous sets of meaning in the paragrammar. *Estonnement* takes place in the continuum of daily labors, hence in a sort of unconscious just below the realm of cognition. "Voicy que j'espreuve tous les jours: suis-je à couvert chaudement dans une bonne sale, pendant qu'il se passe une nuit orageuse et tempesteuse, je m'estonne et m'afflige pour ceux qui sont lors en la campaigne; y suis-je moymesme, je ne desire pas seulement d'estre ailleurs" (372). [Here is what I encounter every day: if I am warmly covered in a good room while a stormy and windy night passes outside, I am astonished and grieve for those who are out in the country; if I am there myself, I hardly wish to be elsewhere.] Testing his "astonishment" through an exercise of style that isolates causes from effects – or that inverts their habitual

Plate 7. Letters "M" and "I" from Hans Holbein, *Dance of Death Alphabet* (ca. 1523), used frequently in the sixteenth century. In the "M," Death stands over a physician and places his hand on the urinal being held up to the light in the upper left corner. With the allegory of the *Danse macabre* and the alphabet the printed letter is conceived as a mark of destiny. Here the scene behind the "M" recalls the opening lines (about the inspection of chamber-pots) of "De la vanité" (946). In the "I," a Duke, despairing at the onslaught of Death, his head arched toward the upper corner of the frame, flees a skeleton cloaked in the garb of an old woman. The mechanical relation of the typographical letter to the human anatomy is implied by the I-like articulation of the left arm over the acute angle defined by the right leg suggesting the presence of the letter A. The skeleton can be plied, the image suggests, into any number of alphabetical letters.

temporal order – Montaigne invites the reader to decipher his verbal register as an extended emblem. The text teaches that the spirit resides "enseveli et endormy" [buried and asleep] in the most battered of bodies. "Et ne pouvois croire que, à un si grand *estonnement* de membres et si grande défaillance de sens, l'ame peut maintenir aucune force au dedans pour se reconnoistre" (375, my italics). [And I could never believe that, with such a great astonishment of members and such a great failing of the senses, the spirit can maintain force enough inside to be aware of itself.]

Through variation on *estonner* Montaigne senses or "tests" the dark of night every day, or "tous les jours," so that diurnal activity will become uncommonly nocturnal. In this quasi-cinematic rendering of day-for-night, because of the effect yielded by *estonner*, the context of storm extends a metaphor ("il se passe une nuit orageuse et tempesteuse") that invokes the sound of thunder. *Je m'estonne* rings of storm, strife, lightning, and brimstone all the while the formula resonates with visual figures that produce images within and beyond the semantic field. In pleading the cause of the utility of beauty, Montaigne compares the description he fabricates of himself to cosmetics that can enhance or embalm a written body. "Encore se faut-il testoner, encore se faut-il ordonner et renger pour sortir en place. Or je me pare sans cesse, car je me descris sans cesse" (378). [Still we must fashion ourselves, even order and arrange ourselves in order to go out in public. Now I bedeck myself endlessly since I endlessly describe myself]. The context would dictate that the strange verb, *testoner*, is close in meaning to what Cotgrave defines as "To curle, entramell, frizle." But *estonner* has been reverberating all through the essay in other words, and its echo makes the limited meanings of *testoner* begin to vacillate. A *teston* was the name given to a piece of money bearing the effigy of the kings of France, circulated when Francis I had the coin struck to commemorate the Milanese campaigns; it held currency in Montaigne's time and all the way up to the reign of Louis XIII.

Now, in endlessly beautifying himself Montaigne strikes his own image on the obverse of the coin that is the very currency of his book. He valorizes himself by means of his lettered medallion of style that acquires the monetary worth. From the clap of thunder to the figure of the coin, the project of self-portraiture acquires the "frappe" – the sound and the image at once – of a head moulded in relief on a heraldic surface. The money of the book will allow its king, the author, to accrue symbolic worth without needing to leave his kingdom or risk falling off his horse. Because of the web of associations generated by the combinations of *estonner* and *testoner*, the birth of the enterprise of visible, almost numismatic, autobiography becomes evident.

But at the same time *estonner* can be followed through Montaigne's particularly graphic appeal to a spectrum of meanings. The sixteenth-century verb goes back to *estonuer* (in the twelfth century), meaning "to shake up" in a physical sense. The verb derives from the Vulgar Latin *extonare* and from the Classical *attonare* and *adtonare*, meaning "to strike with thunder." At the center of the Latin word and its French variant the reader can see the Greek *tono*, meaning to extend, to display, and to make thunder. The two meanings are alloyed in the stormy context of "exercitation," and when drawn to its conclusion, the word opens on to the unconscious of the essay. *Extonare* and *estonner* include in their family the English *astony*, a verb meaning "to paralyze," or "to strike with a thud."[19]

It would be tempting to see the cause of *estonnement* in the stony materiality of the sensation of death as it is inscribed or struck in the chapter. From the beginning. Montaigne noted that he has written his essays through intervals, in moments of pleasure experienced between the pains caused by the urinary stone that had been afflicting him. "Ce fagotage de tant de diverses pieces se faict en cette condition, que je n'y mets la main que lors qu'une trop lasche oisiveté me presse, et non ailleurs que chez moy. Ainsin il s'est basty à diverses poses et intervalles, comme les occasions me detiennent ailleurs par fois plusieurs moys" (758). [This bundle of so many diverse limbs is being made in this condition, by which I put my hand on it only when an overly flaccid idleness presses me, and nowhere else than at home. It has been built at various positions and intervals, as occasion sometimes keeps me away for several months (or: "me's") at a stretch.] Perhaps Montaigne *testonait*, or "tested" and "festooned," his essays when he was not under the pain of the kidney stones passing through his urinary tract or, by extension, when the meaning of his words does not congeal into a bony or stony fixity. His book becomes the simulacrum of a still-born child who will be his only male descendant in the genealogical line reaching back to Pierre Eyquem. One uncanny element of the essay might be seen in the play of a debt owed to Pierre, the synonym of a stone, from whom the author, as son, can never be acquitted, no matter what the production of signs written in the wake of his father. The most immediate reception of the essay has to be supremely ambiguous: a useless and silent *bibelot*, a piece of money without currency, or a shape without a code, it can be figured as the portrait of an author half-paralyzed – *estonné* – by the pain of stones. A hidden term in the symbolic workings of the essay, *Pierre* would equivocate on the money and genealogy that has worth only through self-generated speculation on the future of a past memorialized in printed characters. Or, as he also writes in the essay on the resemblance of children to fathers (II, xxxvii),

Il est à croire que je dois à mon **pere** cette qualité **pierre**use, car il mourut merveilleusement affligé d'une grosse pierre qu'il avoit en la vessie. (763, my italics)

[It might be that I owe this stony quality to my father, for he died horrendously afflicted by a big stone that lodged in his urinary tract.]

The concrete object, the book, would be the best *moyen*, the money or the currency of style and, too, the mediation between health announced at the beginning of the essay – "J'ay passé une bonne partie de mon aage en une parfaite et entiere santé: je dy non seulement entiere, mais encore allegre et bouillante" (372) [I spent much of my life in perfect and entire health: I say not only entire, but even quick and ebullient] – and the dessicated and deadened figure of the *skeletos* at the end.

Skeletos marks the lower edge of the essay's frame and harks back to the *estonnement* of the beginning. Like an extended *sonnet rapporté* of Ronsard's *Amours*, the end of the chapter picks up the letters of the opening sentences, as if it were folding ske**letos** into es**to**nnement. Astonishment at the view of the skeleton refers to the effect of the sight of death precipitated through the words the author is essaying in his narrative. Graphic similarities begin to reveal how the ethics and the practice of style originate through the exercise of visible and concealed writing. Different sets of meanings are born in the expression of what appears to be a clearly defined statement. Style comes forward almost unconsciously, with an uncanny force that virtually catches the reader in the montage of its characters. When Montaigne describes how he regained his health after the trauma of his accident, he rediscovers his sense of style, that is, the wherewithal needed to fashion his verbal portrait:

Mais long temps apres, et le lendemain, quand ma memoire vint à s'entr'ouvrir et me representer l'estat où je m'estoy trouvé en l'instant que j'avoy aperçeu ce cheval fondant sur moy (car je l'avoy veu à mes talons et me tins pour mort, mais ce pensement avoit esté si soudain que la peur n'eut pas loisir de s'y engendrer), il me sembla que c'estoit un esclair qui me frapoit l'ame de secousse et que je revenoy de l'autre monde. Ce conte d'un évenement si legier est assez vain, n'estoit l'instruction que j'en ay tirée pour moy; car, à la verité, pour s'aprivoiser à la mort, je trouve qu'il n'y a que de s'en avoisiner. Or, comme dict Pline, chacun est à soymesmes une très-bonne discipline, pourveu qu'il ait la suffisance de s'espier de près. (377)

[For a long time afterward, and the next day, when my memory began to come back and to show me the state in which I found myself at the instant I had glimpsed this horse bearing down upon me (for I had seen it on my heels and took myself for dead, but this thought had been so sudden that fear had scarcely time enough to be born), it seemed to me that it was a thunderbolt that struck my soul with a jolt and that I was coming back from the other world. This tale of such a slight event is quite vain, were it not for the lesson that I have taken from it for myself. For in truth, to train [*s'aprivoiser*] for death, I find that all that is needed is to be close to it [*s'en avoisiner*]. Thus, as Pliny [*Pline*] says, everyone is for himself an excellent discipline provided that he has what it takes to spy upon himself closely.]

The movement of his reflection begins with the allusion to thunder and lightning. After the storm of war invoked at the beginning of the chapter, where Montaigne fears for those who have no cover in the outdoors, now the bolt of lightning blends with the figure of the sword and stylus that emerges from the last sentences in the contour of a nascent emblem. Spiked, jagged, and pointed shapes give the essay an accidental edge and show where it glides from a consideration of death to a rhapsodic meditation on style and self-study. The horse that knocked the author out of his saddle came upon him like a thunderbolt, an *esclair*. The text alludes to Pliny the Elder (*Natural History*, XXII, 24), as resourceful editors have indicated. Yet, at the same time, any number of ancient authors could be cited to illustrate the same point. "Pline" is quoted as much for the play of characters as for reference to his *Natural History*. Because of the rhyme of *pline* and *discipline*, Montaigne marks exactly where and how he is going to draw his sword of style out of the scabbard of ancient authors. All the connotations of depth and opacity that go with death are turned into a play of surfaces and self-cancelling paradoxes, reflections and refractions abounding among the characters that dance in and through the words:

> Or, comme **dict Pline**, chacun est à soymesmes une trés bonne **discipline,**

shows how the discipline of meditation invests in the play between proper and common names, in paronomasia, but especially in the visible resemblance that one set of letters almost biologically shares with another. Just as *s'avoisiner* inflects *s'aprivoiser*, so does the authority of Pliny ("dict Pline") fold into the art of a discipline ..., that is, one of hidden, inner quotation obtained from viewing the self as a set of interchangeable characters: so says Pliny right here, *dict ci pline*, whence the origin of the self-portrait born and spied upon from within the frame of its own name.[20]

If Pliny dictates the order of a discipline, the play of his signature reveals where and how the sword of style is attached to the sense of sight. In the syntagm that is of a redundant serial order,

> *de* s'**espier** *de* près,

s'espier tends to paralyze movement by its visible identity with *de près*. Its combination of the figure of a (hidden) sword and the thrust of the eye that plunges inward (*espée de près*) beguiles us into following a "deeper" meditation moving away from the surface-effects that are on the page. The relation of redundantly plosive and sibilant vocables heightens the typographical flicker of the poetry. The cadence of the sentences is not a simple effect of alliteration or assonance: they are part of an emblematic mode whose style is developed from the autonomies of language seen and of language heard. Emblems are cast from the given difference, and in this sense the sword that Montaigne loses in his fall is retrieved in a manifold allegory that reflects unconscious dimensions of force, of fear, but also of a will to afford immortality in the shape of his identity of himself as a writer's body set in codes of printed characters.

In the famous addition to the text whose turn of phrase literally essays the inner self, the same verbal emblems penetrate the surface of its words exactly where they keep the eye arrested on the adventitious configuration of writing. "C'est une espineuse entreprinse," he notes, "et plus qu'il ne semble, de suyvre une alleure si vagabonde que celle de notre esprit; de penetrer les profondeurs opaques de ses replis internes; de choisir et arrester tant de menus airs de ses agitations" (378). [It is a thorny enterprise, and more difficult than it appears, to follow such an errant allure as that of our spirit; to penetrate the opaque depths of its inner folds; to choose and arrest so many slight airs of its agitations.] *L'espineuse entreprinse* reflects what it takes to *s'espier de près.* According to the labors of anagrams,[21] *L'espineuse entreprinse* reflects the figure of *s'espier de près,* engaging the visual figure of *l'espée,* both as a lightning bolt and a stroke of writing which penetrate the depths of the self. Spirit or wit is conceived not as a concept or an idea, but as an allure of style, or even a mannequin in a series of other figures that have visible assonance. "C'est une espineuse entreprinse, et plus qu'il ne semble, de suyvre une alleure si vagabonde que celle de nostre esprit": endowed with a style anchored in the recurring bends and bars of his letters, Montaigne glimpses the immortality of his soul in an area neither hidden nor subject to revelation through cognition. A measure, a cadence, a syncopation, the spirit appears to be part of a poetic montage of physical shapes.

In the same fashion we are also tempted to discern another cadence through the labor of amphiboly. If, as Montaigne notes, one must have power enough to *s'espier de près,* one must also scrutinize the formula, as it is printed, at the foot of the letter: also seen and heard are *ses pieds de près* [one's feet from near] by which the sight of one's feet alludes to the measure and pace of the discourse. In the 1592 additions, the text extends the metaphor by insisting on ambulation in the essay of death: "Nous n'avons nouvelles que de deux ou trois anciens qui ayent battu ce chemin" (377). [We have word of only two or three ancients having beaten this path.] The rhythm of the enterprise of style engages an enumeration that connects the "two

or three" souls who have essayed death in Montaigne's own context
of the "third" or "second" − he can't remember which − civil
wars that mark the origins of the Montaigne's inner experience.

In this light the essay binds its visual, graphic and sonorous
elements to the sum of its context. Two or three wars reflect the figure
of two or three attempts at producing a style. In the relation of the
detail and the sum configuration a portrait is born but also, as we
shall discover, a politics of letters. "De l'exercitation" contains
itself in its own conscious and unconscious dynamics, and it maps
a manner or an elegant presence of a self-reflective writing that will
dominate the third volume. Unsolicited effects and new skeins of
meaning are produced through our perception of a syntax of graphic
particles that move in and about the semantic order.[22] The text invites the reader to slide over its surface and to compare the impression
of movement gained in scansion to the meaning articulated in the
grammar. The resulting complexities became endlessly arcane, but
their process is clear. Letters and figures are set in a montage that
might be likened to a mobile or moving architecture. The task at
hand does not involve the need to fix its principles or to formulate
its stylistic laws. Rather, now that an order of movement has been
disengaged from the tale of Montaigne's fall, we must see how the
self-referential operation of the visible writing affects its ideological
and historical latencies.

6

A COLOSSAL ABYSS:
DES COCHES

Montaigne's self-portrait conveys many of its salient traits in good taste, or with *civilité*. The word alludes to social grace, but also to the history of humanity being born out of barbarity.[1] *Civilité* also designates a printing style that had been popular since the middle years of the sixteenth century. Writers possessing civility, therefore, could be expected to be polished, but also cognizant of the new styles of printed writing emerging from the culture of mechanical writing. The essays appear to be written in the wake of Plantin's innovations in print form. They also capitalize on a perspectival interpretation of the letter that Tory had begun with his typographic reform. By the 1580s most reform in orthography had settled and would remain constant into the seventeenth century.[2] The *Essais* exploit typographical forms that had recently been standardized; their innovations work primarily in areas between meaning, paginal format, and equivocations of letter and voice. The *Essais* are sprinkled with Latin citations, in Italic font, that punctuate the chapters. Indentations of paragraph headings are a product of modern editions that interpret falsely where the author's thoughts begin and end.

The order of each essay works much more subtly, according to the graphic and serial distribution of its words, letters, *centons*, or other ciphers. Titles and numbers of chapters accrue special meaning in respect to their text. They mark places where meaning is hidden or nascent, or where letters offer an "oblique view" of the essay and change the tenor of words before our eyes. "J'entends que la matiere se distingue soy-mesmes. Elle montre assez où elle se change, où elle conclud, où elle commence, où elle se reprend, sans l'entre-lasser de paroles, de liaison et de cousture introduites pour le service des oreilles foibles ou non challantes, et sans me gloser moymesme" (995). [I mean that the matter should distinguish itself by itself. It shows enough where it is changing, where it concludes, where it begins, where it is taken up again, without weaving speech into it, linkages, or conjunctions introduced for the service of ears that are weak or nonchalant, and without glossing myself.]

In the same context, when Montaigne announces, "c'est l'indiligent lecteur qui pert mon subject, non pas moy" (994) [it is the indiligent reader who loses my subject and not I], he appeals to an anamorphic wit that bends his words. To read diligently signifies to gather the sense of the essays by patient application. But if the same diligence does not realize that *pert* can infer at once "losing" and "perceiving" or "glimpsing" what is pertinent, or that losing sets meaning in motion, the myriad aspects of the writer's style will be overlooked. The inscrutably rich pages on the poetics of the *Essais* here in "De la vanité" (994–95), in "Sur des vers de Virgile" (874–75) or elsewhere move in dialogue with the printed letter. They suggest that the mechanics of the poetry touch on the political dimensions of Montaigne's self-portrait.

In "De l'exercitation" Montaigne tells how he was knocked off his horse and thrown to the ground. In the third volume at the end of "Des coches" (III, vi), the story is told again, but in the third person and about a South American Indian king. Some Spanish conquerors pull the Emperor of Peru off his litter and topple him over. "De l'exercitation" is placed to the left of the voluminous center of the second book, "Apologie de Raimond Sebond" (II, xii), while "Des coches" figures as a vanishing point of the third volume. Both II, vi and III, vi use the same locus – a seat, a saddle, a position (*assiette*), or throne – to perch figures that are dethroned. Montaigne falls in "exercitation," while his indigenous other, his unknown friend of the Americas, is thrust to the earth in "Des coches." Both essays use the rebus of *sis*, combining a "setting" or a "place," and the number *six* to locate their circularity and axiological play. "Des coches" reputedly counts among the more difficult of Montaigne's later essays.[3] It writes of boats, waggons, war, and locomotion; conquest in the New World; national economic policy under the regency of Catherine de Medici. It ultimately offers its own density as an example of what the essay – again, as evidence of poetry – can marshall to remedy a diseased state of the world. By means of a homeopathic kind of writing, following the synthesis of printing, death, civil war and autobiography begun in "De l'exercitation," "Des coches" links Montaigne's ideological stance of 1588 to the actual *form* of his essay. Where "De l'exercitation" had feigned the trials of its own evolution, "Coches" is written as a totally self-enclosing shape of letters in spatial expression. Its closure maps the diagnostic for a national cure, and it appears that

Montaigne himself is sacrificed in his book for the future of his nation and the world.

At least five different modes of composition appear to produce its aspect of careful chaos. The essay is (1) centered in the third volume so as to fit, like a jewel, abyssally, but also askew, just to the side of the axis of the book, the diminutive seventh chapter tracing a meridian between the zenith and the abyss of kingship or a point around which turns the King's Wheel of Fortune. "Des coches" seems to be an *effect* − or, in visual identity, an *effai* − that anticipates its cause in "De l'incommodité de la grandeur" (III, vii), the central chapter that follows and identifies the seat or throne of power in the book's kingdom. Essays III, vi and III, vii mark the axes of an elliptical, double vanishing point establishing a coincidence of the author and political conditions of the 1580s. The form of the essay (2) follows a practice of textual positioning characteristic of the practice of numismatics. The eye is led to behold a center that is an image or an inscription − as that on a coin − but its enigma can only be solved when the eye scans a superscription − another enigma − and a subscription on the periphery or reverse of its medaillion-like form.[4] Image and text are identical by virtue of their schematic disposition in extensive space, but the displacement, owed to the difference of optical and discursive grounding, forever defers any solution to the problems in the difference that the essay is imprinting.

Discourse (3) continually makes cross-references to itself through play of optical and aural expression. Because the essay seems to be cast as a device, a coin, and a rebus both conveying and figuring its form, the letters transform the implied visual shapes of their referents. One of these is the central component of the vehicle of its title. The letter **o** within the visual axis of *Des coches* (desc-**o**-ches) encircles the intersection of writing and political space. In turn (4), the essay appeals to identities of letters and words which translate each other into meanings so hidden that they are obvious. In this sense Montaigne's writing acquires nuances that distort and complicate statements cast from conventional exempla or banalities. Multiple amphibolies result, such that the style codes *double-entendres* into single words (following the reading of Rabelais above, where words respell themselves or, in the mode of Ronsard, where a signifier of little discursive value is invested into the poetic texture with uncanny poetic intensity). The tactic entails insertion of analogy or association into single digits. We shall see that the letter *o* amounts to a figure of a coin, an open mouth, an anus, a Roman arena, a sign of gold, a wheel, and the barrel of an arquebus aimed at the Amerindian or the reader. Last, as a speculative creation that apposes given geographical and historical knowledge (5), the essay has a cardinal disposition inspired by the allegorical practices of contemporary painting and cartography.

The emblematic form is most striking in the relation that "Des coches" holds with the end seemingly appended to the long and rambling chapter on love, "Sur des vers de Virgile" (III, v), perched just above. A repeated incipit, *il est bien... aisé*, frames the crowning unit of title, chapter, and number:

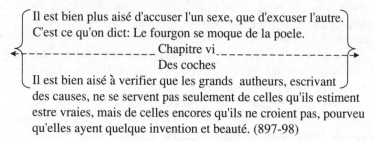

Il est bien plus aisé d'accuser l'un sexe, que d'excuser l'autre.
C'est ce qu'on dict: Le fourgon se moque de la poele.
Chapitre vi
Des coches
Il est bien aisé à verifier que les grands autheurs, escrivant
des causes, ne se servent pas seulement de celles qu'ils estiment
estre vraies, mais de celles encores qu'ils ne croient pas, pourveu
qu'elles ayent quelque invention et beauté. (897-98)

[It is much easier to accuse one sex than to excuse the other.
So goes the proverb: the pot calls the kettle black.
Chapter vi
Of Coaches
It is quite easy to verify that great authorities, writing of causes, do not use only those they esteem to be true, but those indeed they do not believe, provided they have some wit and beauty.]

An initial enigma is produced by the emblematic frame of discourse. The etymology and iconography of *coche* dictate that it be both a boat and a wagon, a *coque* and a *coche*, and all the more in the surrounding context where Montaigne's diction flows freely between Latin and French.[5] The title is as ambiguous as it is amphibious. The mode of transport comes into view in its allusion to an emblem of a ship of state. To a reader of the Angelier edition of 1588 printed in Paris, *coches* would refer to the vessel in the center of the famous escutcheon of the capital that displays a boat on water under a row of *fleur-de-lys*. Below, the motto, *Fluctuat nec mergitur*, "it floats but does not sink," points to an uneasiness that Montaigne associates with seasickness and an urge to vomit. By allusion to the memory-image of the ship of state in the context of the author's discussion of a propensity to be seasick, the title gains a cathartic or emetic virtue that would seem to induce expurgation of illness from one human body in order to precipitate change in the national body in which it figures.

A *colossal abyss:* Des coches

Early in the essay, when confronting the thought of a *mal de mer,* or motion-sickness, Montaigne implies that the same sensation of nausea may be synonymous with "metaphor-sickness," that is, disgust at the ways public language attempts to literalize its referents in lavish show of wealth, and thus to have less physical worth than money. Implicit criticism of the state is made through a mimetic model, by which an authority is seen producing a dazzling display for the purpose of legitimizing its own power. The subjects who observe ostensive public show buy truth on credit. The author soon remarks, "*Or* je ne puis souffrir long temps (et les souffrois plus difficilement en jeunesse) ny coche, ny littiere, ny bateau; et hay toute autre voiture que de cheval, et en la ville et aux champs" (900, my italics). [Now/gold I can't stand for a long time (and used to put up with them with more difficulty in youth) either coach, litter, or boat; and I hate any other mode of conveyance than a horse, both in the city and the country.] The statement mirrors two regimes: one, a wagon drawn by horses, in other words, the effects drawn by their causes; the other, cast in the paragrammar of the sentence, is *or*, or gold, in the balance of syntax, that can be the immediate cause of Montaigne's illness. The two origins of his malaise have to do with circulation of money, with metaphors, and with the plight of international economy.

From the circularity of the diction and the place-names of the essay a carefully drawn cosmography emerges. In a remark poised at the virtual center of the chapter, that hinges between the Old and New Worlds, in a theologically charged discussion of apocalypse, he forecasts, "L'univers tombera en paralisie; l'un membre sera perclus, l'autre en vigueur" (909). [The universe will fall into paralysis; one member will be shrivelled, the other in vigor.] A scheme of cardinal forces dictates the order of the opposition, by which the toponyms acquire a spatial value as if they were stations on a clock, a sphere, or a zodiac. They might be mapped thus:

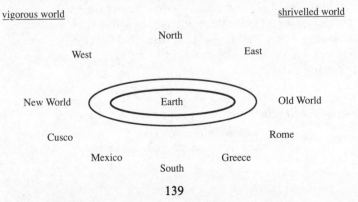

Much of the elliptical order follows the topos of the world in "degeneration,"[6] popular after 1550, that came with the onslaught of civil war and economic depression. It had been associated with renewed readings of the Book of Revelation and with belief in prophecy. With the subjugation of the New Indies, however, came signs of the Second Coming. Europe was said to have to give way to the growth of the Americas that was signalling the return of the Antichrist.

As in the vision of Rabelais, the end of one universe and the birth of another spatialize a sense of renewed fear about the end of seasonal time. Because "coches" comments extensively on the Spanish plunder of Mexico and Peru, the title also points to a discussion of different modes of warfare. "Des coches" can be construed to be about the nock (*coche*) that seats the bowstring propelling its arrow toward a target; but, since wagons also carry culverins, cannon, and muskets, within its array of referents the title implicitly compares archaic and modern technologies of combat; at the same time, a verbal scansion of the letters yields *descoches*, a word that can be read as an imperative because of the unvoiced *s* of the last syllable: *descoche!* With exclamative inflection, the word can invoke the order to "let go," to "release," or to "fire!" a salvo of arrows of gunfire. The essay glides from a general discussion of the causes of unnatural death to the multifarious effects that its title has already suggested. The *effects* of wagons, boats, arrows, cannon, fire, release, and marking go back to the plausible resemblance of *coches* to a plurality of *causes* or *choses*.

The opening lines of the essay provide clues for the decipherment of title, number, and figure heralded in emblematic inscription and superscription. Answers to the enigma are printed within its very form. Authorities, the text confirms – at its most authorative moment, its head, on top of the chapter – speak quite veraciously and usefully if they state ingeniously. The remark seems to be made not only about others but also about itself and the composition below the reader's eyes. Obliquely then, the initial statements point to the number and title that designate a throne, the topic taken up in the following chapter:

Nous ne pouvons nous asseurer de la maistresse cause; nous en entassons plusieurs, voir si par rencontre elle se trouvera en ce nombre,

> *namque unam dicere causam*
> *Non satis est, verum plures, unde una tamen sit.* (899)

[We cannot be assured of the master cause; we pile up several to see if by chance it will be found in this number,

> *For it does not suffice to indicate one cause.*
> *Let us suggest several: one shall be satisfactory.*]

A strange mirroring makes Lucretius' *plures* (*De rerum natura*, VI, 604–05) reflect Montaigne's *plusieurs*, and also has *causam* hark back to *cause*; *satis* forward to *sit*; above all, *sit* to *nombre*, which is *vi* or "six" just above, in the title. *Six* engages bodily pleasure, the art of sitting at the center of the throne, while confusion of six and "seat" fits in the center of the figure of the coach–boat that has the sign of a royal figure at its vanishing point in the field of the coat-of-arms of Paris or its imprint on a French coin.

Somehow a casual cause is forever embowelled in its effect. The tourniquet suggests that the central authority of the text is where it ought to be, that is, literally, at the geometrical axis of the title in name, number and volume. Below is decreed the effect of words giving adequate "cause" to the rebus above. Now because, at the end of the *Essais*, Montaigne writes jokingly about the king on the highest throne of the world who is still sitting on his bottom (1115), a comic regress leads to reflection on a corrective anality needed to keep any political economy from becoming spendthrift or dissolute in its ethics of disbursement.

Me demandez-vous d'ou vient cette coustume de benire ceux qui estrenuent? Nous produisons trois sortes de vent: celuy qui sort par embas est trop sale; celuy qui sort par la bouche porte quelque reproche de gourmandise; le troisiesme est l'estrenuement; et, parce qu'il vient de la teste et est sans blasme, nous luy faisons cet honneste recueil. Ne vous moquez pas de cette subtilité; elle est (dict-on) d'Aristote (899).

[Do you ask me whence comes this custom of blessing those who sneeze? We produce three kinds of wind: what goes out from below is too dirty; what goes out of the mouth carries some reproach of gluttony; the third is sneezing; and because it comes from the head and is without blame, we give it this civil accord. Don't laugh at this subtlety. It is (they say) in Aristotle].

The emblem continues to close upon itself, for the mockery framed in another emblem at the lower edge of "Sur des vers de Virgile" and the upper margin of "Coches" is reflected in *ne vous moquez pas*, while the proverb ("ce qu'*on dict*") about the pot calling the kettle black ("le fourgon *se moque* de la poele, 897) is visibly reversed in the dictum or *dict-on* of Aristotle, an authority no less commanding than that of popular reason resurging from the lower regions of the social body. The essay appears to recall the moments that experiment with death in "Exercitation," in which the greatest human essay involved dying without dying, but by dying in a language that inspires the body to feel the experience (what comes out of death, from *ex-perire*) of reaching beyond the limits of life. It is a topos, to be sure, but one that Montaigne now distorts in figures of ingestion, indigestion, and egestion. No cause is adduced to note why subjects produce the "other" kinds of wind. The broken syllogism explaining why sneezing requires benediction floats on the top of the chapter but remains only partially answered in reference to Aristotle. A subscription to the emblem of the essay itself, the remark simply extends the enigma because Aristotle in no way seems to be an adequate answer to the riddle.

Juxtaposition of reflections on death, flatulence, and intestinal or stoic fortitude suggests that a self-enclosing concatenation of figures is arranged according to plans of multiple closure but also dilation and constriction. Plutarch is said to "render" the cause (in his *Natural Causes*) explaining why seasickness overtakes passengers on the high seas: fear precipitates violent emission (a subject is said to vomit, urinate, or defecate in fear of imminent death), but Montaigne, who is "fort subject" (both subject to fear and himself a subject in the state), counters that experience can tell how far from the truth is Plutarch. Plutarch seems to be as useless as Aristotle. In simple terms, victims are too queasy to fear about why they feel so ill since the effect of the condition makes it impossible to ever think of its etiology. Whatever dangers Montaigne senses (899), are with open eyes, directly, with a "free, healthy, and entire view." Again, almost recycling the experience and discipline gained in II, vi, the author notes that courage is needed for us to gain strength enough to fear. On this score II, vi and III, vi are identical, except that Montaigne's *fuite*, retreat from or sequel to danger, is cast not as cowardice but as a "release" or *lacheté* that gathers paradoxically heroic virtue, the author facing fear *sans effroy et sans estonnement* (899) [without timorousness or astonishment]. The text clearly associates an individual's seasicknesses with the uncertain wafting of the boat-of-state.

A scheme of remarks on political economy is obliquely established. They appear to be based on the relation that an individual's bodily ingestion and expulsion holds with collective policy. Causes are effects of modes of transport – the nation at sea – on or in which nausea is experienced. In the discursive plan these issues are latent. But in terms of the letters of "Coches," another, more pervasive order is put in view. The text offers up its own printed characters as pieces of exchange, as self-struck coins — "testons" — that will establish adequate currency in place of standards devaluating, wavering or being lost at sea in civil war.

The title had alluded to the golden coach or to the filigree of the national emblem but now discloses its golden dimension in the inertia of the central letter of the title that both *is* and *represents* gold, again, that is both the thing and the "piece estrangère jointe à la chose." Scansion of the pivotal **o** in interior duplication unveils a profusion of dense words that contain money in the coin-like shape of the vowel contiguous to the R of royalty. In other words the text renders gold from its own textual body. In the opening sentences, an amber hue shines from words whose aura is owed to their value to the central *o* of the title out of which they seem to pour: p*o*urveu, enc*o*re, v*o*ir, tr*o*uvera, n*o*mbre, s*o*rte, repr*o*che, g*o*urmandise, Arist*o*te, av*o*ir, tr*o*uvé, r*o*ison, pr*o*duire, f*o*rt, p*o*urceaux, h*o*rs, v*o*mir, tr*o*is, tr*o*uvant, t*o*urmente, m*o*rt, tr*o*uvé, c*o*eur, *o*uverts, *o*rdre, eff*o*roy, est*o*urdie and a host of other words glimmer with golden traits in the paragrammar and then determine the subsequent shape of letters in the rest of the chapter. Others fall in cascade: s*o*rt, r*o*y, f*o*rt, *o*rdre, m*o*rt, t*o*rt, au*o*it, emp*o*rter, f*o*rce, f*o*rme, inf*o*rme, r*o*yne, f*o*rtune, p*o*rt, r*o*yal, par*o*le, f*o*rtification, ref*o*rma-tion, pr*o*duction, thres*o*r, b*o*rdereaux deh*o*rs, enc*o*re, *o*rdinaire, end*o*rmir, *o*rdonner and *o*rnement. All inscribe worth into their own form through their visual field, but since they are paper forms, they also amount to promissory notes or junk bonds.

Gold figures as matter inert, dead, static, or indigestible. It is opposed to more active metals that atomize, transform, and lend or adapt themselves to practical labors. According to principles of alchemy that appear to inform the essay, the metal bears specific attributes. Gold resists change. It cannot be easily compounded into other chemicals or, in a metaphorical sense, digested or broken into smaller units. It thus pertains to a high, noble, or timeless order. Yet gold has traits that assign it, unlike more active metals (lithium, potassium, or sodium), to a realm of inactivity. Akin to excrement in the biological world, it responds very slowly to ambient forces of transformation. Since it does not move, the metal lacks the capacity to assure continuity in the cycles of life. These alchemical and biological traits could imply, by way of allegory, that gold has the misfortune of bearing worth solely in visual and signatory appeal. The questionable energetic — as opposed to catalytic or emetic — value of gold inflects the essay at every level of its expression, and to the extent that its stasis or anality offsets the mobility of style that acquires more worth because it is more active than passive. The discourse keynotes words in order to mark their false value in what seems to be the self-containment of letter and meaning. The essay's substantives become identical to the exemplum of Socrates' self-identity and courage (900), displayed to contrast the current condition of deficit spending and buying (with the man named *Lachez*, or *La chaise*, having much to do with the seat of the essay, but also *lâcheté, lâché*, and *l'acheter*) in the national sphere or the colossal waste of European plunder of the New World. Domestic economic policy, lavishly pictured in public pomp, depends on military strength. In accord with Alcibiades' account of Socrates and Lachez (taken from the *Symposium*), Montaigne unwinds the discursive thread along an axis blending questions of thrift with those of warfare and defense.

The 1592 edition provides an insert that connects the riddle of sneezing to the theme of nausea and fear. Tactical changes in logistics come with the ways coaches adapt to newer strategies inspired by use of gunpower. "Si j'en avoy la memoire suffisamment informée, je ne pleinderois mon temps à dire icy l'infinie varieté que les histoires nous presentent de l'usage des coches au service de la guerre" (901) [Were my memory sufficiently informed, I would not spend my time speaking of the infinite variety that histories offer us of the use of coaches in service of war]. The Hungarians put battlewagons to efficient use against the Turks. Each chariot, or *coche*, was armed with a rondellier (a "buckler," a soldier bearing a *rondelle* or circular shield), a musketeer and a stock of loaded arms. The coaches formed a front line, "et après que le canon avoit joué, les faisoient tirer avant et *avaller* aux ennemys cette salve avant que de taster le reste, qui n'estoit pas un leger avancement; ou les *descochoient* dans leurs escadrons pour les rompre et y faire jour" (901, my emphasis) [and after the cannon had played they made them fire straight ahead and have the enemy swallow this salvo before tasting the rest, which was no light advance; or they cockled them in their squadrons to bust and splay them apart]. The foot-soldiers are forced to swallow a volley of lead and grapeshot. Imagined as a deathly salute and salvation, the firing (that which releases, or *lâche*) almost resembles a blast of saliva from a sneezing arquebus that is tasted (or tested, or essayed) as the last instant of life. *Descocher* is also the imperative shouted by the captain to his musketeer: "Descochez!" [Shoot!], or the last shard of sound the troops hear before they see their own death coming with the lead ball approaching their bellies. An infinitesimal gap between the charge to fire, the crack of the arquebus, and the thud of the slug splattering the body is marked in the style. There we "experience" death and nightmare about the future course of things. The beginning would then be an exclamation shouted at the last instant of life, as well as a written scar or mark, *en coche* [checked], inscribed at the moment of death. The verbs which determine the visual order of the account, *descocher* and *avaller*, refer at once back to the title and forward to the last words of the final sentence, in which a conquistador throws a Peruvian king off his palanquin, and thrusts him down so that the earth almost swallows him up (*"l'alla* saisir au corps, et *l'avalla* par terre," 915).

Whereas seasickness was analogous to regurgitation that simulates death, ingurgitation of cannonfire is its opposite, the abusively "real thing," the effect embroiling its cause. To essay death on a boat appears to be the inverse of falling victim to arquebus fire on foot or being tortured at the hands of armored Spanish plunderers on horseback. When he compares chariots and firepower to bows and arrows, Montaigne deals with what by 1580 had become a historical convention about the demise of earlier modes of warfare. The anecdote only "stages" an analysis of logistics in the greater allegory that touches on how quickly the wheels of history are spinning and how, in global production of surplus, gold must be devalued for the sake of the future of an expanding world living in turmoil and travail.[7] This is why the tale obliquely advocates a military policy of renewed fortification as a means of invigorating French domestic policies. Counsel takes place in the literal register of the discourse. The point is most striking when the riflemen kill the enemy on their own terms, by using gunpowder to "release arrows" and to "unseat" them from positions of authority.

Congruence of word and thing and cause and effect establishes a relation between individual and international or collective subjects. They signal that a nation must adapt itself to other military strategies by fortifying its defensive systems and then use a military force of its own subjects — not mercenary soldiers — to contend with movements within the state that legitimate regicide. "De mon temps," Montaigne continues, "un Gentilhomme, en l'une de nos frontieres, impost de sa personne et ne trouvant cheval capable de son poids, ayant une querelle, marchoit par païs en *coche* de mesme cette peinture, et s'en trouvoit très-bien ... Les Roys de nostre premiere race marchoient en païs sur un charriot trainé par quatre boeufs." (901) [In my time a gentleman on the cusp of one of our borders, imposing and finding no horse capable of sustaining his weight, having a quarrel, marched through the country in a coach of this very figure, and did quite well. The kings of our first race marched through the country on a chariot drawn by four steers]. The gentleman in the anecdote is at the boundaries of a nation and a life – on a line of alterity – but succeeds in staying in the country and in peace in a coach. But sedition is at work. Since *lune* is transcripted anamorphically into the text (in *"l'une* de nos frontières"), like the escutcheon of Paris, the sign may allude to the coat-of-arms of Henri II, Charles IX, and Catherine de Medicis, the regent named with praise elsewhere in the essay. The royalty virtually *imposes* in its decision to tax (*impost*). Criticism of a galloping rate of inflation and taxation besetting France in the later civil wars is implied. But so is the actual status – or seat – of kingship itself, since the comparison aligns modern France with its Merovingian ancestors who were known to show their king to the nation by displaying him on a chariot.

But whoever "sits" is subject to being overthrown. Already by the time the first two volumes of *Essais* were published, tyrannicide was argued to be a licit activity in France. The right to knock down incumbent authority informs Du Plessis-Mornay's *Vindiciae contra tyrannos* (1579) but reaches back to François Hotman's *Francogallia* (1573),[8] as well as the political writings of Etienne de la Boëtie to whom the essays are dedicated. Advancing the cause of an estates-general enjoined to elect or change its leaders, Hotman cited the custom of the early Franks who designated their king by elevating him upon the shoulders of those present. "For he who had been chosen by the votes of the people was placed upon a shield, lifted up, and borne three times round the assembly of the electors, or if the ceremony occurred in a military camp, round the rank of the army amid general applause and acclamation."[9] "Des coches" exploits the same circular motion. Allusion is made to early leaders in a moment of transition in the chapter – where transitions or modes of conveyance are everywhere – that resembles the figure of the Peruvian king thrown off his palanquin. These obliquities still point to the latent argument for overturning a social order, akin to the revolution of a wheel, where Montaigne observes, "Des tyrans ont esté sacrifiez à la hayne du peuple par les mains de ceux mesme lesquels ils avoyent iniquement avancez" (904). [Tyrants have been sacrificed to the people's hate at the hands of the very persons whom they had unjustly put forward.] Perhaps the warning of Protestant ideology serves as a corrective to practice of excessive show in Catholic realms. Whatever the view, the author, unable to state the issue directly, would be required to use arcane expression

and to suggest that an unconscious register of the writing will conflate into its shape other political views.

Circumlocution appears to dictate a discursive and allegorical
order of the essay. A common axis among the superimposed circular
figures evoked – of wheels, coins, letters, coaches – is the horse.
In the mediation between the figure and the function of the coach, the
horse, the second half of the unit of vehicle and tenor of Montaigne's
analogy, defines the "system" of the *coche*. The animal links old
and new modes of defense, transports cannons and machines and,
as *cheval*, supports the national emblem and keeps its troops from
falling to the ground, *aval*.

The final sentences bind the figures of horse and coach, wheel and
foot, support and cadence, center and circumference and respond
to the initial inquiry of the essay:

Retombons à nos coches. En leur place, et de toute autre voiture, ils se
faisoient porter par les hommes et sur leurs espaules. Ce dernier Roy de Peru,
le jour qu'il fut pris, estoit ainsi porté sur des brancars d'or, et assis dans
une cheze d'or, au milieu de sa bataille. Autant qu'on tuoit de ces porteurs
pour le faire choir à bas, car on le vouloit prendre vif, autant d'autres, et
à l'envy, prenoient la place des morts, de façon qu'on ne le peut onques
abbatre, quelque meurtre qu'on fit de ces gens là, jusques à ce qu'un homme
de cheval l'alla saisir au corps, at l'avalla par terre. (915)

[Let's fall to our coaches. In their place, and in preference to all other car-
riages, they [leaders] had themselves carried by men and on their shoulders.
This last King of Peru, the day he was taken, was carried thus on golden
stretchers, and seated in a golden throne in the middle of his battle. For as
many as these porters were killed to knock him down (for they wanted to
take him alive), so many others willingly took the place of the dead, in a
way that they could never beat him down, whatever butchery was imposed
upon those people, until a horse man went to seize him around the body
and toppled him down to earth.]

The emblem of the title is reproduced in a narrative of a juggernaut
wrought in visual symmetries. The Peruvian King sits in the middle
of battle and finds himself in a position, at a point of focal inversion
or dissolution, exactly inverse to that of the "imposing" gentleman
(901) of Montaigne's time. In the absolute center of the slaughter,
the King is immobile until he is either swallowed or thrust into his
own chasm. The gold of which the Peruvian king was a human sign
on the immobile palanquin, separated from the subjects, was displaced by the mobile, dexterous soldier on his horse. By circularity,
the concluding anecdote leads the essay from its own placement at
the end, back up to the top. The latter was marked by the mouth

of the person sneezing, while the former connotes the ethical and biological bottom of the world. The essay moves back and forth from one end to the other.[10] The *coche* on which the reader falls at the terminus becomes an uncanny *coche/cause/chose* of vicious reasoning emblazoned in the collapsed origin and finality of the self-enclosing form. In its given shape the essay baits and enervates its reader through the perfection of its symmetry.

"Coches" is apparently written to be read by a national body or, in relation to the author, as microcosm, to a French macrocosm. Here the critique of national economy appears to be decisive in its play of the letter, where two bundles of characters ostensibly reflect differing views of religion and political practice. Gold is likened to the sign of the thing (the effect or the coach of the *cause*... or *coche*) just as Protestant ideology had seen in the Eucharist only a *sign* of the sacred body of Christ. The *chose*, however, of the King's body, is displaced into the stamp of Montaigne's language which assails — hence corrects — the gap opened by the accruing distance between sign and referent or the leader, his attributes, and his subjects. Commentary on monetary policy is bound to the same issue insofar as currency is being debated in terms of its real or speculative value.[11]

Causes become graphic extensions of the letter **o**, both sign and identity of the nation and the writer. Coaches are royal modes of conveyance plated with gold, as are the litters footmen bear on their shoulders; in the context, boats carry ore from mines to European shores, and artisans fashion figures of the same vehicles under royal contract. Montaigne's incipient autobiographical statement about nausea experienced during languorous motion refers to gold by the proximity of the commanding figure of a national coach emblazoned in the coat-of-arms of Paris: horses are more practical than wagons because they are living, moving bodies and figures associated with style. They are naturally suited for use among all social classes, in Paris or in the provinces, in war or in peace, and among both the nobility and the peasantry. The horse mediates contradiction between classes at war over the unequal taxation, and its active status, in contrast to the deadness of gold, can help to shore up the economy within French borders. As *cheval* connotes *aval*, the letters invoke the state body and its alimentary passage from mouth to sphincter of both the civic body and the essay itself.

The chain of signifiers, like the harness connecting golden coach and horse, leads back to the enumeration of the author's reflections on movement: palanquins, less commodious than coaches, apparently sway with the deliberate movement of feet below them; rocking over

turbulent water, like riding a horse at full gallop, is more settling
than the lazy drift of a ship of state on a suspiciously placid sea in
momentary calm during civil war.[12] Yet the litter is not driven by the
wheel, the western invention that goes with the development of the
Christian ideology that colonizing nations had been using to rational-
ize plunder and slavery.[13] The remarks concerning Montaigne's
preferences for travel are set in autobiographical and political
dialogue. The sensation of a sudden lurch provoked by a wagon or
boat would be less "seatful" or sedious than that of a ship sailing
with a false sense of security: better an efficient economy of overt
exchange than one of constipated pomp set over a trembling center
of authority. "Par cette legere secousse que les avirons donnent,
desrobant le vaisseau soubs nous, je me sens brouiller, je ne sçay
comment, la teste et l'estomach, comme je ne puis souffrir soubs
moy un siege tremblant" (901). [By this light jolt that oars give,
slipping the vessel away under us, somehow I feel my head and
stomach turn, just as I can't stand a trembling seat below me.] The
modes of locomotion are not those driven by horses; reference to
oars implies that the author is referring to galley ships that employ
slaves to row them. Slaves, we shall observe below, will return, like
the repressed, to haunt the essay.

The tales of vehicles, transport, of modes of combat, and of
Socrates' courage (899–900) entail a critique of deficit spending.
Because the king emblematizes the most precious matter of the state,
his presence must be made manifest not just at the upper and lower
ends of the social order, in both cities and the provinces, but also
in the median regions of the national body. Discussion turns from
modes of transport to visible play on **or** insofar as it is embodied in
roy. Anagram and amphiboly convey the underside of the essay's
policies. Once again, the power of Montaigne's words to absorb
things allows his *style* to become the analogical standard of measure.
His verbal performance is far more adequate to his chosen subject
than state policy is to its economy. Counting among his "effects,"
his clothing becomes a favored figure of his wit, and its presence in
the temporal order of the essay yields an equivalence of time and
money. Montaigne recalls his youth, as a soldier, when he made a
grand display of his clothed body. "J'aymois à me parer, quand
j'estoy cabdet, à faute d'autre parure, et me sioit bien; il en est sur
qui les belles robes pleurent. Nous avons des comptes merveilleux
de la frugalité de nos Roys au tour de leur personne et en leurs dons;
grands Roys en credit, en valeur et en fortune" (902). [I enjoyed
bedecking myself, when I was a cadet, for the lack of other ornament,

and it sat well with me. There are people who have looked elegant in fine clothes. We have marvelous accounts on the frugality of our Kings around their person and in their gifts; great Kings in prestige, in value and in fortune.] The indeterminate *pleurent* refers both to Montaigne's sight of pleasure in youth and to the dazzle of golden embroidery in ermine and velvet robes. The word reflecting Montaigne's military past, *cabdet*, also refers to an adolescence of letters, the theme that will soon be taken up in the discussion of the new World (908). *Cabdet* reflects **b** and **d** against a central mirror splitting the word into halves, and it contains the humble beginnings of the initial moments of writing as seen in the word's anagram, in a, b, c, d, e. Is something implied about national educational policy? Are great kings in "credit, value, fortune" those who keep *or* contained in *fortune* and earmark funds, perhaps, toward programs of nationalized education? Here and elsewhere a program of alphabetization surges forward and becomes part of the counsel offered to the contemporary reader who would, ideally, be Montaigne's king.

Up to this point it appears that keeping precious goods in French coffers would not be remedy enough for current fiscal crisis. Vessels should not just hold the sign of production but constitute production itself, or even become, as the essay exemplifies, self-engendering.[14] Signifier and signified must coalesce in the figure of the boat circulating in and on the periphery of the state. The 1592 insertion summoning Theophrastus (880) for arriving at the contrary conclusion in *Des richesses* underlines this part of Montaigne's argument: pomp and ceremony, because they waft away from memory as soon as the spectator's eyes are sated, are less important than provisions that set current surplus aside for future need. Thus the choice of nouns circumscribing gold and praising the regent Catherine de Medici uses anagram to advance counsel within a standard form of encomium:

L'emploitte me sembleroit bien plus **ro**yale comme plus utile, juste et durable, en **po**rts, en havres, **fo**rtifications et murs, en bastiments somptueux, en eglises, hospitaux, colleges, re**fo**rmation de ruës et chemins: en quoy le pape Gre**go**ire treziesme a laissé sa mem**oi**re **re**commandable de mon temps, et en quoy **no**stre **Ro**yne Catherine tesmoigneroit à longues années sa liberalité naturelle et munificence, si ses moyens suffisoient à son affection. La **Fo**rtune m'a faict grand desplesir d'inter**ro**mpre la belle structure du Pont-neuf de **no**stre grand'ville et m'**o**ster l'espoir avant de m**o**urir d'en v**eo**ir en train l'usage. (902, my italics)

[Spending would seem to me a good deal more royal and just as worthy and lasting in ports, in harbors, fortifications and walls, in sumptuous buildings, and churches, hospitals, colleges, renovation of streets and roads. In which Pope Gregory XIII left his noteworthy memory in my time, and which our Queen Catherine would leave testimony of her natural liberality and munificence for long years, if her means were the equal of her desires. Fortune has given me the displeasure of interrupting the beautiful structure of the New Bridge of our great city and to remove from me the hope of seeing it in use before I die.]

Gold is within the words, each substantive being the cause, process, container, result and sum of the precious metal of writing. Yet in the text an excess of gold is turned into paper, into useless display, but with the difference that it is only within itself and not in objects and institutions foreseen in the future. A scheme of construction, a practical vision of harmless waste − writing − replaces an allegory of a second coming or of an apocalypse that would be associated with myth or ideology. Allusion to the incomplete "new" bridge (begun shortly before publication of the *Essais* in 1578 and terminated sixteen years after his death in 1608) is an analogue to the author and text: the book is still an incomplete shape that will, in the situation of a finite process, bind together the state and provide circulation between the opposite sides of the city.[15]

Because the allegorical and historical currents of the essay are joined, we are encouraged to associate coaches with the bridge on which they roll, on cobblestones and over the waters running through and dividing the capital of Paris. But since coaches are causes bound to effects, they concretize tropes of metonymy as well as of metaphor. Where today a pedagogical distinction tends to be drawn between form and content, what I.A. Richards called a "tenor" and a "vehicle,"[16] Montaigne conflates the two elements into one. The puzzling jumps and startling transitions are set forward to contrast the uneasy languor of metaphor associated with the ideology that the text reformulates for the design of its own allegorical autobiography. Emblematic inscription replaces imaginary movement of metaphor, requiring attention to the letter to supersede the drift of words or meaning.

For the sake of the figural and fiscal cartography, the author has recourse to the cliché of the "allegorized landscape" that had been the stock of contemporary emblematists who were fabricating visions of the New World. They used the tradition of medieval panel-painting to frame new information coming with gold and other imports from the West. Montaigne copies the same stereotypical plan in comparing Mexico to Rome:

Quant à... cette premiere abondance de richesses qu'on rencontra à l'abord de ces nouvelles terres (car, encore qu'on en retire beaucoup, nous voyons que ce n'est rien au pris de ce qui s'en devoit attendre), c'est que l'usage de la monnoye estoit entierement inconneu, et que par consequent leur or se trouva tout assemblé, n'estant en autre service que de montre et de parade, comme un meuble reservé de pere en fils par plusieurs puissants Roys, qui espuisoient toujours leurs mines pour faire ce grand monceau de vases et statues à l'ornement de leurs palais et de leurs temples, au lieu que nostre or est tout en emploite et en commerce. Nous le menuisons et alterons en mille formes, l'espandons et dispersons. Imaginons que nos Roys amoncelassent ainsi tout l'or qu'ils pourroient trouver en plusieurs siecles, et le gardassent immobile. Ceux du Royaume de Mexico estoient aucunement plus civilisez et plus artistes que n'estoient les autres nations de là. Aussi jugeoient-ils, ainsi que nous, que l'univers fut proche de sa fin, et en prindrent pour signe la desolation que nous y apportames. (913–14)

[As to this first abundance of riches that were encountered upon meeting these new worlds (for while much is drawn away, we see that it is nothing at the cost of what was to be expected), there the use of money was entirely unknown, and that consequently their gold was found all together, having service for no more than show and parade, as furniture reserved by father to son through several powerful Kings who always exhausted their mines to make this great pile of vases and statues for the ornament of their palaces and temples, in place of our gold that is all in spending and in circulation. We piece it up and alter it into a thousand forms, spread and disperse it. Would our Kings have piled up all the gold they could find in several centuries and kept it immobile? Those of the Kingdom of Mexico were a bit more civilized and craftsmanlike than were other nations over there. Hence they judged, like ourselves, that the universe was nearing its end, and took for its sign the ruin we brought to them.]

Two economies are paired in this picture, one expansive, the other self-contained. The latter appears to suggest a remedy for the excesses of the former. In the New World inert metals seem to be respected for their *rigor mortis*, where the reverse is the case in the Old. Excremental fantasy of touching and caressing gold makes the European display of golden coaches the inverse to Mexican statues. The "**or**nement" of the Aztec nobility is grounded in the stable economy of the artisan class giving the illusion of a static historical order existing prior to development of overseas trade. Nostalgia for an age of gold affronts its own impossibility, since the Indians themselves, the text adds, saw the end of the world at the moment the mercantile conquerors inscribed a void into their own traditions.

Through quotation of Calpurnius, Montaigne praises the eternal city for its containment of excess within the Coliseum (905–07).

A *colossal abyss:* Des coches

Extensive descriptions of circularity are then counterpoised by the linear beauty of the road from Quito to Cusco (909). The round shape of the arena is compared to the orthogonal extension of the South American highway; where the Romans had placed artificial rivers inside their world, the Indians dug rivulets along the shoulders of theirs; the ornamental mountains and seas of the theatrical decor in Rome contrasted with trees planted to the left and right of the South American way. Romans made use of wheels and chariots to carry their King, while Peruvians used to elevate and displace (*charrie*) theirs on palanquins. Romans used a *coche-d'or* and the Americans a *cheze d'or* (894). Enumerating comparisons that juxtapose classical sources to the more recent accounts of New Spain by López de Gómara, the essay situates itself resolutely *between* the Old and the New, the East and the West, Rome and Peru, circular and linear configurations. A proto-typical discourse of ethnohistory is begun, suggesting that the past must be examined in order to establish a focal distance that can discern events or other peoples,[17] and that at the end of its consumption, the present spirals into the past and cannibalizes itself, eating the entire superficies of its former condition until neither land, gold nor solid worth can remain.

At the vanishing point of the reversible tableau is another emblem synthesizing the memory-image of Father Time. One of the most popular mythographical *topoi* of the Renaissance, Chronos depicted the world in its regress and degeneration.[18] No better an image of plunder could have been used to make a moralized interpretation of the colonization of the New World. A picture of Saturn eating his children could typify a mythography of the Americas. In the allegorized landscape, the countryside to our left of Saturn looks withered and bleak, while what is on the right promises new growth and luxuriance. Bruegel put the god on an hourglass poised on a "coche" (or boat–wagon) carrying the globe with stations marked by the signs of the zodiac. In one hand Saturn brandishes his symbol, a snake eating its tail, while with the other he devours the limbs of his children. The standard image of Saturn had no doubt been confused with the imagination of cannibalism. Practice of anthropophagia could be offered through an accessible icon that portrayed the ravages of time.[19] The fear that the image elicited could, in turn, be used to account for uncertainties seen in the context of civil war and in projections of the future. "Des coches" varies on the themes of cannibalism, Saturn, the end of the world, and the destruction of time, in both conception and execution. Its center denotes a fulcrum between the worlds, as noted above, balanced in the kernel remark,

153

Plate 8. Engraving of *The Triumph of Time or Saturn* by Pieter Bruegel the Elder (1530–60), printed 1574 (Bibliothèque Albert I, Brussels). The allegorized landscape uses elements – living and dead trees, lands rich and devastated, Saturn squatting on the hourglass, the amphibious coach on land and sea – with which Montaigne also depicts relations of the Old and New Worlds.

"L'univers tombera en paralisie; l'un membre sera perclus, l'autre en vigueur" (909).

But the allegory seeps into the words far less representatively than a standardized tableau. In the world of time arrested in the allegorical landscape a figure that acquires force is *montre*, signifying on the one hand the elaborate display of regal procession used to forge memory-images, and on the other, the time-piece, a somewhat recent invention, like the compass, linking new sciences and new worlds. An entire convention had been established for the decoration of clocks, such that the inlay of gold and metal in filigree designs decorating them would amount to a *montre* of *montre*, a display of the world's cycles, heretofore seen only with seasonal change, popular almanacs, and the sight of growth, decay, and regeneration of trees in tableaux of the cycles of the four seasons.[20] In these allegories the effect of the condensation of time and energy into *or* and *montre* is likened to entropy, where the difference between the seasons assuring a reliable calculation of the rhythms of the world, now displayed, like printed writing, is arrested in final form.

In Montaigne's figural diction, where gaps are caulked between the sign and the referent, the display literally and figuratively runs out of space and time. Monstrosity and passing time are marked with reference to public show and thus entail a critique of political economy. The Aztecs had used their gold to delineate orthogonal and circular perspectives, parade and passing time, "n'estant en autre service que de *montre* et de parade" (913), contrasting with European practices reaching back to Calpurnius' description of Roman show. Lavish display of money had the virtue of "stopping" cannibalistic Time, keeping it immobile, in representation, out of circulation. Because gold is figured in the context of time and anthropophagia in the allegorical landscape, Saturn becomes a figure metamorphosed from a deity into both an attribute of time and a convenient symbol of Spain's "black legend."

When Montaigne imagines the sight of the conquistadors before the eyes of the Indian population, the text almost assumes the point of view of the native facing the armed conquerors and leads to what appears to be a willful confusion of horses and time-pieces.[21] The soldiers were "*montez sur des grands monstres incogneuz*, contre ceux qui n'avoyent non seulement jamais veu de cheval, mais beste quelconque duicte à porter et soustenir homme ny autre charge" (909, my italics) [mounted on great unknown monsters, against those who had never seen either a horse or any kind of beast led to carry and bear anything: whether man or any other burden]. The horse is a veritable *monstre* on which sit these deadly avatars of Saturn – unlike the clearly homeopathic cannibals that Montaigne had defended in "Des cannibales"[22] – who will eat children and plunder the wealth of the planet. Time is set in cadence according to the hoofbeats of desire to possess and contain all the world's gold. To display the force of avarice, the text suddenly assumes the point of view of the Amerindians who face the Spaniards.

They face the onslaught of death in a fashion identical to the Turks seeing the Hungarians aiming their arquebuses at their faces. In the eyes of the natives – whose "nudity" had been a stigma for them no less than their purported "cannibalism" – the Europeans arrive no less nude, "garnis d'une peau luisante et dure" (909) [garnished with an enduring and shiny skin] of steel. Where their natural state is contrasted with the metallic dress of armored horsemen, the alterity of each culture is displayed on the pupils of the other. As the essay percolates meaning through the form of the words and their letters, adjacent enumeration of festivities in the Coliseum forces the image of alterity to turn back upon the **o** that had been heralded in **or**. Gold and gun barrels, printing, and Roman architecture coalesce in the figure of the letter through allusion to the mechanics of writing inherited from Tory and the Humanists of the 1530s. The student of the *Champ fleury* learning Roman orthography was told to compare the **O** to the Coliseum because the intrados was to be slightly off-center and drawn as an ellipsis, while the extrados was to be a circle.[23] As if mocking Tory's idealizing propensities, the text takes up the A, B, Cs as elements no longer of reform, but of global strategies used to take over the Indies.

If the Indians were to be converted, their bodies would have to be lettered. How a world without writing could be profitably redeemed by Christian religion figured in the center of the colonial enterprise. Here Montaigne's critique of ideologies inflects *coches* as wounds that leave scars on the bodies of native subjects. In the greater allegory the *coche* designates a difference traced between a world of written characters and an oral culture,[24] and for this reason the convention comparing the effects of gunpowder and printing is used because the compelling *form* of the metaphor masks the more immediate consequences of brutality levelled against populations in Africa and the New World:

Nous nous escriïons du miracle de l'invention de nostre artillerie, de nostre impression; d'autres hommes, un autre bout du monde à la Chine, en jouyssoit mille ans auparavent. Si nous voyons autant du monde comme nous n'en voyons pas, nous apercevrions, comme il est à croire, une perpetuele (c) multiplication et (b) vicissitude de formes. ... Nostre monde vient d'en trouver un autre (et qui nous respond si c'est le dernier de ses freres, puis que les Daemons, les Sybilles et nous, avons ignoré cettuy-cy jusqu'asture?) non moins grand, plain et membru que luy, toutesfois si nouveau et si enfant qu'on luy aprend encore son a, b, c; il n'y a pas cinquante ans qu'il ne sçavoit ny lettres, ny pois, ny mesure, ny vestements, ny bleds, ny vignes. (908)

[We were heralding the miracle and invention of our artillery, of our printing; other men, another end of the world, in China, enjoyed them a thousand years before. If we see as much of the world as we do not see, we should glimpse, in most likelihood, a perpetual (c) multiplication and (b) vicissitude of forms. ... Our world has just found another (and who answers us whether it is the last of its brothers, since the Demons, Sybils and ourselves, we have been unaware of it until now?) no less great, full, and strapping, always so new and so childish that we are still teaching it the *abc*s. Not even fifty years ago it knew nothing of letters, weights, measures, clothing, crops, nor vines.]

Letters are seen carrying an "artificial" order inscribed over "nature". From the relation of the figure of the former to the ground of the latter the comparison draws an identity of artillery and writing, but only so as to enable differences to settle over the course of time. Addition of *multiplication* in 1592 (in what follows, the words interpolated after 'c') opens the text (b) of 1588, making the expansion of written words fold both outward and inward. The abecedarium is precisely the European axis, and the American limit the outer circumference. And *a, b, c* is encoded, it appears, to transliterate the author's critique of the expansive European economy and its subjugation of the New Indies. Indigenous populations were in control of a world ostensibly having neither writing nor history, but only with the introduction of Western modes of writing and exploitation of gold are they enslaved or, in Montaigne's amphiboly, both *a–b–c* and *abaissé* [knocked down]. The childish stuttering, what Montaigne calls the *balbucie* of the New World (911), sets into the essay an already mastered writing, an a, b, c, falling at rhythmic intervals in the harmonic system of b-*a*-l-*b*-u-c-i-e. His reference to ideogrammatic writing in China reflects, it appears, an intention to establish his own "hieroglyphic" style as a remedy to worlds and letters in expansion.[25] It is dense, thrifty, self-contained, and enduring. Despite the allegorical oppositions, Mexico, Rome, and *Chine* beckon a spatial and temporal foil to the present moment of colonial expansion. The text suggests how China, like (and unlike) the invention of printing, can give perspective to the overseas policies the West undertakes for short-term profits. Repeating in part the lesson learned from the effects that writing brought to the self-contained, oral culture of Lahontan in "De la ressemblance des enfans aux peres" (778), Montaigne uses *Chine* to call in question the wont to divide the world into a body and soul based on the distinction between Orient and Occident or voice and writing. The printed letters of "Des coches" are evidence everywhere of a critique of the spiritual position investing authority in a spoken, originary voice above a political body or even a written text. The identification of that voice, it will be seen below, is contained in the initial riddle of the essay that we have yet to solve.

But first it remains to be seen how, in the anagrammar of "Des coches," *Chine* also offsets policies that favor colonizations. Plunder is associated with cowardice. The Amerindians' protection against artillery comprises scarcely more than "bows, stones, sticks, and wooden shields" (909); the soldiers' deployment of gunboats, arquebus, mortar and cannon is enough to rival the devil. "Contez, dis-je, aux conquerans cette disparité, vous leur ostez toute l'occasion de tant de victoires'' (910). [Relate, I say, to the conquerors this disparity, and you take from them the occasion of so many victories.] Insistence on the facility of victory and the devaluation of heroism elicits an interjection associating mastery with slavish adherence to mechanical systems. The Spaniards are ''si vilement victorieuses'' (910) [so vilely victorious]; their extermination of cities and nations ''pour la negociation des perles et du poivre'' [for barter of pearls and pepper] prompts a calm rejoinder eradicating all cause for exclamation: *mechaniques victoires* (910) [mechanical victories].[26] Final retribution takes place when the conquerors systematically plunder themselves in intestinal dispute, practice the very cannibalism they abhor, or sink into the Hellish mouth of the sea. The saturnine ''machine of the world'' is invested in the visible identity of China to the time-piece and wheel (*la machine* or, implicitly, ''there my China'') microcosmic of larger patterns of connotation: the cogwheels and springs of the essay would move plates and figures of the planets in perfect proportion with the algebra of the universe. But the fundamental contradiction has the print of the essay take part in a mechanical victory insofar as its letters figure in the same currency of waste in bookish commerce.

And second, a vanishing point of the chapter, once more in the middle of the letter **O**, between Occident and Orient, is the sea which figures as a perspectival object where Montaigne tests the rapport of the body to language. An abyss and a passage, the sea carries analogies with an open cavity of unknown origin. Docile movement of the sea causes seasickness in such a manner that the mouth vomiting liquid is microcosmic of the ocean swallowing the swine colonizing the Americas. Imaginary retribution takes place when ''Dieu a

*mer*itoirem*ent perm*is

que ces grands pillages se soient absorbez par la *mer* en les transportant, ou par les guerres intestines dequoy ils se sont en*trem*angez entre eux'' (913). [God meritoriously permitted that their great pillages be absorbed by the sea conveying them, or through intestinal strife by which they were intereaten among themselves.] The portmanteau *mercadence* (Cotgrave: ''small traffick'') that describes the colonial ventures (913) reduces the Spanish economy to something, in the network of the essay's figures, tantamount to having the gold seekers swallowed *down* into the sea, in a movement rhyming with the end of the essay (''*Retombons* à nos coches ...,'' 915).

An expansive economy eating the world is undone when the distance thought to exist between the two continents is reduced to zero. The sea is the crevasse into which the ignoble monsters must fall. Cartographers had dotted the surfaces of maps with wind roses, decorous serpents and scaled creatures to give visual variety to the image of the world, and Montaigne's *mer* is no doubt used with the same pictographic motives. Monsters find their representative lairs in the Mexican and Roman seas of artifice in either the bowels of the Coliseum, "une mer profonde" (906) [a deep sea], or the royal garden, among "les animaux qui naissoient en son estat et en ses mers" (909) [among the animals that were born in its state and in its seas].

The New World throws the Old out of kilter. Montaigne uses a tale of the King of Mexico to fashion an emblem of courage off-setting the cowardice of the colonizers. Burning at the stake after having been swindled, the king enjoins a suffering compatriot chained to an adjacent pole not to wilt in the flames. The companion looks at his leader and asks for an equivocal *mercy*, a sign of death and watery salvation inversely identical to what swallowed the Spaniards. "Ce seigneur, se trouvant forcé de la douleur, environné de braziers ardens, tourna sur la fin piteusement sa veue vers son maistre, comme pour luy demander *mercy* de ce qu'il n'en pouvoit plus" (912, my italics). [This lord, finding himself enslaved by his pain, surrounded by ardent coals, at the limit turned his eyes with pity toward his leader, as if to ask grammercy of him for what he could no longer bear]. The example coincides in epigrammatic opposition with what Montaigne says about his own intestinal fortitude when he travels on rough waters. The two accounts are identical in shape to the anecdote concerning the heroism of Socrates on foot, and each echoes the exemplum of Pyrrho's stalwart *cochon* related by Plutarch.

The whole spectacle begins with the most flaccid descriptive, *chose*, apparently chosen at first to herald the pomp of Roman plumbing. The least significant word, close to *cause* that inaugurates the essay,[27] introduces the passage on the Coliseum and also replaces the o of *or* in an abyss between *ch* and *se* marked at the center of the title:

C'estoit pourtant une belle chOse, d'aller faire apporter et planter en la place aus arenes une grande quantité de gros arbres, tous branchus et tous verts, representans une grande forest ombrageuse, despartie en belle symmetrie, et, le premier jour, jetter là dedans mille austruches, mille cerfs, mille sangliers et mille dains, les abandonnans à piller au peuple; le lendemain,

faire assomer en sa presence cent gros lions, cent leopards, et trois cens
ours, et, pour le troisiesme jour, faire combatre à l'outrance trois cens pairs
de gladiateurs, comme fit l'Empereur Probus. C'estoit aussi belle chOse à
voir ces grands amphitheatres encroustez de marbre au dehors, labouré
d'ouvrages et statues, le dedans reluisant de plusieurs rares enrichissemens,
Baltheus en gemmis, en illita porticus auro. (905, my emphasis).

[It was however a pretty thing, to have brought and planted in the place
of arenas a great quantity of thick trees, their limbs all green, representing
a large, shady forest, set in pretty symmetry and, on the first day, throw
inside a thousand ostriches, a thousand deer, a thousand wild pigs and a
thousand reindeer, letting the people pillage them; the next day, to have
slaughtered in its presence a hundred fat lions, a hundred leopards, and
three hundred bears, and for the third day, to have three hundred pairs
of gladiators fight to the limit, as did the Emperor Probus. It was also a
pretty thing to see these amphitheatres encrusted with marble on the outside,
inscribed in relief with works and statues, the inside glimmering with several
rare ornaments,
*Here is the periphery decorated with precious stones, here is the portico
in gold.*]

The Latin quotation carries in *illita porticus* a translinguistic,
almost anamorphic reminder of a golden palanquin on which a noble body is seated, at once marking the axis of a kingdom's limits
and announcing other worlds surging out of the past. The superimposition of different times and spaces becomes visible only when
a discursive reading is poised against the emblematic balancing of
letters, figures and images in their spatial relation to each other.
It is repeated not only in the multiplication of things and curiosities,
but also in the verbal identities of causes, coaches, *coches* and *choses*,
whose anagram pivots about the letter **o**, the vowel that pulls the
vocal "vehicle" of the consonants.

It would appear that the self-referential aspects of the essay isolate
its form from the political remarks located in the discourse, or that
the author's tour de force of analogy supersedes the political design.
A key to the rapport of poetics and politics is evinced when the
beginning or mouth of essay is apposed to its lower end. A median
focal point is located in Calpurnius' description of the Coliseum,
where four stages of artifice are set in montage. In the first day of
festivity a fake forest is filled with 1,000 ostriches, 1,000 boars, and
1,000 stags left for the people to pillage. On the second day 100 fat
lions, 100 leopards, and 300 bears are placed inside, while on the
third 300 pairs of gladiators battle each other, in view of 100,000
spectators. The public is the fourth element in the series, just as

four orders of games are then enumerated in the same numerical progression (1: crevasses vomit beasts; 2: a sea with ships and monsters drowns the spectacle; 3: gladiators combat on a dry surface in daylight; 4: vermilion and storax bedeck the palace, where an infinite number of people can play in a rink). The spectacles that Montaigne finds "excusable" (907) only because of their invention and "novelty" (like specious causes attributed with wit to explain common effects, 898–99) are mobilized according to a logic of fours.

Sets of thousands bring forth a millennarian moment of the text that is juxtaposed to the cosmology of the New World, taken from López de Gómara's account of the Mexican world-view (913–14), listing the five stages of the planet. Four of them had "already furnished their time": (1) a universal flood killed all living creation; (2) the sky fell and crushed all life that had since then been reborn; (3) a fire burned the next world. In the fourth, a blast of wind and air (an *émotion d'air et de vent*, 914) knocked the mountains down, and men were turned into monkeys. After the death of the fourth sun, the world was in shadows for twenty-five years, but at the end of the fifteenth a man and a woman were conceived to rebuild the human race. Ten years later the sun returned, inaugurating a digital or clock-like sense of time. The old gods died on the third day of creation, while the new, it is reported, have been since born, but only from day to day. The fourth change met with a conjunction of stars that about 800 years ago produced great disturbances and "novelties" in the world (914).

Montaigne abbreviates Gómara's account and places it next to the description of the demise of the Peruvian king that ends the chapter. Arguably the Mexican apocalypse varies on Revelation. But more crucially, in the circularity of "Coches," Montaigne's "émotion d'air et de vent qui abbatit jusques à plusieurs montaignes" [blast of air and wind which flattened up to several mountains] refers back to the mountains in the center of the Coliseum, forward to the Andean kingdom around Cusco, and downward to the France about and around Montaigne's own name.[28]

The apocalypse of civil war is invested with a strong political bias coloring the enigma about sneezing that inaugurates the essay. Seen thus, the infinitely small becomes infinitely great. The riddle that Montaigne posed under the title was "Me demandez-vous d'où vient cette coustume de benire ceux qui estrenuent?" (899) [Do you ask me whence comes this custom of blessing those who sneeze?]. Following the visual and discursive logic of the letter, the response cannot follow the question but has to be located within its formulation and seen between typography and meaning. *Estrenuent*, a portmanteau creation that conjures up gift-giving or liberality (*estrener*, as Cotgrave notes, meaning: "to handsell; or, that hath had a New-Yeare's gift; also, to beat, swindge, cudgell, correct"), invokes too a will to make a great display (*esternir*), but also − thanks to the abyssal presence of the **O**, the wheel of *des coches*, to have commerce with indigenous nations, that is, to deal in slaves. *Estrenuer* can also be held to mean *estre-nue(r)*, "to be naked persons." In the oblique evocation of slaves and Indians, bodies are paraded, swapped, bought, beaten and sold. But what of those who like to *benire* or "bless" those who *estrenuent*? It was Pope Alexander IV, years before, who had *blessed* the Spaniards' conquest of the New World and, in so doing, legitimized slavery, a commerce that Montaigne is condemning. Any authority which can adduce a noble cause to such inhuman effects − whether Catholic Popes or Aristotle − is to be abhorred.[29] Aristotle, the authority whose heritage had been used to advance genocide, is quashed in the secret style of the essay. Aristotle is aligned with orthodoxy, and used by popes who place their benediction on the murderous "sneezers," that is, armored criminals who traffick in slaves. Casual or pragmatic use of causality is severely impugned (as it was in III, i and will be in III, xi) by the self-containment of the writing and the play of the letter. The emblematic closure reverses the discourses that legitimize the butchery in contemporary time.

The chapter is thus cast for posterity as a fragment of political discourse that uses the "logic of the mark," a *logique de coche*, to propose a more sensible historical relation of man and nature. The way the essay lets its letters float in a visual field to make a veiled critique of a global economy in expansion or development offers a model of hidden writing admonishing the way censors − popes, Catholic belief, Aristotle, or others[30] − go about destroying the planet. In the graphic areas of his style, Montaigne shunts the contents on to the letter, a letter visible only to Montaigne's "diligent" readers, coequals, who read words with the same sense of force and motion as he writes them.

CONCLUSION

In the dazzling play of the letter in "Des coches" we discover a critique of political economy marked all over the surface of its printed discourse. The text of the essay reveals dimensions of meaning in the form, movement, shape and placement of its characters. They shunt to and fro between lexical and emblematic functions. They unveil the inscription of a caustic view of papal orthodoxy in the very place where its praise is offered. The letter acquires a demonic force, indicating in turn how a highly invested writing coordinates poetics and politics. The title, number, and initial riddle of "Des coches" suggest that the letter can complicate what we believe may be the symbolic efficacity of the *Essais*. When the style writes with productive duplicities, we realize that the paragrammatical dimension of the text provides a verbal substance joining characters to representations of things or, metaphorically, words to things, or causes to *choses*. "La piece estrangère" is, despite the assertions at the beginning of "De la gloire," attached "à la chose." A beginning (or a *cause*) and a printed letter or typographical effect are one. The text affirms that a new adequation of language and matter is put forward as a different standard of exchange.

The practice of the letter in "Coches" responds to the style and tenor of the last pages of its companion-piece in the first volume, "Des cannibales" (I, xxxi). In that essay a similar critique of political economy is launched, which the eighteenth-century *philosophes* would soon deploy to impugn social injustice in the *ancien régime*. In "Cannibales" Montaigne projects two critical views of class conflict onto the eyes of the other. He has reputedly encountered two Amerindians on display in Rouen. They reported three things (*choses*) to their interlocutors but Montaigne, his memory no doubt blurred by the impact of print culture, only recalls the first two and notes either with sarcasm or seriousness, "et en suis marry" [and I'm chagrined about it, too]. Why, they ask, does the nation obey a child-king (Charles IX, who was hardly an adolescent at that time, in 1562)

163

surrounded by huge bearded soldiers bearing arms (that is, Swiss mercenaries whom French taxpayers subsidize)? Why, too, are there a few men "stuffed with all kinds of commodities" amidst a populace of fellow humans stripped bare by hunger and poverty? These homeless souls who are begging at the doors of their brothers would have reason, add the natives, to take the rich by their throats or set fire to their houses (213–14). The tactic that puts social criticism in the eyes of the other will be the focal substance of the *Lettres persanes* two centuries later. But the art of "Des coches" may be more arcane than what Montesquieu made of it, since its highly wrought analogies of the letter, that disappear with the demise of analogy in seventeenth-century discourse, make its style and enunciation become the very *content* of a political economy. As we remarked at the beginning of chapter 5, we are *sur la maniere, non la matiere du dire*. "Coches" performs through its literal and figurative imprint what had been projected through complex mirrorings in the discursive order of "Cannibales."

The call for parsimonious use of signs and money reflects Montaigne's conservative view of the institutions of his time. But, with the protean dimension of the letter, it also shows where printed characters are seen engaging homeopathic and mimetic relations with readers. What we discern in the letter, no matter how fantasmatic our impressions may be, can circulate back into the discourse and continue in dialogue with it. At the same time, the letter, as both a saturated and an empty sign, reflects a state of language charged with bearing remedies to cure the diseases of the world in civil war and general degeneration. *Style*, the *Essais* seem to wager, will extract ills from the social body and neutralize their toxins. The writing encloses a severe critique of papal orthodoxy at the same time as it tells the world to prepare for the future by slowing down and conserving its resources. "Des coches" entails a view of prophecy and of the "end of the world" in order to imply that *man* will be the cause of the demise of the planet, and not God. The density of the manner of "Coches" and its form become figural prescriptions aimed at curing some of the national diseases. Slippages of words will redirect national energies away from civil conflict over belief or paper issues and toward more materially consequential problems. Not the least of which (as in our own time) is *escrivaillerie*, profusion of flaccid writing, hackwork, a "symptom of a century going overboard" that needs "coërction" (946) [coercion or correction] by means of style. Everywhere Montaigne's practice of the letter envisages a dynamic relation with future time, not

counted in seconds, days, or months, but in hundreds of years.[1]
His call for an active balancing of words, actions, and form is
aimed at preserving the diversity of world history and in this sense
does not reflect the static view of social institutions.[2] "Des coches"
argues for a long-term global ecology, and thus returns, like the
unconscious, to our present day with uncanny force and currency.
The politics of its style aver to be humane in respect to the other
and, as it were, *auto-bio-graphical* in the commitment the writer
shares with a plan using language to preserve natural wealth threat-
ened with extinction.

If we heed Montaigne's style in this way, we begin to envisage
how the letter of early modern literature touches on our notions
of the unconscious. Nicolas Abraham and other analysts have
remarked that any genuine work of literature has an unconscious,
and that this uncontrolled and uncontrollable dimension drives
it across oblivion and makes it contemporary at all times.[3] A work
of any such origin can be contemporary because it acquires power
enough to change the ideological contexts in which it surfaces.[4]
In contrast, most work that we encounter tends to reproduce what
might be called a "designer-unconscious," that is, a carefully
articulated order of limited effects of contradiction that are aimed
at making the reader a primarily buying subject. Critical relations
with objects are discouraged in favor of quantifiable returns taken
from relations of desire written into style and format. "Marketed"
thus, readers or viewers are offered limited fields of perplexity
that can be resolved by further purchase of the same effects (or
causes). They are not, however, *marked* by uncanniness or arcane
opacities or other resistance.

In the same light, following the work of Raymond Williams,
Fredric Jameson, in *The Political Unconscious* and subsequent
writings, has shown that the dominant culture in the age of "late
capital" has sought to remove from the world everything that
cannot be subject to corporate control.[5] Included is nature and,
with its analogue, in bodily terms, the unconscious. In a period
of electronic and cybernetic technology, the market fabricates
communicational designs that can be likened to what Jameson
calls "strategies of containment." These strategies intend to control
the desires, the dreams, and even the daily habits of entire populations
of consumers. Narrative units, brand-names, slogans, and "info-
tainment" (patently mediated interpretations of events scaled to
equate news with television ratings and to coordinate distribution
of literature with programming) are used to explain what in earlier

historical phases had fallen under the aegis of chance or destiny. According to this view, the rhythms of life can be monitored by corporate agencies through informational webbings stretched all over and above the globe.

One of the most important threads in the fabric of the designer-unconscious entails coded articulations of moving letters and images. High-speed transmission of emblems and image-texts has become a crucial element in its rhetoric.[6] Early in our century advertisers and market analysts discovered that a subliminal writing could produce an unconscious and make it obey carefully crafted commands. Proper names, trademarks, emblems, or pithy imperatives ("drink coke," "die," "x," etc.) are tipped into moving images in order to entice viewers to act out or respond directly to their signals. If a death's head were cast in the frame of an image, a brief shudder would be prompted by its spell, effectuating purchase of a product. The act of buying – and hardly the object or commodity itself – would assuage or defer the menacing fantasy elicited by the subliminal image-writing.[7] Despite its novelty, the strategy has been well known at least since early Christian times, in which the process of reading, that is, of following a text and translating its signs into meaning, is interrupted by the sight or cast of its individual letters. These graphic units arrest the activity of cognition, produce other meanings, or even cast a momentary "spell" upon the reader. In the age of cinema and television the strategy has led people to believe that a fundamental freedom of vision is being twisted by malicious and demonic agencies.[8] No matter what the ethical implications of these rhetorical ploys, effects are solicited by coordinations of images and figures that appear and disappear in movement. The image is detached from but conjoined to a shard of writing in order, on the one hand, to show us that an image *is not* writing while, on the other, the placement begs us to transgress the opposition. We are momentarily led to believe one *is* the identity of the other.[9] By offering complex codes of binarities the strategy engages a spectatorial relation that solicits, on the part of the reader or viewer a feeling of deficiency or lack. A sense of sin and guilt is imposed where none needs to exist. In the imbalance that is offered the medium wills to control or channel the energies of its public. Both affirmation and denial of the analogical relation of pictures and of writing are established in the passage of printed forms before our eyes.

Now it appears that the approach we have taken to analyze the letter of early modern writing might be compared to the ways that the unconscious is conceived for limited ends. From our view of French writers of the sixteenth century, the unconscious is stretched out and in fact impugns all strategy of limit. Virtues of analogy reside in the letter, and analogy is so strong that it can put in question all forms of control that wish to regulate unconscious and conscious registers of language. In this respect the archaic, difficult, or opaque qualities of the works we have studied play with and against literal, pictural, and semantic orders. They yield to the unconscious, and they let it play out its effects in and about its own forms. Marot, Rabelais, Ronsard, and Montaigne are, in this respect, exemplary: each articulates pictural patterns of words whose random distribution casts doubt on any overriding order of our time or of our social practices, and the resulting play of shapes allows a timeless unconscious to be glimpsed in the flicker of verbal and graphic forms. Each of the writers works with the letter differently, but all tap into the same drive and leave us with unsettling impressions.

From the perspective of our time, when the unconscious is said to be losing ground as a concept or a working principle in everyday life, these four writers of the Renaissance bring it back to us. They render the unconscious graphically. Their writings illuminate through ploys of the letter that turn their works into movements of surfaces. Because they resist designs of thought or of verbal form that we know, their political force becomes evident: not only do they provide *other* ways of working with the materials of language, they also tell us about the history of mediation that informs print culture from the sixteenth century to our day.

NOTES

Introduction

1 Cambridge: Cambridge UP, 1988, 173. He looks to Walter J. Ong's "From Allegory to Diagram in the Renaissance Mind," *Journal of Aesthetics and Art Criticism* 17 (1959), whose hypotheses are developed at length in *Ramus, Method, and the Decay of Dialogue: From the Art of Discourse to the Art of Reason* (Cambridge: Harvard UP, new edn 1984). Scott adds that the graphic imagination goes much further back, as he shows in reference to Jack Goody's *Domestication of the Savage Mind* (Cambridge: Cambridge UP, 1977).

2 Here I rely on the findings of Lucien Febvre and Henry J. Martin, *L'apparition du livre* (Paris: Albin Michel, 1958); Elizabeth L. Eisenstein, *The Printing Press as an Agent of Change*, 2 vols. (Cambridge: Cambridge UP, 1979); Roger Chartier, *The Cultural Uses of Print in Early Modern France* (Princeton: Princeton UP, 1987); Frances Yates, *The Art of Memory* (Chicago: U of Chicago P, 1966).

3 "Transmission" is chosen here in place of "tradition." Freud reminds us that tradition constitutes "incomplete and blurred memories" of the past. In the same vein, he notes that the inaccuracies of "tradition" offer "a peculiar attraction" to the artist who, better than others, can caulk "gaps in memory according to the desires of his imagination." He subverts tradition in order to make historians both archivists and creators: "Latency Period and Tradition," in *Moses and Monotheism, Standard Edition of the Complete Psychological Works* 23 (London: The Hogarth Press, 1960), 71. Further reference to this edition will be abbreviated to *SE* and followed by the volume and page numbers.

4 Michel de Certeau uses "heterology" to mean the activity that inserts alterity of the past into the present, or that seeks foreignness in familiar space. It perspectivizes what we take to be invisible or ineffable, and it thrusts unconscious forms into consciousness. The rapport of the discipline to early modern studies is taken up in *Heterologies* (Minneapolis: U of Minnesota P, 1985), 67–115. Roger Chartier refines the issue in "Le passé composé," in *Traverses* 40 (1987). I would like to add that experience offers a litmus test for the problems we face when we attempt to use medieval or Renaissance literature to

change received ideas about culture. I have been professionally trained in Renaissance studies but do concurrent research in cinema. Analyses of sixteenth-century texts and twentieth-century films follow similar methods [e.g., the relation of my *Film Hieroglyphs* (Minnesota P, 1991) to chapter 2 below]. Yet enrolment in a film curriculum, adjacent to sixteenth-century literature, remains at a ratio of about 50:1, even when students are implored to learn early modern literature if they wish to gain a working sense of *montage*, visual composition, or even screenwriting. One can easily fear that the specificity of Renaissance literature risks being dissolved in a pabulum of monolingual "culture studies" in current and future planning in many American universities.

5 See Claude-Gilbert Dubois, "Taxinomie poétique: compositions sérielles et constructions d'ensembles dans la création esthétique en France au seizième siècle," in Lawrence Kritzman, ed., *Le signe et le texte* (Lexington: French Forum Monographs, 1990), 131–45. He grafts theological and sexual functions on to odd and even numbers to show how the Renaissance conceived of generation in a "manner hardly evident to our modern eyes" (131). The critic suggests that the period saw writing as the "result of an elaboration, not as a pre-fabrication; a scaffolding of relations, of proportions and linkages that make an apotheosis of calculation, the splendor of constructive intelligence, and not the affirmation of a power refusing to admit contestation" (136). Proscriptive forces that limit analogy of this sort indicate the advent of the absolutism of Louis XIV, a period that pushes the Renaissance out of its field of view.

6 Michel de Montaigne, *Les Essais*, ed. Pierre Villey, 3 vols. (Paris: PUF, Série Quadrige, new edn 1988), II, 618. All subsequent references to the *Essais* will be taken from this edition and noted between parentheses in the body of the text above. Here and elsewhere all English translations from French sources are my responsibility and will be placed between brackets following quotation of the original material.

7 Many studies take up the relation of letters to analogy and provide a grounding for the work that follows. Classic is Etienne Gilson, *Les idées et les lettres* (Paris: Vrin, 1942); Ernst Robert Curtius, *European Literature and the Latin Middle Ages*, tr. Williard R. Trask (Princeton: Princeton UP reprint, 1971), 301–57; Michel Foucault, *Les mots et les choses* (Paris: Gallimard, 1966), chapters one and two; Michael Riffaterre, *Semiotics of Poetry* (Bloomington: Indiana UP, 1978), 80ff.; Terence Cave, *The Cornucopian Text* (Oxford: Clarendon Press, 1979); Roger Dragonetti, *La vie de la lettre au Moyen Age* (Paris: Seuil, 1980); François Rigolot, *Le texte de la Renaissance* (Geneva: Droz, 1982); Yves Delegue, *La perte des mots: essai sur la naissance de la "littérature" aux XVIe et XVIIe siècles* (Strasbourg: Presses de l'Université de Strasbourg, 1990). Dragonetti sums up the relation of analogy and the letter when he remarks, apropos of Isidore

of Seville, "Cette 'imaginative compréhension' de la lettre, qui forme, dans le champ des virtualités du savoir, de nouveaux entrelacs symboliques des signes graphiques, n'est rien moins que la pensée analogique au travail" (67). [This "imaginative comprehension" of the letter that in the field of the virtual power of knowledge forms new symbolic weavings of graphic signs is nothing less than the work of analogical thinking.] Thought is *literal*, and *movement* of knowledge transforms the graphic shape of writing. The graphic force of writing "implique une dialectique lecture–écriture, c'est-à-dire un jeu de liaisons visant, consciemment ou inconsciemment, à nouer sans cesse, dans le tissu anagrammatique du langage, des rapports de similitude entre les signes graphiques des mots et leur sens, à percevoir par conséquent le semblable dans les différences, l'un à travers l'autre, en direction d'une synthèse dont la force, qui le meut tout entière, est le mode analogique de circularité" (66–67) [implies a dialectic of reading–writing, that is, a play of linkages aimed, consciously or unconsciously, at endlessly binding, in the anagrammatical tissue of language, relations of similitude between graphic signs of words and their meanings, thus perceiving resemblances in differences, unity through multiplicity and indetermination, the same through the other, all in the direction of a synthesis whose force, that moves it entirely, is the analogical mode of circularity]. We must note that Isidore of Seville is not solely an inspiration for the Middle Ages. Geoffroy Tory theorizes the printed letter through Isidore and Martianus Capella, and thus invests analogy into print culture where it had reigned in manuscriptural traditions.

8 In *L'imaginaire de la Renaissance* (Paris: PUF, 1985), Claude-Gilbert Dubois writes of knowledge in the sixteenth-century world, insisting that by mid-century "chaque détail graphique a son importance et renvoie à un signifié au moins double, dans l'ordre physique et dans l'ordre de la foi" (64) [every graphic detail has its own importance and refers to a referent split in at least two ways, in the physical order and in the order of faith]. Throughout "il y a l'inlassable volonté de vaincre l'écart entre l'ordre des choses et l'ordre des mots, entre le signe et le référent, sans lequel il n'y a pas de langage possible" (76) [there is the tireless will to overcome the gap between the order of things and the order of words, between the sign and the referent, without which language would be impossible]. But the same distance, he adds, is increased as the century draws to a close, and generative traits of figure and sign or things and words become attenuated.

9 Claude Lévi-Strauss believes that the average person of the early modern age was aware of most systems of material production. See *La pensée sauvage* (Paris: Plon, 1962), chapter 1.

10 Erwin Panofsky suggests that at given historical moments characters carry a principle of disjunction within themselves. In the Carolingian and twelfth-century renascences of classical culture, the abyss between

the present and the past is obvious: Roman characters were practically illegible for medieval scribes who were obliged to rewrite them in Gothic script. By the sixteenth century readers comprehended both recent and antique graphic styles. See *Renaissance and Renascences in Western Art* (Stockholm: Almquist & Wiksell, 1960), 130–31. By the sixteenth century the classical past had been internalized. Nonetheless an overriding sense of separation or disjunction from a mother-culture appears to have motivated the relation that contemporary life held with what it was seeking to revive. Otherwise, any attempt at revival would have been pointless.

11 In the same vein Freud offers a daring theory of the origins of the smile: the two ends of our lips curl upward when, flipping an electric commutator, we recall that we are saving ourselves from labor we formerly expended to light a gas-jet. The pleasure that the memory brings forth is based on economy. The memory-image of the gas-jet tells us that we used to go about our daily business more cumbrously – especially, as Freud implies so ironically, in matters of "illumination" or "enlightenment." *Jokes and their Relation to the Unconscious*, SE 8, 157.

12 The erotic dimension of the metaphor of inscription is commonplace in late medieval literature, notes David Kuhn in *La poétique de François Villon* (Paris: Colin, 1967), 26–27), whether in terms of a plume on paper or a plow in the fields. In R. Howard Bloch, *The Scandal of the Fabliaux* (Chicago: U of Chicago P, 1988), the same metaphor is seen prevailing in popular medieval literature. Freud inherits the same material, but he also dissimulates it by using his own manner to display what his meaning will not dare to utter. The imagination of the patient who experiences difficulty in donning his socks, we note in "The Unconscious" (1915), could be likened to a sixteenth-century reader who beholds as many percussive inscriptions on one printed page as there are characters allotted to it.

13 Jean-François Lyotard telescopes its history from Rabelais to Freud in *Discours, figure* (Paris: Klincksieck, 1971), 296–7, especially note 31: the timeless play of the word-picture links Mallarmé, Freud, Cézanne, and the avant-garde in a "play of deconstruction of linguistic and plastic space; upheaval of orders of writing instituted one over the other."

14 *Champ fleury* (Bourges, 1529), ed. J.W. Jolliffe (Paris: The Hague: Mouton and Johnson Reprint, 1970), ff. xiiii–xviii. This edition reproduces a first edition (British Museum 60.e.14.). Available in English translation (first printed in a limited edition by the Grolier Club, 1927, and republished New York: Dover, 1967).

15 *La figure et le lieu* (Paris: Gallimard, 1967), 40–60. He shows how the works of the time must be sifted both through our world and theirs, but in terms of an "imaginary," a "perceived" (or symbolic area

of only ostensively stable languages) and a "real," or an objectal dimension that is impervious to language.

A case in point would be the letter "F" that becomes Jean Lemaire's alphabetical vanishing point in his *Concorde des deux langages* (1512): the poet wants to bring "concord" to debates over the value of French and Italian and peace to two nations at war. To do so he conflates the letter of *F*rance with that of *F*lorence. Some of his verbal flourishes are couched in fricative alliterations that display a synthesis that ultimately tips in favor of the letter heralding France:

> François faictiz, franz, fortz, fermes au fait,
> Fins, frecz, de fer, feroces, sans frayeur,
> Telz sont voz noms concordans à l'effect.

> [French fair, frank, forceful, firm in fact,
> Fine, fresh, ferric, ferocious, and fearless,
> Such are your names concording in effect.]

(In *La Concorde des deux langages*, ed. Jean Frappier, Paris: Droz, 1947, lines 583–85. It is worth noting that the editor takes up Lemaire to deal with "concord" toward the end of the Second World War, thus displacing his own time, concerned with the desire to end European discord, into that of the Renaissance.) F becomes a visual rhyme, the reality of a mute cipher of "pictural speech" that bears the imaginary concord all the while it motivates real poetry. François Cornilliat traces the same contradiction elsewhere through Lemaire, in "La couleur et l'écriture: le débat de peinture et de rhétorique dans *La Plainte du désiré* de Jean Lemaire," *Nouvelle Revue du Seizième Siècle* 7 (1989), 22–23. In *Le texte de la Renaissance*, François Rigolot uses Lemaire to show how the elaborate allegories of graphics and meaning tend, on a structural level, to deny "the arbitrary nature of the syntagmatic dimension of language" (56), and how the *Concorde* writes over a fundamental discord, such that a violence of ambivalence indicates the emergence of an "unconscious of the text" (104), a notion he takes from Jean Bellemin-Noël's *Vers l'inconscient du texte* (Paris: PUF, 979), a study of Proust and the modern canon. The pictural or "paradigmatic" axis of the text brings us into a problematic field of mixed means of representation. Their "discord" becomes a resistance, and hence a symptom of our unconscious.

16 See the background developed in "I primi lumi: Italian Trecento Painting," in *Renaissance and Renascences in Western Art*, 120–31.

17 See Erwin Panofsky, *Meaning in the Visual Arts* (New York: Doubleday, 1955), on perspective and the human body, as well as note 7 above. Michel de Certeau's study of the mystical figuration of Hieronymous Bosch in *La fable mystique* (Paris: Gallimard, 1982), 35–64, sees bodies and ciphered forms in dialogue with "Northern" and "Southern" visions. The relation of ocularity, mysticism, and cardinality is taken up in

"The Gaze of Nicholas of Cusa," *Diacritics* 17.3 (Fall 1987), 2–38, in which the same Northern and Southern traditions are viewed as being displaced into each other (13–14).

18 Jurgis Baltrušaitis explores the affinities and ramifications of the style in *Le Moyen Age fantastique* (Paris: Colin, 1955), and *Réveils et prodiges* (Paris: Colin, 1960). The flamboyant remains a calligraphic architectural style that shares much with form and meaning of literature. François Rigolot compares its tortuous forms to the Grands Rhétoriqueurs in "1496," a chapter of the *New History of French Literature* (Cambridge: Harvard UP, 1989), devoted to the eve of the sixteenth century (132). And at the other end of the Renaissance, in *La littérature de l'âge baroque en France* (Paris: Corti, 1953), Jean Rousset wonders if the arcane meanders of Montaigne's style reach back to the memory of flamboyant gothic inspiration (80–100).

"Saturated" is a double-edged term that betrays a will of denial in Johan Huizinga's famous *Waning of the Middle Ages: A Study of the Forms of Life, Thought and Art in France and the Netherlands in the XIVth and XVth Centuries*, tr. Frederick Hopman (New York: Doubleday, 1956). The author tries to resist being fascinated by what he wants to show as symptomatic of an order in decay. He devotes the entire book to enumerating negatively these profusions of detail. Erich Auerbach follows Huizinga to the letter – *verbatim* – in his reading of the "suffocating" and "saturated" allegories of Antoine de la Sale in the chapter of *Mimesis*, tr. Williard Trask (New York: Doubleday, 1956) on "Madame de Chastel."

19 The play of the two systems tended to lose influence as the sixteenth century advanced. In *L'orthographe française à l'époque de la Renaissance* (Geneva: Droz, 1968), Nina Catach determines that typography settled down by the time of Montaigne, and that the ferment of the great periods of activity (1520–40 and 1540–60) was done. Direct manipulation of the letter became more and more a problem of metaphor. Such, for example, was the relation of Montaigne to print. In "De la vanité" (III, ix, of 1588), when the author gently compares his writing to excrement, he also implies that the typographic style implicitly equates ink with waste. The autobiographer avows, "Ce sont icy, un peu plus civilement, des excremens d'un vieil esprit, dur tantost, tantost lache, et tousjours indigeste" (946). [Here are, a little more civilly, excrements of an old mind, sometimes hard, sometimes soft, and always undigested.] Could *civilement* refer not only to the code of decency his metaphor is straining, but also to *civilité*, the typeface that will help him move along "une route par laquelle, sans cesse et sans travail, j'iray autant qu'il y aura d'ancre et de papier au monde" (945) [a road along which, endlessly and without travail, I shall go as long as there are ink and paper in the world]? And could the *excremens* be what is excreted, on paper, from the *mens* or mind of the author? The direct

relation of typography and meaning had been somewhat attenuated by the 1590s. (See also chapter 6, note 1).

20 Guy Rosolato studies the concept of the *objet de perspective* through clinical practice and analysis of painting in *Eléments de l'interprétation* (Paris: Gallimard, 1985), 123–33 and 305–6.

21 In *The Cornucopian Text*, Terence Cave studies the paradox thematically, through the figure of vacuity and proliferation. He often calls upon the letter to serve in the double role conceived as a juncture of *res* and *verba*, of thing and movement: "Allegories and erudite allusions, scaffolded as *res* on the colourful surface of *verba*, point back towards a supposed *sententia* or *sensus* whose hidden presence would give plenitude to *copia*" (35). Things are thus "word–things" on a "landscape of discourse" (36) and have, if we substitute "page" for "landscape," an uncannily familiar relation with the letter.

22 In "De la vanité," horizontal play is so stressed that the definite article ("la") of the title splinters into *l-a*, forcing *a* to slip into *vanité*, thus suggesting an echo of a strange ...*avanité*, an *avan(t)-ité*, a "before-ness" or degree to which vanity deals with the curiosity humans have to study what is before them, *avant*, in configurations of history. The montage that Montaigne makes of the title is confirmed when later, in the same essay, comparing ancient and modern Rome, he is inspired to wander in the wind, the *vent*, of his time, to *suyvre le vent* (994) [follow the wind], *à l'advanture* (993), with the writing of adventure and chance.

23 "De la vanité" again serves as an example. A certain "beforeness" pervades the essay. It comes with the autobiographer's tales of travel from France to Rome in the later pages (996–1001). Montaigne discovers that he is happening upon what he has known for a long time. Nothing is new, even under Italian sun. The theme of beforeness or *avantité* is also encoded in the number of the essay in superscription. The digits of *ix* yield a pun on "things new" and "nine." "Neuf" fits well above the chapter on age, on *novelty*, things new ("neuf"), and on the curiosity that prompts humans to dig into their past. Its hieroglyph confirms again what Montaigne suggests poetically when he soon remarks, "les noms de mes chapitres n'en embrassent pas tousjours la matiere; souvent ils la denotent seulement par quelque marque ..." (994) [the names of my chapters don't always embrace their matter; often they only denote by some mark ...]. The amphiboly is grasped in the vertical scansion of the chapter.

24 Gisèle Mathieu-Castellani notes that emblematic literature displays images resisting the reductive discourse of explanation, and that its configurations are thus far more complicated than they appear. Her use of a cinematic metaphor implies that the emblem inscribes division and breakage into its process: "the sound track isn't always in synchrony, and the image track takes liberties ... Between the two, three, or four

units correlated to produce one meaning, hierarchical relations are struck with instability.'' Words and images in a vertical relation seem to be part of a montage: ''A mute speaker, the image often says more than the letter, and it says more in other ways. Symbolic representations manifest the humanistic desire to make the world speak, to restitute the mute language of signs. ... In the course taken from meaning to representation ... the ideal figurability of the intelligible is postulated: is there not written into the very project, like the worm in the apple, the program of its failure from the moment when the compulsive question of meaning is put forward unaware of the modes of meaning pertaining to each art?'' ''Le retour de l'emblème,'' *Littérature* 78 (May 1990), 6–7.

25 In the introduction to his forthcoming *Screening the Text* (Baltimore: The Johns Hopkins UP, 1992), T. Jefferson Kline studies how a glyph of images, titles and letters produces effects of ''misprision,'' a ''locus of conflict,'' of a ''graphic unconscious'' in cinema. ''They institute a complex and highly mobile configuration of meanings, memories, and associations'' that owe much to ''productive repressions of image and writing'' (3–4). Seen in this light, the mobility of the letter *already* practices what film will exploit three and a half centuries later.

26 For the authors of the French Renaissance, ''words are things, their poems reflect the sensuality of forms, their prose adheres fully to thought or to experience. To read the ancients does not mean being confined in prison or a library, it entails preparation *to seize better the present time*.'' Without stating the point unequivocally, Jeanneret argues for the immediate timelessness of the Renaissance text. Furthermore, literature ''gives itself to be seen as such: a labor of the letter, a *montage* made from all pieces.'' *Des mets et des mots* (Paris: José Corti, 1988), 249 and 251 (my italics).

27 Literature on the topic is legion. In *The Legend of Freud* (Minneapolis: U of Minnesota P, 1982), Samuel Weber links Freud's formulations about the unconscious to the hieroglyph and *Bilderschriften* of his own writing in the *Interpretation of Dreams* (27–33). François Roustang reminds us that for Freud the unconscious is not a truth but an *invention* or a poetic trait that allows him to use myth and destiny while working as a scientist: ''On the Epistemology of Psychoanalysis,'' *MLN* 99 (September 1984), 929.

1 A secret space: Marot's *Rondeaux*

1 Frank Lestringant, ed., preface to *L'adolescence clémentine* (Paris: Gallimard/Poésie, 1987). Where possible, reference to the *rondeaux* and other poems will be made to this edition and cited in the text between parentheses containing the number of the poem, line and page in that order. Where sixteenth-century orthography must be reproduced, other editions will be cited.

2 Lestringant associates the process with tropes, especially *antanaclasis*, or repetition of one word taken in different meanings, and *syllepsis*, in which the same word is understood in literal and abstract registers (337–38). Use of these tropes is clearly related to typography.

3 Huguet, in the *Dictionnaire de la langue française au XVIe siècle* (Paris: Didier, 1925–67) lists *clavier* as "keyring," "keychain," "lock," or "buckle" (II, 310). Randle Cotgrave, in *A Dictionarie of the French and English Tongues* (London, 1611 [Columbia: University of South Carolina Press reprint, 1968]), enters "A key-chaine, or chaine for keyes, or chaine whereat keyes are hanged," whereas a *claviere* is "a key-keeper, or key-carrier; a woman that hath charge of all the keyes in a house."

4 Tory insists on the myth of IO to marry straight and curved lines. See introduction above, n. 14. The printer appends a moral meaning to the tale of the goddess IO. "I et O sont les deux lettres, desquelles toutes les autres Attiques sont faictes & formees. Le A est faict seulement de le I. Le B est faict du dict I & de le O, brise ... (f. viii v°). [I and O are the two letters from which all the other Attic letters are made and formed. The A is made only with the I. The B is made from the said I and from the O broken ...]

5 Lestringant uses the concept to put forth the modernity of Marot in his preface, 12ff.

6 X, 180–81. Because of the emblematic presence of the ampersand and the confusion of inner and outer voice in this poem that comes when inverted commas are omitted, orthography follows what is given in *Œuvres diverses: rondeaux, ballades, chants-royaux, épitaphes, étrennes, sonnets*, cr. edn by C. A. Mayer (London: Athlone Press, 1966), 75–76. Subsequent *rondeaux* quoted in their entirety will be taken from this edition.

7 The confusion of fish and crustacean is partially due to homonymy. In the sixteenth century, [u], [y], and [o] were conceivably quite close in pronunciation. *Ouisme* prevailed in the sixteenth century, as Ferdinand Brunot notes in *Histoire de la langue française de ses origines à 1900*, vol. 2 (Paris: Colin, 1905). Charles Beaulieux takes up the point in matters of typography. In *L'histoire de l'orthographe française*, vol. 1 (Paris: Champion, 1967 reprt) he adds, "L'ouisme, qui est au XVIe siècle plus florissant que jamais est, on le verra, bien plus un fait de prononciation que de graphie" (167). It may supersede print, but the only access to it is by way of written documents.

Furthermore, the *escrevice* figures prominently in emblem books, notably La Perrière's *Théâtre de bons engins* (1538) and others, noted in Arthur Henkel and Albrecht Schöne, *Emblemata* (Stuttgart: Metzlersche Verlag, 1967), columns 722–28. The quatrain that describes La Perrière's emblem can apply to the movements of Marot's life: "L'escrevice est à cheminer habile, / Tout en avant qu'en arrier' s'il fuyt / Changer noz

meurs est chose tresutile, / Quand nous voyons, que ce faire nous duit"
[In movement the crayfish is deft, / If he flees he goes forward and
backward / When we change our ways from right to left / In what for
us is toward]. According to Cotgrave, the *escrevice* is "A crevice, or
crayfish." while an *escrevice de mer* is "a lobster; or, (more properly)
a sea-crevice."

8 So amphibian are the signifiers that one might be tempted to see the eel
(*l'anguille*) figured in **ll** pressed into the serpentine **ss** of the subjunctive.
Another shape of transformation, the eel embodies a sign of language
and of movement. The pun on *languisse/langue isse* is common in the
Rhétoriqueurs, as François Cornilliat shows in "Equivoques générali-
sées," *Poétique* 83 (September 1990), 299.

9 *Clément Marot and the Inflections of Poetic Voice* (Berkeley: California,
1974), 65–66.

10 Pauline M. Smith, *Clément Marot, Poet of the French Renaissance*
(London, Athlone Press, 1970), 148–49. See also C. A. Mayer's notes
in his critical edition of the *Œuvres diverses* (London, Athlone Press,
1966), 58 and 93–94.

11 See C. A. Mayer and D. Bentley-Cranch, "Clément Marot, poète
pétrarchiste," *Bibliothèque d'Humanisme et Renaissance* 28 (1966),
32–51 and Daniel Poirion, *Le poète et le prince* (Paris: PUF, 1965).
Verdun Saulnier remarks of the poem, "Nous sommes toutefois plus
proprement dans le temps du prépétrarchisme français. Avant de sacrifier
à Pétrarche, la lyrique française d'amour s'inspire en fait d'une tradition
composite, qui relève de la tradition médiévale et courtoise, et du *jardin
de plaisance*, autant qu'elle doit à l'Italie. Cette définition très composite
de l'amour poli réussit pourtant à donner l'impression, dans le poème
de Marot, d'un sentiment des plus racés." [We are still anchored more
in the time of pre-Petrarchan French lyric. Before devoting itself to
Petrarch, French love lyric is inspired in fact from a composite tradition
that goes back to medieval and courtly tradition, and to the pleasure-
garden no less than to Italy. This very composite definition of refined
love nonetheless succeeds, in Marot's poem, in giving the impression of
one of the raciest feelings.] In his preface to *L'adolescence clémentine*
(Paris: Armand Colin, 1958), xxxii–iii.

12 See Lestringant, 335–38, and Thomas Sébillet, *Art poétique françoys*, in
Francis Goyet, ed., *Traités de poétique et de rhétorique de la Renaissance*
(Paris: Livre de poche, 1990), 109ff.

13 Geoffroy Tory noted that the sibilance of the letter **S** comes from a Greek
proverb describing the sound that red-hot iron makes when plunged into
cold water. Its silence evokes temperance and conviviality, f. lvii r°
(English translation, 139).

14 See Rabelais, *Gargantua*, chapter ix, where *espoir* is a rebus of the
globe, and chapter two below, note 1.

15 Randle Cotgrave: "*Sente*: f. A hollow path, a narrow (and well beaten)

way.'' David Kuhn takes up the medieval connotations – also Marot's of *sente* – in his reading of Villon's *lubres sentemens* in *La poétique de François Villon*, 141.

16 *Antre* or *antre obscure*, that is, the analogy of the imperfect world to the human body in a platonic system contemporary to Marot's, is implied here. Inflections of the term are studied in Jacques Derrida, "La Double séance," in *La dissémination* (Paris: Seuil, 1972), 240–41.

17 This resembles the order of disorder that Natalie Z. Davis has traced in "The Reason of Misrule" and "The Rites of Violence" in *Society and Culture in Early Modern France*, 97–123 and 181ff.

18 Identity of genitals and eyes was fairly standard in sixteenth-century iconography. Montaigne uses the same vocabulary to parody the emblem of Cupid at the onset of "Sur des vers de Virgile," where the loss of a generative organ spurs a desire for a presence which must be apparent but also visibly absent. Like Marot, he notes how the will has to be aroused and tempered "avec reláche et moderation: elle s'affole d'estre trop continuellement bandée" (841) [with ease and moderation: it is maddened by being too continually banded (or erected)].

19 It could be noted that, following Emile Benveniste's essay on pronouns, "De la subjectivité dans le langage" in *Problèmes de linguistique générale*, vol. 1 (Paris: Gallimard, 1966), 258–66, the play of *moy, pere* (*il*) and the unspoken term, the reader (*tu*), in the second stanza the voice eluded intersubjectivity and becomes a cipher in a play of graphic, lyrical, and metaphysical forces.

20 M. A. Screech poses them along historical and thematic lines in *Marot évangelique* (Geneva: Droz, 1967). A later view, embracing poetry-writing and religion, is advanced in his "Marot and the Face of the Gospel," in Jerry C. Nash, ed., *Pre-Pléiade Poetry* (Lexington: French Forum, 1985), 65–75, where he notes, "Marot saw his face reflected in a stream of truth" (70) that can be construed to be paginal and typographical.

21 J. Berchtold, "Le poète-rat: Villon, Erasme, ou les secrètes alliances de la prison dans 'l'épître à son amy Lyon' de Clément Marot," *Bibliothèque d'Humanisme et Renaissance* 50.1 (1988), 57–76, studies the event and its transmission before arriving at similar conclusions: "Le discours hérétique apprend ... à crypter son texte, profitant non seulement de la duplicité des mots, mais s'ouvrant aux galeries de lacunes qui l'aérent et le strient, et qui, le déchirant, créent la mystification" (69–70, my italics). [Heretical discourse learns how ... to encrypt its text, profiting not only by the duplicity of words, but by opening on to galleries of lacunas that aerate and striate it and which, by tearing it up, create mystification.]

22 In this sense Marot's relation to the *Rhétoriqueurs* follows Walter Friedlander's famous "grandfather law," by which artists of one generation work through their œdipal relation with their masters by adopting the codes of their fathers' fathers, as coined in *Mannerism and Anti-Mannerism in Italian Art* (New York: Columbia UP, 1957 repr.), chapter 1.

23 For cause of orthography, the text of Lyon: A l'enseigne du Rocher, 1544 (*Les Œuvres de Clement Marot, Vallet de chambre du roy. Plus amples, et en meilleur ordre que paravent*), is reprinted, taken from Albert-Marie Schmidt, éd. *Poètes du XVIe siècle* (Paris: Gallimard-Pléiade, 1953), 25. It can be compared to the previous version, of 1538, in C. A. Mayer's edition, 104. In 1538 the poem was titled "Des Nonnes qui sortirent du Couvent pour aller se recreer," but it was written prior to 1527.

24 The poet wishes to enter into an erotic space other than his own. The same themes are handled in *rondeaux* XLV and XLVI (202–03), and recall folklore and narrative. Sight of the beautiful nun is patent in Boccaccio (*The Decameron*, third day, first novella) and in Bonaventure des Périers, *Nouvelles récréations et joyeux devis* (tale 62), reprinted in Pierre Jourda, ed., *Conteurs du seizième siècle* (Paris: Gallimard-Pléiade, 1965).

25 The etymon, *cuvens*, had developed into both *convent* and *couvent*. Both spellings are represented in the dictionary of the French Academy of 1684. "*Convent*. Some write *couvent*, and that is the way it should be pronounced," cited in *Trésor de la langue française*, 6 (Paris: CNRS, 1978), 390.

26 The identity of *or* as both gold and a conjunction will be studied further through Montaigne's "Des coches" (chapter 6 below). *Or* figures as what another poet of incarceration, Jean Genet, calls a "universal equivalence" of desire and interchangeable beings, in "Ce qui reste d'un Rembrandt," *Œuvres complètes* 4 (Paris: Gallimard, 1968), 24–25.

27 The reminder is most clearly scripted into the pull of the fourth line of the quatrain spoken by the poet-criminal at the gallows:

> Je suis François dont ce me poise
> Né de Paris empres Ponthoise
> Or dune corde dune toise
> Mon *cou* saura que mon *cul* poise

> [I am Francis and this hangs heavy
> Born in Paris near Ponthoise
> Now from a cord long as a levey
> My neck will know my bottom is heavy].

28 The *rondeau* of Marot is located at an axis of two traditions that first intersect in the verses of Charles d'Orléans. "Artistes et lettrés abandonnent la conception du lyrisme lié à la fête de cour. L'échange avec le public n'a plus le même caractère. Dans le cas du rondeau, c'est la sentence initiale qui sert de médiation entre le poète et la société. Le refrain rend au public ce qu'il a prêté: la doctrine commune ... Or justement la situation équivoque de l'homme de cour, l'opposition ou la juxtaposition du monde extérieur et du monde intérieur, vont trouver la structure même du rondeau, dans sa dualité originelle, la forme idéale d'expression." [Artists and men of letters abandon the conception of lyricism linked

to courtly entertainment. Exchange with the public no longer has the same character. In the case of the *rondeau*, it is the initial sentence that serves to mediate between the poet and society. The refrain gives to the public what he has borrowed: common doctrine ... Then, to be sure, the equivocal situation of the courtly man, the opposition or the juxtaposition of the exterior world from the interior world, will find in the very structure of the *rondeau*, in its original duality, the ideal form of expression], notes Poirion, *Le poète et le prince*, 339–40. The author insists on the *incipit* which returns "under different lighting effects," similar to a face first seen frontally and then from profile. The novelty of the *rondeau* after Charles d'Orléans is due to the literary artifice consisting of adapting one formula to different contexts.

29 Such as Apollinaire's

pupille   Christ   de l'œil

in "Zone" (*Alcools*, 1913), a poem owing much to Villon, Marot, and other medieval writers.

30 The same visual system inspires the second and most celebrated *rondeau* in the *Adolescence clémentine*, "A ung creancier," in which the poet fabricates a *rondeau*-as-I.O.U. while staving off the bill-collector. The poem becomes a fake "rond" or coin all the while it puts in question the belief (or "creance") of the public agent,

A UNG CREANCIER

Un bien petit de près me venez prendre
Pour vous payer; et si debvez entendre
Que je n'euz onc Angloys de vostre taille;
Car à tous coups vous criez: baille, baille,
Et n'ay dequoy contre vous me deffendre.

Sur moy ne fault telle rigueur estendre,
Car de *pecune ung peu* ma bourse est tendre;
Et toutefoys j'en ay, vaille que vaille,
      Un bien petit.

Mais à vous veoir (ou l'on me puisse pendre)
Il semble advis qu'on ne vous vueille rendre
Ce qu'on vous doibt; beau sire, ne vous chaille.
Quand je seray plus garny de cliquaille,
Vous en aurez; mais il vous fault attendre
      Un bien petit.

[To a Creditor

A little bit you come to take, near to me;
In order to be paid, you must know your fee
Exceeds the English coins that you require;
For you're yelling *Pay up!* over and over,
And I'm helpless in defending against your decree.
To me you should never extend all this rigor,
For my purse is empty, tender, without vigor,

And I always have, more or less, my sir,
A little bit.

But in seeing you (be I hanged or burned in fire)
It seems clear that no one will ever tender
What is owed to you; stately sire, never tire
In knowing that when I am rich with tender
You'll have some. For now wait, dear lender,
A little bit.]

The center is spotted by the movement between *pecune* and *ung peu*, in which alliteration betrays the worth, p-e-u, that spins off *pecune* to the left of center. Its resulting composition becomes, for what little worth it may have upon cursory glance, far more heavenly than that of worldly money.

31 Rudolph Arnheim was shown that gridded space plays on relations of center and circumference in *The Power of the Center* (Berkeley: U of California P, 1988), 9ff. His conclusions can be extended to writing. The rapport of center and periphery also entails problems of selfhood and conquest, as implied in Marot's poem. The theme is taken up in Samuel V. Edgerton Jr., "From Mental Matrix to Mappamundi to Christian Empire: the Heritage of Ptolemaic Cartography in the Renaissance," in David Woodward, ed., *Art and Cartography: Six Historical Essays* (Chicago, U of Chicago P, 1987), 10–50, especially 6–17. It can be added that once again nothing radically new occurs in the movement of characters. Charles d'Orléans had practiced the same visual and graphic sense of reversible writing in his *rondeaux*, especially in those which blend metaphors of nature and of writing. The point is developed in my "Jargon d'Orléans," *The New Orleans Review*, 12 (1985), 12–26. In his edition of the text, Geoffroy Tory published the *Adolescence clémentine* (Paris: Roffel, 1532) to launch spelling reform (adding the accent on the final *e* and the cedilla) but also to share an affinity with Marot's art. See Pauline M. Smith, "Clément Marot and the French Language," in P.M. Smith and I.D. McFarlane, eds., *Literature and the Arts in the Reign of Francis I* (Lexington: French Forum, 1985): 163–65.

32 See Angus Fletcher, *Allegory: Theory of a Symbolic Mode* (Ithaca: Cornell UP, 1964), chapter 2, on the mode's "daimonic agency."

33 On 5 February 1526, Robert Knecht reports, in reponse to the excesses of the *Réforme de Meaux*, "The French Parlement issued a decree in which heresy was defined so broadly as to include any deviation, however slight, from orthodoxy. Censorship was carried to greater lengths than ever before, printers and booksellers being forbidden to publish or even stock translations of works." *Francis I* (Cambridge: Cambridge UP, 1982), 180–81 (pp. 250–51 take up Marot's continued harassment).

34 The ways by which writing tends to silence voice are taken up in Gérard Defaux, "Clément Marot: une poétique du silence et de la liberté," in

Nash, *Pre-Pléiade Poetry*, 44–64: "Lorsque Marot parle, c'est au fond toujours en rêvant qu'il vaudrait mieux se taire. La liberté qu'il espère est en dehors des mots" (61). [When Marot speaks, it is basically by dreaming that it would be better to remain silent. The freedom he yearns for is outside words].

35 The practice of inscribing a figure of death across an image or a text is probably more pervasive than our memory of Holbein's painting might lead us to believe. It was part of the tradition of tapestry (see below in the analysis of Ronsard, "Comme un chevreuil ...," chapter 3, n. 19), and it is evident in both the historiated alphabets and the emblems. Holbein scattered them through various vanishing points in his illustrations that were printed in the *Simulachres de la mort* (1538), and he printed a handsome alphabet in the frame of the *danse macabre*: Francis Douce, ed., *Holbein's Dance of Death* (London: Henry G. Bohn, 1858), 218ff. (See Plate 7.) See Gisèle Mathieu-Castellani, *Emblèmes de la mort: le dialogue de l'image et du texte* (Paris: Nizet, 1988), 33–46, in which she argues that death is effectively what *cannot* be represented. It can therefore be added that death marks a progressively visible relation in a text because of its own ineffable qualities that are better lent to pictures than to discursive language.

36 The initial *rondeau* fixes the poet in a social space of print. It reproduces the birth of the subject through the social use of the proper name. François Rigolot studies the ways that the proper name becomes set or "fixed" in the fabric of the early sixteenth century in *Poésie et onomastique* (Geneva: Droz, 1978), 24–28.

2 The Rabelaisian hieroglyph

1 *Gargantua*, in François Rabelais, *Œuvres complètes*, ed. Jacques Boulenger (Paris: Gallimard-Pléiade, 1955), 48. All subsequent references will be made to this edition and cited between parentheses.

2 That reads:

> Cy gist, repose et dort léans
> Le feu Evesque d'Orleans:
> J'entends l'Evesque en son surnom,
> Et frère Jehan en propre nom.
> Qui mourut l'an cinq cens et vingt,
> De la verolle qui luy vint.
> Or affin que sainctes et anges
> Ne prennent ces boutons estranges,
> Prions Dieu, qu'au frère frappart
> Il donne quelcque chambre à part.

> [Here lies, sleeps and within remains
> The former Bishop John of Orleans:
> I mean, yes, Bishop in the surname,
> And Brother John in proper name,

Who died in the year fifteen twenty
Of pocks of which he had a plenty.
Now, so that saints and angels
Won't be spotted with these pimples,
Let's pray to God for this Brother Knocker
That He'll put him in another locker.]

In *L'adolescence clémentine*, ed. Frank Lestringant, 143−44. See chapter 1, n. 1. The poem is taken from the 1538 edition but includes materials dating back to 1515.

3 Typographical change in the sixteenth century affirms the "principle of disjunction" at work in cultural change − by which practices of one time and space are either able or unable to read those of another. We recall again Erwin Panofsky's point in his comparison of Roman and Gothic styles in *Renascence and Renaissance in Western Art*, 107−08. He notes that in the Italian Renaissance the eye fixes a distance between itself and its object and thus begins to see its history in and across time. "Our own script and letter press derive from the Italian Renaissance types patterned, in deliberate opposition to the Gothic, upon Carolingian and twelfth-century models which in turn had evolved on a classical basis. Gothic script, one might say, symbolizes the transitoriness of the medieval renascences" (108).

4 Mireille Huchon has traced the history of typography and punctuation in two studies of Rabelais. In one, "Pour une histoire de la ponctuation 1532−1553," *Nouvelle Revue du Seizième Siècle*, 6 (1988), 15−28, she shows how variety in form and punctuation among the editions, widespread before 1534, settles quickly from 1534 to 1540, before finding regularity upon the impact of Etienne Dolet's *La maniere de bien traduire d'une langue en aultre. D'avantage. De la punctuation de la langue Françoyse* of 1540. She traces neologisms according to similar vectors in "Rabelais et les genres d'*escrire*," in Raymond C. La Charité, ed., *Rabelais's Incomparable Book* (Lexington: French Forum, 1986), 226−47.

5 Some of the graphic compulsions of the early Rabelais are studied in Eva Daddesio, "Le bruissement silencieux de la graphie dans 'Les Fanfreluches antidotées,'" *L'Esprit Créateur* 28.2 (Summer 1988), 48−57.

6 In *Eléments de l'interprétation*, Guy Rosolato affirms that the relations that writing, because it does not transcribe speech, opens with the unknown are owed to an optical distance it takes from what it is supposed to mediate. Entailed thus are interdictions which configure the invisible, or whatever pertains to Eros or to Death (175−76). Interdiction, he adds, is already written into writing. The same double-bind will dominate *Gargantua*.

7 Michel Jeanneret, "Du mystère à la mystification: le sens caché à la Renaissance et dans Rabelais," *Versants* 2 (Winter 1981−82), 17. For Humanists, the substance of a message had to be taken in act of faith without any allegorical or exegetical mediation. The Humanist had to reveal the totality of the world's secrets in an Esperanto of instantaneity.

8 *Champ fleury*, f. xlii r°. Georges Ives, in the English edition, remarks, "The play on words can hardly be reproduced in translation" (104).

9 The problem of typography and meaning in Rabelais is vast and does not settle by the time of the fourth book. Samuel Kinser shows how ambiguity is a function of typography, in *Rabelais's Carnival* (Berkeley: U of California P, 1990), 136–38.

10 *Champ fleury*, f. viii v°.

11 François Rigolot observes that Rabelais, like Dante, builds his book upon numerological codes. He shows that "numerological *conjointure* is only the signature, the literal 'cipher' of a much deeper conjunction that we recognize in thematic, structural, and metaliterary levels of the intertextuality of *Purgatory* and *Pantagruel*," in *Le texte de la Renaissance*, 162. He uses the cipher in order to work toward a broad comparison of organizational schemes that bind the two great authors. From the standpoint of typography, we should note that early modern writers do not supersede their creations so easily. The letter pulls them into common and collective practices that complicate the status of the author. In the lexicon of Michel Foucault, who has impugned the status of the "author," we note that these are proper names that function according to an *epistemè* that structures what can be said or thought in a given time. Thus the vanishing point that Rigolot locates at the center of *Pantagruel* may indeed be there, but as cipher it points to other frames of closure that are not simply determined by bilateral symmetry. *Other* letters come into play, and so does what the reader construes to be a frame productive for interpretation. Centers will thus proliferate in the quest of meaning. Rabelais, Guy Demerson has argued in *Rabelais* (Paris: Balland, 1986), gives readers tremendous latitude to invent forms from figural latencies in the text. Thus it is not unwarranted to see Tory's IO in 10, the number of the chapter on hieroglyphs.

12 In *Des mets et des mots*, Michel Jeanneret observes that a psychogenesis takes place. A dialogic condition, without border or sense, but of universal frivolity, gives way to a reasoned conviviality. Flow becomes measured where the characters learn that they cannot speak and eat or drink at the same time. Biological measure happens when a balance of ingestion and speech is attained (20ff.). Alfred Glauser invents a convincing order in the first chapter of *Fonction du nombre chez Rabelais* (Paris: Nizet, 1984), 25–35. He emphasizes the infinite possibility of *engendrement* through phonic repetitions of syllabic figures. The selection is derived by typographic means.

13 Alfred Glauser suggests that the moment, in the manner of Proust, moves "from time lost to time regained." *Rabelais créateur* (Paris: Nizet, 1966), chapter 2.

14 The open-ended allegory is no doubt a convention of decorative schemes that were current in the 1530s. Dora and Erwin Panofsky argue that the Galerie François Premier rewrites the past life of Francis I but with

an eye open to the possibilities of change in his future. It is hence historiographical at the same time as it carries a sibylline dimension. See their "Galerie François Premier at Fontainebleau," *Gazette des Beaux Arts* (1958), 11–113.

15 The Egyptians, noted Alberti, made use of secret symbols in order not to lose knowledge that, if couched in ordinary language, would fritter away over time. He used the Etruscan language, which resembled the hieroglyphs, as an example of a secret idiom. "For among the ruins of several towns, castles and burial places I have seen tombstones dug up with inscriptions on them ... in Etruscan characters which nobody ... can understand." *Ten Books on Architecture*, vol. 8, cited by Rudolph Wittkower, "Hieroglyphics in the Early Renaissance," in Bernard S. Levy, ed. *Developments in the Early Renaissance* (Albany: State University of New York Press, 1972), 69.

16 Roland Barthes reviews the genre in his essay on Archimboldo in *L'obvie et l'obtus* (Paris: Seuil, 1982), 120–30. In his *Art poétique françoys* (1546) Thomas Sébillet writes of enigma as a genre whose form is designed to put forward a mystery (in Goyet, *Traités*, 134–40). The secret or invisible dimension is not innate or a simple truth of truth; rather, it remains a product of artifice that merely feigns mystery.

17 The chapter is reminiscent of a totally modern literature, in which, as Natalie Sarraute argued in *L'ère du soupçon*, description is free from the regulations of point of view commanded by a "dit-il" or a "dit-elle," markers that deprive a work of its richer dimensions that confuse voices and promote ambiguities of perspective.

18 Psychoanalytical meanings of regression would help clarify the speech of the *bien yvres*. In a clinical situation, regression or "the regressive moment" catalyzes the action of transference (in this instance, reading) which, in turn, forces patient and interlocutor to discern in their movement of dialogue a recurring number of word-figures that are not confined to the semantic structures of communication. Their sensory range allows a letter or a pictogram to emerge from the analysand's conscience that, up to that point, had repressed its visibility. See Claude Sylvestre, "Le moment régressif," *Topique* 25 (1980), 27–30.

19 With footnotes indeed! *Rabelais* (Ithaca and London: Cornell UP, 1980), 134. Pages 137–43 take up Tory and emblematic writing in detail.

20 In "Titre à préciser," *Parages* (Paris: Galilée, 1986), Jacques Derrida studies how the title engenders a law in respect to itself. A work without a title is an impossibility. The title (of a book, a painting, a film, or a chapter) establishes a binding relation between itself and the body it crowns, such that in the eyes of the reader a quasi-contractual obligation has to be sought. The title verifies the work and vice versa. If one does not "bind" the other, then the reader's or viewer's imagination will supply enough meaning to do so in the gap between one area and the other. Our compulsion to make things mean fabricates orders everywhere.

21 As Donald Frame and others have shown, the work indicates a transition from comedy to seriousness. The Alcofrybas of 1533–34 becomes the Rabelais of 1548 and after. See Raymond C. La Charité, "Narrative Strategy in Rabelais's *Quart Livre*," in Barbara C. Bowen and Jerry C. Nash, eds., *Lapidary Inscriptions: Renaissance Essays for Donald A. Stone, Jr.* (Lexington: French Forum, 1991), 195–97 and 203.

22 See François Rigolot, "Dichotomie épistémologique chez Rabelais," in *Poétique et onomastique* (Genève: Droz, 1977), 92–93.

23 This process of "federalized" responsibility, by which the author has the reader complete the book by playing with it, indeed recalls many of the precepts of the avant-garde. We recall the Surrealists' definition of the author as an *exécutant*, a figure constructing unfinished designs that invite extended interpretation. Using Max Ernst, Claude Lévi-Strauss stresses how this activity works in archaic thought in "Une pensée méditative," in *Le regard éloigné* (Paris: Plon, 1983), 327. He is close to Guy Demerson, who studies the same function of puns in "Les calembours de Rabelais," in *Le comique verbal au XVIe siècle* (Warsaw: Cahiers de Varsovie, 1981), 90ff.

24 See Terence Cave's remarks in *The Cornucopian Text*, on the rapport of *res* and *verba* and on the relation of writing to the seasons, especially in the pages on Ronsard's *Hymnes*, 242ff. Seasonality and writing will be taken up in chapter 3 below.

25 The allegorical Y is something of an icon in the early 1530s. See the "moralized" Y of the *Champ fleury* and François Rigolot and Sandra Sider, "Fonctions de l'écriture emblématique chez Rabelais," *L'Esprit Créateur* 28 (Summer 1988), 38–39.

26 Rosolato, *Eléments de l'interprétation*, ch. 3.

27 The way that a space is animated in the *propos des bien yvres* roughly follows the model of motivation that Frank Lestringant fashions in "Rabelais et le récit toponymique," *Poétique* 50 (April 1982), 207–25.

28 The combination of ham and poetry was no doubt a convention developed through Villon, whose work infuses *Gargantua*. In the "Ballade de la Grosse Margot," the narrator-pimp and his bawd clash and love "en ce bordeau ou tenons nostre estat." [In this house where we hold our court.] In winter, they sleep together snug as a bug in a rug ("Tous deux ivres dormons comme un sabot"), but when spring comes, she wakes him up and strikes him on his fat thigh: "Gogo me dit et me fiert sur le *iambot*." [Gogo she says and hits me on the *jambot*.] As in Rabelais, the figure releases a music of cacophony that signals a time of collective rebirth.

29 See the special number (12) of *Corps Écrit* (Paris: PUF, 1984) devoted to silence in the arts. In *The Symposium* Socrates arrives at the party, as proverbs go, "late and loaded," but full of wit and vision inspired by good company and plenty of drink.

30 As Floyd Gray notes in "Ambiguity and Point of View in the Prologue

to *Gargantua,"* *Romanic Review* 56 (1965), 19—25. In a more recent study, the critic observes how, in "the conventions of printing serving to undermine, even contradict, the fiction or oral presentation," the prologue to *Pantagruel* embodies a divided relation that alienates voice and script. As in the work of Henry James, Gray remarks, the reader of Rabelais remains a spectator of a scene from which he is increasingly excluded. *"Rabelais's First Readers," Rabelais's Incomparable Book*, ed. Raymond C. La Charité (Lexington: French Forum, 1986), 15 and 25. The study pertains at once to prologues, the *propos des bien yvres*, and the tension of script and voice.

31 See Michel de Certeau, *L'écriture de l'histoire* (Paris: Gallimard, 1975), 102, citing J. M. Lévy, "L'écriture en miroir des petits écoliers," *Journal de Psychologie Normale et Pathologique* 32 (1935), 443—54 and J. de Ajuriaguerra *et al.*, "L'écriture en miroir," *La Semaine des Hôpitaux de Paris* 2 (1956), 80—86.

32 "Sigma doncques signifie & denote Silence, a la cause de quoy les Anciens bien souvant lescripvoient toute seulle au dessus de lhuis du lieu au quel on mengeoit & beuvoit acompaigne de ses bons amys. Pour mettre devant les yeulx que les parolles & propos quon tient a table doivvent estre sobres & gardes en silence. La quelle chose ne peult estre faicte sil y a exces de trop boyre & menger ..." (f. lviir°). [Sigma thus signifies and denotes Silence, because the Ancients often wrote it alone over the door to the hall where everyone ate and drank in the company of good friends, in order to put before our eyes the words and conversation that are held at the table must be sober and kept in silence. Which cannot be done if there is an excess of drinking and eating.]

33 See Gisèle Mathieu-Castellani on Montaigne as "coprographer" in *Montaigne, l'écriture de l'essai* (Paris: PUF, 1988), 198.

34 François Rigolot has argued that the "invention" mimes and exceeds the indeterminate erotic dimension of Michelangelo's painting of Leda and the Swan. The chapter recognizes the new patronage of Francis I, absorbs the figure of Leda making love to the downy bird, but casts it along a regressive axis – it is implied from the standard Freudian model of sexual development articulated in the *Three Essays* – that moves from insinuations of homoeroticism, in Michelangelo's depiction of the myth, to a collective laughter of Platonic obscenity. "Léda and the Swan: Rabelais's Parody of Michelangelo," *Renaissance Quarterly* 38.4 (Winter 1985), 488—700.

35 Another model is found at Châteaudun but is enclosed. Jean Guillaume notes that the spiral staircase at Blois (1515) attests to a "complete renewal" of the basic theme of the structure. Blois (and Bonnivet) are two principal creations that "constitute the achievement of all research conducted in France since the fourteenth century: the great spiral comes to perfection at the moment it is about to disappear." "L'escalier dans l'architecture française de la première moitié du XVIe siècle," in

L'escalier dans l'architecture de la Renaissance (Paris: Picard, 1986), 30. The documentation suggests that Rabelais's inspiration comes from the new building campaigns that modified the late-medieval spiral staircase for use in the château.

36 See Rigolot, *Le texte de la renaissance*, 114−15.

37 Given the hieroglyphic dimension of the words, the syntagm invites a translinguistic reading which ventures into the international space evoked by the Canary Islands: *son* (English: son) *filz* (French: son), and yields a rebus with international affinities and filiations that move from France back and forth over the North Atlantic. This reading would modify François Rigolot's provocative study of the relation of birds to scholasticism, punning on the Affaire des Placards, in what he calls *une affaire de canards*, "Rabelais et la scolastique (*Gargantua* 12)," in Raymond C. La Charité, ed., *Rabelais's Incomparable Book*, 119. If his study of the rumpwiper and Michelangelo (above) is compared to that of the same invention and the world of Duns Scotus and Ockham, it follows that the chapter becomes something of a pervasively "floating signifier" that can distort any number of cultural traditions.

38 In an unpublished doctoral dissertation (Minnesota, 1991), Martine Sauret argues that Tory's rebus is crucial to the play of perspective and proportion in *Gargantua*. The work suggests, it can be added, that Lacan's famous "objet petit-*a*" that codes the fortunes of desire might have origins in Rabelais's *a-petit*.

3 Ronsard's sonnet-pictures

1 Donald Kelley sketches a history in chapter 1 and 2 of *The Beginnings of Ideology* (Cambridge: Cambridge UP, 1982).

2 Louis Marin develops an extended comparison of the king and his artistic programs in *Portrait of the King*, tr. Martha Houle (Minnesota: U of Minnesota P, 1988). He argues that the king's real power was located in the esthetic effects he fashioned and imprinted upon his subjects. In the time of Francis I, Henri II, Charles IX, and of course the era of the Wars of Religion, the relation of the artist to the king appears to have been less unilateral or immediately propagandistic.

3 In 1542 Meigret published his *Traité de l'escriture françoise*, in which he argued for a phonocentric reform of orthography: letters ought to translate directly the verbal texture of words. Meigret criticized the practice of verbal *diminution* (*chef* or head does not spell "chief" as the word is commonly heard), *superfluité* (one writes *aorné* while pronouncing "orné"), and *usurpation* (in *façon c* is pronounced as *s* but has the value of k). Verdun Saulnier traces the history of the debate and its heritage in Georges Grente, ed., *Dictionnaire des lettres françaises: le XVIe siècle* (Paris: Fayard, 1951), 507−08. Charles Beaulieux studies Meigret's phonetics in detail in *L'histoire de l'orthographe en France*, 2, 43−49.

4 With Ronsard, we are in a world where allegory is the median area between speech and writing or discourse and picture. Angus Fletcher noted that in allegory, every single mark within its field can be appropriated to represent not the world but an abstraction. It uses *every possible detail* for its overriding order and carries with it a quasi-Freudian obsession with minutiae. See *Allegory: Theory of a Symbolic Mode*, 149–50.

5 See Margaret M. McGowan, *Ideal Forms in the Age of Ronsard* (Berkeley: U. of California P, 1985), a comprehensive study of the parallel creations of art and literature of the middle years of the sixteenth century.

6 Music is therefore a function of spacing. Already scholars have shown how little Ronsard has to do with music as an effect of voice. In "The Idea of Music in Ronsard's Poetry," Brian Jeffrey notes that music plays little importance in the overall œuvre, except as a figure of beauty in a general sense. In Terence Cave, ed., *Ronsard the Poet* (London: Methuen, 1973), 208–38.

7 Henri and Catherine Weber, critical edition of *Les Amours* (Paris: Garnier Frères, 1963), 39. All references to material of 1553 will be made to this edition and cited between parentheses in the text here and in the following chapter.

8 Such is Leonard Barkan's conclusion to his comparison of the two poets in *The Gods Made Flesh: Metamorphosis and the Pursuit of Paganism* (New Haven and London: Yale University Press, 1986), 215.

9 The sonnet is studied at some length in Henri Weber, *La création poétique au XVIe siècle en France* (Paris: Nizet, 1956), 238–42. The author restricts his reading to a comparative appreciation of the various renderings and insists on the supple rhythm of the sonnet which evinces creative effort invested in the image. Weber searches for the effects of description in melting snow and "voluptuous savor." He notes an "excessive research" in line two that we shall project, to the contrary, to be its visible virtue. Michel Dassonville shows how Scève's "Libre vivois en l'Avril de mon age" (*Delie*, vi), a "gem," may be much closer to Ronsard's sonnet than the official model of Bembo that Estienne Pasquier had first specified in *Recherches de la France*. Dassonville suggests that all Ronsard takes from the Italian is the shell of the sonnet while following the place, moment, motivation and expression of errant love from the dreamy discourse of Scève. His point – in *Ronsard: étude historique et littéraire, vol. 3: Prince des poètes ou poète des princes* (Geneva: Droz, 1976): 35–36 – moves away from that of Weber who had compared the text to *Si come suol, poiche'l verno aspro e io ... .* No matter what its sources, the sonnet confirms what Alfred Glauser had already noted in passing. "Il s'empare d'un thème; en échange il donne des vers mieux écrits, un chant inconnu du modèle" [He steals a theme; in exchange he offers lines that are written better, in song unknown in the original], in *Le poème-symbole* (Paris: Nizet, 1967), 41. All of these readers tend to

use esthetic criteria to judge the value of the sonnet, whereas it remains a piece of currency in the context of its production.

10 Marcel Raymond, in *Baroque et Renaissance poétique* (Paris: Corti, 1955), 78, notes that Ronsard owes as much to his French heritage as he does to Italian models.

11 See Leo Bersani, *The Culture of Redemption* (Cambridge: Harvard University Press, 1990), ch. 1.

12 With attention to the periodicity not of the poem but of its tempo of writing, Glauser demythologizes the idea of a melancholic or meditative Ronsard: "The sonnets will be good or bad according to the weather ... Ronsard is not a poet of geneses. He likes inhabited and cultivated places." *Le poème-symbole*, 42. Expanding on these remarks, François Rigolot indicates how Ronsard jostles the mimetic system of the sonnet. The play of comparison and compared opens up the poem and gives it mobility: "L'hyperbole des 'Mille traitz' tirés 'd'un coup' renvoie paradoxalement à la nature du comparant, comme si l'amant désirait se faire tuer 'comme un chevreuil': mort souhaitable, car mort plus que les 'mille mortz' renouvelées par le pétrarquisme." [The hyperbole of the "thousand arrows" taken "in one blow" refers paradoxically to the nature of the comparative term, as if the lover wanted to be killed "like a shammy:" a desired death, for the death is softer than the "thousand deaths" renewed by Petrarchism.] *Le texte de la Renaissance*, 190.

13 Huguet provides copious samples that generally compare the diminutive to spring and to little women. He omits *herbette* by alluding to it simply as variant of *l'herbelette: Dictionnaire de la langue française du XVIe siècle*, 4, fasc. 35 (Paris: Didier, 1949) 468. Noteworthy is Littré's omission of *herbelette*, a rather odd diminutive; he favors *herbette* in a strictly pastoral sense developed among precious poets – we witness Antoinette Deshoulières – of *rocaille* two centuries later:

> Vous qui, gras et beau,
> Me donniez sans cesse,
> Sur l'*herbette* épaisse,
> Un plaisir nouveau.

[You who, plump and of handsome view, / Gave me forever, to the quick, / On the little grass so thick, / A pleasure ever-new.] *Herbelette*, almost a homonym of *arbaleste*, is repressed in favor of a less frequently used variant, *herbette*, for reasons that would combine allusions both to grass and an errant beast or, in a more physiological sense, grazer and pasture.

14 That Baïf rewrites the same poem by having the deer felled by arquebus fire comes as little surprise. The paradigm of the poem is used to enumerate methods of killing. In the context of the civil wars, the occasion is ripe for updating the sonnet with a heavier instrument in the meter of twelve feet. We obtain a blunderbuss of a sonnet:

Comme quand le printemps de sa robe plus belle
La terre parera, lors que l'yver depart,
La bische toute gaye à la lune s'en part
Hors de son bois aimé, qui son repos recele:
De là viander la verdure nouvelle,
Seure loin des bergers, dans les champs à l'écart:
Ou dessus la montagne ou dans le val: la part
Que son libre desir la conduit et l'appele.
Ny n'a crainte du trait, ny d'autre tromperie,
Quant à coup elle sent dans son flanc le boulet,
Qu'un bon harquebouzier caché d'aguet luy tire
Tel, comme un qui sans peur de rien ne se defie,
Dame, j'alloye le soir, que vos beaux yeux d'un trait
Firent en tout mon coeur une playe bien pire.

[As when the Spring with its prettiest dress displays the earth, when winter goes away, the spritely doe goes off to the moon, out of her beloved woods, that her repose conceals. To eat the new grass, safe far from the shepherds, in the faraway fields: Or on the mountain or in the valley: she leaves when her free desire drives and calls her. She fears no arrow, nor other deceit. When all of a sudden she feels a bullet in her side, that a good musketeer hidden in ambush shoots at her, such, like one without fear who suspects nothing, Lady, I went in the evening, that your handsome eyes, in one shot, made in my heart a wound much worse.]
Les Amours de Francine, ed. Ernesta Calderini (Geneva: Droz, 1966), 152.

Esthetic and technical traditions coincide, as the newer mode of warfare generates a different version of the sonnet with flint and thunder. The lady's eyes now shoot not arrows but balls from the orbit of her musket. Conversion from crossbows to flintlock and gunpowder seems to be slower in strategies of metaphor than in reality. The time-lag notwithstanding, we must remember that the printer's studio was filled with metallic objects – puncheons, springs, levers – that bear analogy with the gunsmith, whose triggers, bored barrels, and flashpans are crafted from the same matter. If a technology of weaponry were charted across the sonnets, Ronsard would probably have *already* accounted for Bembo's *inganno* (line 9) that literally generates the *engin* of Baïf's version. For Ronsard there seems to be little anxiety of influence. Extended comparison would have to include Ronsard's rewriting of "Comme un chevreuil …" in the *Continuation*, XVII: "Le vintiéme d'Avril couché sur l'herbelette, / Je vy, ce me sembloit, en dormant un chevreuil" (ed. Weber, 181), and Pasquier's version in *Recherches de la France* in the 1580s.

15 See de Certeau, *L'écriture de l'histoire*, 102, and chapter 2, note 30, above.

16 The money obtained from the "Oroison" is exemplary, as in Molinet's "Oroison sur Maria," "Oroison à la Glorieuse Vierge Marie," "Devote Louenge," "Glorieuse Vierge Marie," and "Oroison à Nostre Dame," etc., in *Les Faictz et dictz*, 3 (Paris: SATF, 1937), 454–90, which lead

"Au plain chemin de l'éternelle gloire" (467). This recoups the work of Marot, too, in "Hors du couvent," studied in chapter 1 above.

17 The confusion of a quasi-copulative *or* allowing the eye to exchange words or concepts in a verbal contract, in which the useless term binds the units of a syllogism identical to a measure of a precious metal reifying a commodity, has been an almost timeless ruse among modern poets. Molinet plays on the term in "Le Cri des monnoies" (*Faictz et dictz*, 766–67); Marot in his *rondeau*, "Au roy" (XXXIV, 195–96); Montaigne all over the surface of "Des coches" (see chapter 6 below); and of course, in later literature, with Balzac, in "La Fille aux yeux d'or."

18 In *Freud, Proust, and Lacan: Theory as Fiction and Fiction as Theory* (Cambridge: Cambridge UP, 1987), 47, Malcolm Bowie recalls that Proust had summed up "theory" as a price tag a person unwittingly leaves on a gift. Similarly, Henry James often writes sensuous descriptions of landscapes before he tells the reader how much they are worth. Unlike Proust or James, Ronsard leaves a price tag on his poems, but he incorporates it within the printed letters and figures.

19 It would be tempting to align the relation of exchange at the basis of the writing of a courtly sonnet with innuendo of fear of castration. In the imaginary world of the poem, it is implied that to be short of money is tantamount to living in a condition of castration. But when the equivalence is studied closely in the text, it appears that Ronsard is suggesting that the effect of castration is simply that: an effect or pose. The staging of the fear of loss thus functions in a dynamic that wills to gain capital from the effect produced in the poem. The "fear" that comes from unrequited love or the "Cassandra-scenario" of the *Amours* would seem to compound biological, poetic, and economical conditions in the fourth line of the printed text of 1553. Since *boys* in the sixteenth century is synonymous with *andouiller*, or horns, *Hors de son boys* evokes a buck whose antlers have been pruned, or else a deer so horny that he is unable to copulate. Without his rack the deer has no sexual queue or "code"; alliteration of the median lines – the lure of onomatopoeia of dogs barking melodies over hill and dale – dresses the poet in a travesty of a castrated cervine, an image that will be set in relief in the 1587 version. That castration is neither here nor there in the play of distortion gives proof to the force of the poem and the unconscious that refuses castration as an essence or a guiding concept. It is hence not a truth but a condition of wit.

20 The anamorphic inscription of a deadly sign in the center of a work, in the manner of Holbein's "Ambassadors," has been the topic of more modern readings than classical ones. We know, according to Jean Parrot, that Henry James dealt with half-letters of death when he entitled his novel of the same name after Holbein's portrait: "L'Anamorphose dans les romans de Henry James," *Critique* 383 (April 1979), 330–51. Mannerist artists and, before that, late-medieval tapestry-weavers inserted

signs of death within signs. In the Cleveland Museum of Art, the Chaumont tapestry of Charles II of Amboise (1500–10) displays three parts that allegorize eternity, youth, and time. In the central tapestry, two death's heads are woven into the attire of two youths who move about a maiden in the center. The death's heads shimmer on the surface of the composition. One of the skulls is illustrated in Geneviève Souchal, *La tapisserie en France au XVe et au XVIe siècles* (Paris: Catalogue de l'Exposition au Grand Palais, 1976), 166. Gisèle Mathieu-Castellani remarks the same process at work in Holbein's emblems, in *Emblèmes de la mort: le dialogue de l'image et du texte*, 36–37.

21 The issue of *trace* overriding the "unconscious" of such a text is so fruitful that it allows comparison with Jacques Derrida's "Retrait de la métaphore," *Poésie* 6 (1979) (in English in *Enclitic* 4, 1979, 13–26), that also depends on the identity of pictural and discursive orders (*écart* being *tracè*).

22 It is latent in the poem but will be amplified in the rewriting of the *Amours* in much of the *Continuations*, what Ronsard will call his "style bas." See Louis Terreaux, "Le style 'bas' des *Continuations des Amours*," in *Lumières de la Pléiade* (Paris: Vrin, 1966), 313–16.

23 *Les Œuvres de Pierre de Ronsard. Texte de 1587*, ed. Isodore Silver, 1 (Chicago: Published for the Washington UP by the U of Chicago P, Librairie Marcel Didier, 1966), 145.

24 Louis Terreaux, *Ronsard correcteur de ses œuvres. Les variantes des "odes" et les deux premiers livres des "Amours"* (Geneva: Droz, 1968), 630.

25 Ronsard develops the same scene of a birth of historical autobiography in his "Response aux injures et colomnies de je ne sçay quels predicans et ministres de Geneve" (1563):

> Je vy que des François le langage trop bas
> Se trainoit sans vertu, sans ordre, ny compas:
> Adoncques pour hausser ma langue maternelle,
> Indonté du labeur, je travaillé pour elle,
> Je fis des mots nouveaux, je rapellay les vieux:
> Si bien que son renom je poussay jusqu'aux cieux:
> Je fis d'autre façon que n'avoient les antiques,
> Vocables composés, et frases poëtiques,
> Et mis la poësie en tel ordre qu'apres,
> Le François s'egalla aux Romains et aux Grecs.

[I saw that for the French an overly common language dragged behind, without force, order, or bearing. Thus to pull up my maternal tongue, unafraid of the labor, I worked for her, I made new words, I recalled the old ones so well that I thrust its renown as high as the heavens: I did this in a way other than the classics, with composed vocables, and poetic clauses, and I arranged poetry in such order that French became the equal of the Romans or the Greeks]

Discours et derniers vers, ed. Yvonne Bellenger (Paris: Garnier-Flammarion, 1979), 149–50, lines 1017–26.

The revision of the past amounts to a "screen-memory" of the kind that Freud detected in Leonardo da Vinci rewriting the past through the written distortion of a recollection that had no graphic form (*SE*, 11, 79ff). In his famous study of the artist, Freud notes that the "writing of history" begins from these deformations. When Ronsard revised his sonnets and his own past, he moved from poetry to historiography. That the letter was again pivotal in this shift of activity shows how typography "settled" from 1552 to 1587, and how form became the subject of a political view of the past.

26 By this it is meant that the body is transformed from a landscape into a book of lettered pages. It anticipates mystical discourse, by which the text is a trace of a speaking body. It goes against what the mature Ronsard advocates in the *Discours* of 1564 (just above) and later. See Michel de Certeau, *La fable mystique*, 103–06.

27 In his explanation of the move from limited to a general discourse entitled *From Telling to Talking: A Study of Style in Rabelais*, Etudes Rabelaisiennes XIV (Geneva: Droz, 1978), Jeffrey Kittay shows how a narrowly defined descriptive system of blockages gives way to a gratuitous flow of words. We could liken this to Ronsard in the shift from the April scene in the poem to its flow of letters that run all about and everywhere in the paragrammar. Thus a breakage of that initial system is witnessed, but with the difference that a Rabelaisian free-for-all, like what we have seen above in the *propos des bien yvres*, now works in terms of a twisting flow of letters throughout "Comme un chevreuil..." The poem amounts to salutary visual noise which, syncopating and correcting the imperfect measures of the disturbed body of the cosmos, dialogically induces a healthy death and regeneration of the body. Global animation is precipitated from the engagement of the silent dimension of words and characters. The *chevreuil* is forlorn, but the sonnet is noisy and brimming with wit.

28 We are tempted to recall that in "Comme un chevreuil..." Ronsard, one of the more narcissistic poets of his time, parades his own narcissism in what we are likely to understand in Lacanian terms. "The effect of mimicry," Lacan notes, "is camouflage in the strictly technical sense. It is not a question of harmonizing with the background, but against a mottled background, of becoming mottled – exactly like the technique of camouflage practiced in human warfare." Cited by Joan Copjec, in "The Orthopsychic Subject: Film Theory and the Reception of Lacan," *October* 49 (Summer 1989), 70–71. Letters are hence part of the "retz effect" that produces a poem of mottled figures of venery or desire itself.

29 I have attempted a study of the relation of "Comme un chevreuil" to emblem-pictures in greater detail in "Le sonnet-emblème: Scève et Ronsard," *Littérature* 63 (October 1986), 24–37.

4 The turn of the letter: from Cassandre to Hélène

1 Roland Barthes, "L'Esprit de la lettre," in *L'obvie et l'obtus*, 95.
2 These aspects of sixteenth-century life are studied in Eisenstein, *Printing Press* and Ong, *Ramus*. See also Introduction, notes 1 and 2. Particular emphases on the status of education are offered in François Furet and Jacques Ozouf, *Lire et écrire: l'alphabétisation des Français de Calvin à Jules Ferry*, 2 vols. (Paris: Minuit, 1970). One thinks of Bruegel's print, "The Ass at School," in H. Arthur Klein, *The Graphic Worlds of Pieter Bruegel the Elder* (New York: Dover, 1963), 143.
3 A tradition of exegesis grows from the hermetic aspect of his style. In fact, both Rémy Belleau's and Muret's *Commentaires* now appear as prototypical "critical editions" which give proof to the relation of the teacher (or poem) to the student (the reader) deciphering the verse. That they deal thematically with the poetry shows either that the graphic elements may have been too obvious for commentary or that even in the sixteenth century they remained unnoticed. See the commentaries appending the poems taken up in Gisèle Mathieu-Castellani, ed., *Les commentaires de Muret et de Belleau*, 2 vols. (Geneva: Droz, 1985–86).
4 According to Piera Aulagnier, the pictogram forms the basis of the future relations that a subject will hold with the symbolic world. The child's graphic dreams have the effect of framing later relations in intersubjective spheres. *L'apprenti-historien et le maître sorcier* (Paris: PUF, Série "Fil rouge," 1984), 203–04. Her conclusions derive from clinical practice in the psychotherapy of children. Similar results are studied in her essays collected in *Un interprète en quête de sens* (Paris: Ramsay, 1986), 329–58. In literary theory Gabriele Schwab reaches similar conclusions in "Genesis of the Subject, Imaginary Functions and Poetic Language," *New Literary History* 15 (Spring 1984), 453–74, where she superimposes Lacan's theories of psychogenesis (developed in "The Mirror Stage") on to Bakhtine's notion of dialogic language. Malcolm Bowie sorts through psychogenesis and literary language in *Freud, Proust and Lacan: Theory as Fiction*, 105–07 and 120–24.
5 Emphasis can be placed again on Guy Rosolato's terminologies. See chapter 2 note 6, above, and "L'objet de perspective dans ses assises visuelles," *Nouvelle Revue de Psychanalyse* 35 (Spring 1987), 143–64.
6 Ronsard's frequent allusions to the plastic arts inspire comparisons of verbal and visual media. Margaret McGowan, *Ideal Forms in the Age of Ronsard*, follows the figures throughout the work.
7 According to Tory in the *Champ fleury*, where S denotes silence, R inscribes the barking of dogs. Quoting Persius, he notes, "*Sonant hic de nare canina litera*," or "*La lettre canine resone en cest endroict cy, dung coste du nez*" (f. lv r°) [The canine letter resounds in this place, from the nostril]. In his program rage must effectively give way to silence, just as *r* must give way to *s* in the alphabet.

8 Robert Cottrell develops the point through an extended comparison of the genre with Lacan's notion of the mirror-stage in "Scève's *Blason* and the Logic of the Gaze," *L'Esprit Créateur* 28.2 (Summer 1988), 68–77.

9 In *The Gods Made Flesh*, Leonard Barkan uses the sonnet to show how Petrarch's vision of the pagan world, intellectual and rhetorical in sum, gives way to one of sensuality. Flow and sensuous dissolution take over: "*Vague* plus *ondes* equals *vagabondes*; and the sense of aqueous motion quite naturally introduces the figure of love who rises from the sea. Yet just as the words dissolve, so do the myths," which lead to "erotic pleasure itself" (216–27). Apropos of the sixteenth sonnet, he argues that Ronsard's only real objective (at least in the self-consciousness of the sonnets) is a wish to obtain fame and glory that reveal " 'the myth of signature' " (216). Margaret McGowan studies how Ronsard fuses "the motifs of waves and hair, waves of the sea, and those of the body" (*Ideal Forms*, 199). She notes that the Venus we associate with Botticelli is seen *indoors* in this sonnet and brings into view, because of the bonnet on her head, "a copy of Léonard Limousin's coiffed and bonneted Venus" seen on an enamelled dish in the Louvre (201). Hair is used in the poem because of "its power to hide or reveal" (202). In a reading of the *Amours* that emphasizes "a charade that dissimulates profound sexual ambivalence," Lawrence D. Kritzman argues that in this poem two genders are present, and that each "is at the same time the dividing force and support of the other." *The Rhetoric of Sexuality and the Literature of the French Renaissance* (Cambridge: Cambridge UP, 1991), 113 and 127–28.

10 As Rosolato notes, "un plaisir à distance, qui s'enrichit d'une multitude d'informations, plus riches, à ce stade qui précède l'acquisition du langage, que celle qui viennent de l'ouïe" [a pleasure in distance, which is nourished by a multitude of information richer, at this state prior to the acquisition of language, than what comes from hearing], "L'objet de perspective," 151.

11 *Champ fleury*, f. xxvi r° and f. xlix r°.

12 It could be said that here we glimpse what Anton Ehrenzweig calls the "inner fabric" of art, especially in our momentary or reduced awareness of its form. "We are forced," he notes, "to observe the unconscious structure of art with the gestalt techniques of the (conscious or preconscious) secondary process which will automatically infuse a more solid and compact structure into it." *The Hidden Order of Art* (Berkeley: U of California P, 1971), 78. When the letters dissolve into meaning of movement, they are "revised" in our secondary operation of reading.

13 An element basic to the rhetoric of classical cinema, the term seems appropriate to explain the relation of letters and space that we engage in the sonnet. In film the lap-dissolve designates a brief superimposition of two shots, one ending a sequence and the other beginning the next,

that usually denotes a transition of time and space. Yet when two images are melded, unconscious effects are often produced. The relation of the unconscious to the lap-dissolve is taken up in my *Film Hieroglyphs* (Minnesota: U of Minnesota P, 1991), xx and illustrations, 36 and 182–83. In Ronsard's poem the letter appears and disappears into the figure of the woman's body and vice versa.

14 *Noud* also appears to allude to current debates about Venus naked versus Venus clothed. The word invokes orthographic issues that play on nudity (*nu*) and human collectivity. Its form is, like Freud's mark of the uncanny ("un"), cast as a doubling of the same or a symmetry of *u* and *n* (inversions of each other) that describes the beauty of a body without a code. In the *Amours* we recall the *Elegie à Janet peintre du roy*:

> Je ne sçay plus, mon Janet, où j'en suis,
> Je suis confus, & muet je ne puis,
> Comme j'ay fait, te declarer le reste
> De ses beautés, qui ne m'est manifeste:
> Las! car jamais tant de faveur je n'u
> Que d'avoir veu ses beaus tetins à nu
> Mais si l'on peut juger par conjecture,
> Persuadé de raisons, je m'asseure
> Que la beauté qui ne s'aparoist doit
> Du tout respondre à celle que l'on voit.
>
> (lines 123–32, 161)

[I no longer know, my dear Janet, where I am, I am confused, and mute I cannot, as I have done, tell you about the rest of her beauties, that aren't so manifest: Alas! For never had I so much favor than in seeing her beautiful bare breasts, but if one can judge by conjecture, persuaded by reason, I must be assured that beauty which does not appear may entirely match what one beholds.]

The masterful narrative about visibility and Eros has its hidden order in *nu*, a typographical variant on *n'eus*, that almost – were it not for the apostrophe – makes a perfectly symmetrical figure of a bare line. Apropos of the same poem, André Tournon remarks that the description of the imaginary portrait is the "sign of a sign." In the place of the body is the "pictural representation of the body": "Palimpsestes, échos, reflets: le dédoublement dans la poétique de Ronsard," in Philippe de Lajarte, ed., *Aspects de la poétique ronsardienne* (Caen: PUC, 1989), 33. He stresses a poetics of imitation that, in our reading, seems to be complicated by the materiality of Ronsard's verbal practice.

15 But also keep her from being any of a number of things happening or having come (*venus*) upon the stage of the sonnet...

16 *Studies in Iconology* (New York: Harper, 1967), 126–28.

17 Montaigne cultivated the same ambiguity when he placed "Sur des vers de Virgile" under the monogram of the Roman numeral V (chapter 5) of the third book of *Essais*. The essay on sexual difference has Difference itself crowned in the device-like *v* placed above it.

18 Regression to ambiguous origins, signalled so clearly in this poem, may remind a reader of Freud's *Dora*, the case history in which he reminds his audience of the mythic origins of the human species: "*inter urinas et faeces nascimur*'" (*SE* 7, 31). Ronsard is effectively returning to the same origin, but through coy and comic means. Freud reminded his readers of those origins once again in his study of Leonardo da Vinci, written soon after *Dora*.

19 The notion of the *bas corporel* inspires much of Mikkaïl Bakhtine's *Rabelais et le Moyen Age sous la Renaissance* (Paris: Gallimard, 1968). The relations of sadism, narcissism, and pleasure are sketched in Leo Bersani and Ulysse Dutoit, *The Forms of Violence* (New York: Schocken, 1985), 37–39.

20 The king's travels are documented in R. J. Knecht, *Francis I*, 174–75.

21 Charles Beaulieux recounts the fortunes of the cedilla in sixteenth-century France in his *Histoire de l'orthographe française*, 2, 41.

22 The letters resemble what Montaigne calls the "testes" of death, that are both death's heads and typographic characters: "Pour en renger davantage, je n'en entasse que les testes" [To put more in place, I only pile up heads]. "Consideration sur Cicéron," *Essais*, 1, xl (251).

23 In *Œuvres complètes*, vol. 2, ed. Gustave Cohen (Paris: Gallimard-Pléiade, 1950), 1007. In "Le Palimpseste de *l'Abbregé de l'Art Poétique françois*," Mireille Huchon demonstrates that Ronsard cribs Sébillet, and that Ronsard leaves in shadow his own working principles of creation. For Huchon the history of the text, its borrowings, and its politics indicate that the second half of the sixteenth century still depends on work accomplished in the 1550s. In Lajarte, *Aspects de la poétique ronsardienne*, 113–28.

24 "Remonstrance au peuple de France" (1563), lines 133–34.

25 The graphic dimension seems to engage silence, the ground for the mute gaze or birth of desire. Claude-Gilbert Dubois traces themes of silence in "L'Impossible à conter et l'inter-dit du silence: problèmes de la profération dans le discours de Ronsard." In Lajarte, *Aspects de la poétique ronsardienne*, 41–54.

5 Montaigne's test of style: *De l'exercitation*

1 In his *Essais sur les "essais"* (Paris: Gallimard, 1968); Patrick Henry, *Montaigne in Dialogue* (Stanford: Anma Libri, 1987), 90. In *Le texte de la Renaissance*, François Rigolot studies Montaigne's self-marginalization to the degree that the writer literally goes to the margins of his own page. "Montaigne translates this predilection not only in the order of his images but also in the order of the structure of his books. Paradoxically he chooses the center of his books to affirm his taste for decentering" (224).

2 André Tournon also wonders how and where the uncanny forms of

Montaigne's book originate. Some of its traits, he notes, can be recognized in the "lesson," glosses, and *centons* where the erudition and wisdom of Humanism were scattered. In *La glose et l'essai* (Lyon: PUL, 1983), 10.

3 Initial work is undertaken in Claude Balavoine, "Une écriture emblématique?" in Frank Lestringant, ed., *Rhétorique de Montaigne* (Paris: Champion, 1985), 59–72. *Sententiae* figure in quasi-parataxis, as do titles and subscriptions, that promote an "associative play" of figures. Beyond identification of tropes, more extensive comparison of emblematic style to verbal montage needs to be made. Appeal can also be made to Jacques Derrida's critique of fixed schemas in "Force et signification," in *L'écriture et la différence* (Paris: Seuil, 1968), 3ff.

4 The theory of division inhering in the emblem is developed in Robert Klein, *La forme et l'intelligible* (Paris: Gallimard, 1970). Barry Lydgate deals with the difference in the forms of the essay and print in "Mortgaging One's Work to the World: Publication and Structure of Montaigne's *Essais*," *PMLA* 96 (March 1981), 210–23.

5 In *Le texte divisé* (Paris: PUF, Série Ecriture, 1981) Marie-Claire Ropars-Wuilleumier sketches a theoretical picture of divided, "hieroglyphic" writing through Freud's concept of *Zusammensetzungen*, Eisenstein's filmic ideogram, Benveniste's figure of "plastic" languages, and Derrida's concept of *différance*. She shows how a hieroglyphic style can be based "upon a virtual demotivation of the image in respect to the object that it represents: a dissociation, therefore, of figuration from meaning" (71), that thresholds division. A multiplication of meaning comes with the gap opened between vocal and printed tracks. The subversive dimension of the sign divided into figure and inscription is studied in her *Ecraniques: le film du texte* (Lille: PUL, 1990), 26–29. Madeleine V. David's *Le Débat sur les écritures et l'hiéroglyphe aux XVIIe et XVIIIe siècles et l'application de la notion de déchiffrement aux écritures mortes* (Paris: SEVPEN, 1965) provides a historical complement to the same problem.

6 Throughout *The Matter of my Book* (Berkeley: U of California P, 1977), Richard Regosin shows how Montaigne's style is in material transformation consonant with the mutation of the writing subject, the I, in the time and space of the work. Our reading will specify some of the graphic means deployed in this process.

7 Floyd Gray studies the protean definition of the essay in terms of both gravity and change in *Montaigne et la balance: exagium/essai* (Paris: Nizet, 1982).

8 I have attempted more detailed readings of III, iii and II, xi in this fashion in "Montaigne's Gascoigne: Textual Regionalism of 'Des boyteux,'" *MLN* 92 (1977), 710–23 and "*De capsula totoe*: lecture de 'trois commerces,'" *L'Esprit Créateur* 28.1 (Spring 1988), 5–12.

9 Nicolas Abraham notes that any work of art − that is, any *real* work of art − has an unconscious dimension. Elements that betray or contradict statements within their own enunciation yield rich paradox. "An inauthentic work has no unconscious," he underlines in *L'Ecorce et le noyau* (Paris: Aubier-Flammarion, 1978), 18. For him ineffable rhythms of speech are folded into authentic literature; we should emphasize that those rhythms owe much to the scansion of visible shapes that work with and against the flow of discourse.

10 Informative studies concerning style and portraiture include Floyd Gray, *Le style de Montaigne* (Paris: Nizet, 1958); Albert Thibaudet's remarks on Montaigne's metaphors in the last section of his posthumous *Montaigne* (Paris: Gallimard, 1963); Michel Beaujour, *Miroirs d'encre* (Paris: Seuil, 1980); Marc-Eli Blanchard, *Trois portraits de Montaigne: essai sur la représentation à la Renaissance* (Paris: Nizet, 1990). Pictogrammar and psychogenesis are treated in Aulagnier, *Un interprète*, while self-fashioning is the topic of Stephen Greenblatt, *Shakespearean Negotiations* (Oxford: Clarendon Press, 1988), 3−20.

11 *The Cornucopian Text*, 298.

12 In *Emblèmes de la mort* (155−56), she notes that Montaigne exhibits a *jouir du mourir* in II, vi, and that the process engages life and death insofar as each represents the other in alternative roles of image and text (166). The relation touches on poetry, she adds in *Montaigne: l'écriture de l'essai*, when signification goes "beyond (*au-delà*) the single meaning of the vocables" (96).

13 It is worthwhile to recall that in *A la recherche du temps perdu* the narrator begs the reader to evaluate the meaning of an event by heeding the verbal sign that heralds the tale that follows. *Toujours, parfois, souvent, le samedi*, or *une fois* mark the beginnings of paragraphs in *Combray*. *Une fois* is always a capital moment in the search for lost time. No less complex in his representation of a traumatic event, Montaigne hides the unity of his example by framing it within a seemingly "faulty" memory that his bookish project has generally forced into oblivion. For Montaigne the sign of "bad memory" indicates that the moment is often reported with uncanny exactitude: the book is a memory-machine that makes up for whatever loss he might have experienced without printed words and pictures. Hence, all memory is consigned to the characters printed on the page.

14 It would be redundant to compare the identities that Montaigne's formula shares with Maurice Blanchot's speculations on death and writing in *Le pas au-delà* (Paris: Gallimard, 1973). One author is a variant of the other. Already Blanchot had scripted the order of movement and visibility of Montaigne in "Parler, ce n'est pas voir," in *L'entretien infini* (Paris: Gallimard, 1969), 46ff.

15 Montaigne always prefers the "softness" of a serene death to less attractive, or more manly, demises. Natural death that comes from weakening

and gravity "me semble molle et douce" [seems to me soft and sweet] he notes later (but in the same turn of style) than by way of sword or arquebus fire (*harquebousade*). ("De la vanité," 983.)

16 After "De l'exercitation" Montaigne often establishes an identity of the essay with an effect, not only in the broken logic he uses (as charted by Erich Auerbach in *Mimesis*), but also in the multiple visual amphiboly owed to the resemblance of the medial *s* to the *f* in the spelling of *effai* and *effet* in his orthography. "De conclurre par la suffisance d'une vie particuliere quelque suffisance à l'usage public, c'est mal conclud; tel se conduict bien qui ne conduict pas bien les autres et faict des *Essais* qui ne sauroit faire des *effaicts*" (992, my italics). [To conclude through the sufficiency of an individual life some sufficiency for public use is to conclude badly. Such a person conducts himself well who does not conduct others and makes *Essais* that could not leave any effects.] The effect of the essay is bound to the title of its cause.

17 In this sense the writing is mystical, where the signature or style of the text is proof of the writer's body. See Michel de Certeau, *La Fable mystique*, 14ff., or his "Lecture absolue," in *Problèmes actuels de la lecture* (Paris: Clancier Guénaud, 1982), 76. The anatomy lesson that Montaigne offers has a background in illustrated books that span from Holbein in the 1530s to Ambroise Paré at the end of the century. Some of the verbal and visual relations of the genre are developed in Devon L. Hodges, *Renaissance Fictions of Anatomy* (Amherst, Mass: U of Massachusetts P, 1985), 1–19.

18 See François Jacob, *La logique du vivant* (Paris: Gallimard, 1970), chapter 1.

19 The Old Testament, Webster reports, verifies the physical sense of *astony*: "Then Daniel was astonied for one hour" (Daniel, 4:19); "I rent my garment and mantle ... and sat down astonied" (Ezra, 9:3). *Astonish* is identical: "Enough, Captain, you have astonished him" (Shakespeare) and "he had his wits astonished with sorrow" (Sidney). The verb conjures up lapidary meanings. The ostensive origins of *estonnement* are motivated by the ciphers folded into the word, at least through the presence of a foreign element, like the virtue of Saussurean *Langue*, contained in Montaigne's orthography. Would it be legitimate to see *stone* in **eston**ner? Does the reader's interpretive eye go "too far" or *trop au-delà*, beyond the limits of Montaigne's diction by seeking a stony fragment of Engish buried in the Gascon history of *teston*? The diction would tend to show that indeed the ramification of meanings is licit.

20 The psychoanalytical consequence of chosing a proper name from an arbitrary ensemble of letters or characters inflects the relation of names of things throughout the *Essais*. Piera Aulagnier reminds us that the history of any subject is made when he or she creates the fiction of a necessary *non-interchangeability*. When the subject does not fabricate a

history to dispel human indifference, he or she risks falling into atrophy. Health depends on the creation of a fiction made by selecting figures, metaphors, shifters, and even characters to designate difference. Montaigne's reader follows the birth of the subject and his history in a way that is developed in her *L'apprenti-historien et le maître-sorcier*, 8–11.

21 Noted in the introduction above, but depending on Saussure's notes, edited by Jean Starobinski, in *Les Mots sous les mots* (Paris: Gallimard, 1974).

22 The way that Montaigne's writing articulates a montage is studied in more detail in my "Montaigne en montage: Mapping 'De la vanité' (III, ix)," *Montaigne Studies* 3 (1991): 208–34.

6 A colossal abyss: *Des coches*

1 Roger Chartier, "A Concept and its Books: *Civilité* between Aristocratic Distinction and Popular Appropriation," in *The Cultural Uses of Print in Early Modern France* (see Introduction, note 2), 76.

2 In *L'orthographe française à l'époque de la Renaissance*, Nina Catach follows reform in sixteenth-century orthography, grammar, and spelling through developments of print that begin with Robert Estienne and Tory in the 1520s and 1530s and lead to Plantin in the 1560s. After that moment typography settled into shapes that have continued until now. Montaigne appears to inherit the work of the 1560s and exploits typography not for itself but for what it can do in its relation to visibility and meaning.

3 Its composition is festooned with a string of enigmas that have left a critical legacy. A first reading that aligns itself with art history is R. A. Sayce, "Baroque Elements in Montaigne," *French Studies* 8 (1954), 1–15. René Etiemble, in "Sens et structure dans un essai de Montaigne," *Cahiers de l'Association Internationale des Etudes Françaises* 14 (1962), 263–74, treats the economic themes from a general point of view. Robert Griffin's "Title, Structure and Theme of Montaigne's 'Des coches,'" *MLN* 82 (1967), 285–90, suggests that hidden forms are at work. Dain A. Trafton studies carefully the cartography of times old and new in "Ancients and Indians in Montaigne's 'Des coches,'" *Symposium* 27 (Spring 1973), while Marcel Gutwirth mediates a thematic and quasi-psychoanalytical element in his " 'Des coches,' ou la structuration d'une absence," *L'Esprit Créateur* 15.1–2 (Spring–Summer 1975), 8–20. John O'Neill extends Etiemble's, Sayce's, and Gutwirth's readings in "Civilization, Literacy, and Barbarism" at the end of his *Essaying Montaigne* (London: Routledge and Kegan Paul, 1982), 188–201. One of the pioneer studies of ethnographic history is Marcel Bataillon's "Montaigne et les conquérants de l'or," *Studi Francesi* 9 (1959), 353–57. Some of the broader implications of III, vi can be found in Peter Burke,

"Montaigne as Ethnographer," in his *Montaigne* (New York: Hill & Wang, 1982), 44–51.

4 Louis Marin accounts for some of the relations of the emblem and numismatics in "Sur une médaille et une gravure," in *Etudes sémiologiques* (Paris: Klincksieck, 1972).

5 It would be tempting, too, to see in the relation of *coche* and *coque* (or boat) something of an originary problem of causality. What came first, the chicken (the *poule*) who makes such a cackle in the last sentences of III, v ("ce notable commentaire, qui m'est eschappé d'un flux de caquet" (897) [this notable commentary, that has escaped me in the flush of cackling] or the egg (the *coque*), that begins III, vi? The question of causality is posed between the two chapters, in the words and form that link the end of one and the beginning of the other.

6 See Margaret Hodgen, *Early Anthropology in the Sixteenth and Seventeenth Centuries* (Philadelphia: U of Pennsylvania P, 1964). Firsthand elaboration of the theme is marked in Pierre Boaistuau, *Histoires tragiques*, ed. Richard Carr (Paris: Champion/STFM, 1977), 123.

7 See Eric R. Wolf, *Europe and the People without History* (Berkeley: U of California P, 1982), 82, who discusses how analogies of feudalism with Chinese or Asiatic modes of production are "usually treated as enduring and unchanging opposite," or as "ahistorical, hence ideological views of history." Even if Montaigne's presentation of a steady-state culture in the East appears mythic or ideological, both then and today it has, at least within the overriding allegory of "Des coches," political impact in its imperative that asks the world to slow down, or to reject economies of expansion or whatever promotes geocide.

8 David Parker, *The Making of French Absolutism* (New York: Saint Martin's Press, 1983), 44.

9 *Francogallia* (9), 231–33. (The selection and translation belong to Robert Knecht.)

10 The synthesis of narrative and allegory produces a continous movement in which all parts of the essay turn simultaneously. For this reason our view must dispute Jean Starobinski's reading based on a logic of progression that articulates a political view over the passage of time. "Adhérer étroitement à la vie sensible, *puis*, par sympathie, *étendre* cette adhésion au-delà des limites de la vie personnelle, c'est vivre dans la non-violence, où, dans la moindre violence," he notes about "Des coches" in *Montaigne en mouvement* (Paris: Gallimard, 1984), 301 (my italics). [To stick closely to affective life, then, by generosity, extend this adhesion beyond the limits of personal life means to live in non-violence, or in the least violence possible.] Delay allows his reading to bind social criticism with what appears to be the *Essais*'s thematically conservative view of political institutions. The optical facets of the text and the self-contained structure of the chapter do not allow such protracted evolutive movement to emerge from the writing.

11 In the "Remonstrance au peuple de France" (1563), Ronsard explained the problem of sign and embodiment in similar terms. Addressing God, his equal and rival, he explains,

> Tu as dit simplement d'un parler net & franc,
> Prenant le pain & vin, *C'est cy mon corps & sang,*
> Non signe de mon corps.

> [You simply said in a speech both clear and frank,
> Taking the bread and wine, *This is my body and blood,*
> Not a sign of my body].

Œuvres complètes 11, ed. Paul Laumonier (Paris: STFM/Didier, 1946), 69, lines 113–15.

12 "De mesnager sa volonté" (III, x) ends with the same uneasiness. It translates its fear of calm through the *Aeneid* (V, 849–51), and projects a sense of learned ignorance into the next chapter, "Des boyteux," as another superscription of an emblem:

> *mene huic confidere monstro,*
> *Mene salis placidi vultum fluctusque quietos*
> *Ignorare?* (1024)

> [Should I take confidence in this strange calm?
> Would I be able to forget what the face of the sea and
> its wafting waves might conceal?]

13 Wheels were used to distinguish Christian from pagan orders. Cultures without wheels, R. W. Bulliet notes, were seen as nomadic, or "fomenters of trouble on the frontiers" of a society. The wheel was associated with rational planning, while those who did not use the pivoting axle were not. They were inclined to use pack animals or pallbearers and did not need central turnabout areas in urban design. The wheel bears the same connotations in "Coches." See "The Camel and the Wheel," in Marc Ferro, ed., *Social Historians in Contemporary France* (New York: Harper, 1972), 58.

14 The paradox of self-engenderment acquires both political and literal aspects. Gisèle Mathieu-Castellani, in *Montaigne: l'écriture de l'essai*, takes it up as a premise to the entire autobiographical project which may or may not include commentary and counsel (32ff.).

15 In *Les métamorphoses de Montaigne* (Paris: PUF, 1988), 35–60, François Rigolot determines how the *Essais* mediate history and allegory in order to compromise difficult options. His reading leads to a conclusion that can be directed toward the structure of both "Des coches" and the ways that information we receive in most news and reporting is mediated and allegorized.

16 *The Philosophy of Rhetoric* (New York: Oxford UP, 1959), 49.

17 Anthropology, in this respect, owes much to the birth of perspective in the Italian Renaissance, at least as Panofsky argues in *Renaissance*

and Renascences. However, the gap between symmetries and information shows where experience of alterity goes back to the models of detailed observation in Northern European painting. The birth of an anthropological distance in Montaigne's "Cannibales," that applies to "Coches," is taken up in Michel de Certeau, "The Savage 'I,'" in *Heterologies*, 67–79.

18 See Erwin Panofsky, "Father Time," in *Studies in Iconology*, 155–82. In the same vein, his *Early Netherlandish Painting*, 1 (Cambridge: Harvard UP, 1953), 47, takes up the same problem. The divided landscape shares much with what social historians have discovered in the oppositional configuration in sixteenth-century festivals. Different classes acted out their conflicts in the play that spatial allegories staged for the participants. Roger Chartier notes that "with its rituals, its actions, and its objects," the *fête* "becomes a grammar of symbols that enables the articulation in a clear or implied manner of a political project" (*The Cultural Uses of Print in Early Modern France*, 27). Since "Des coches" is no less a verbal *fête* of its own kind, Chartier's word can apply to the overall landscape of the chapter.

19 Bruegel's allegory, dated 1574, is in H. Arthur Klein, *Graphic Worlds of Pieter Bruegel*, 177. Early representations of anthropophagia in the New World intertwine with Saturn. In Sebastian Münster's 1540 (Basle) edition of Ptolemy's *Geographia*, representations of the "novae insulae," Brazilian lands, are illustrated with a clump of trees from which hang an amputated leg and a man's head. See R. A. Skelton's new edition, third series, 5 (Cleveland and New York: World Publishing, 1966), f. 45.

20 Montaigne had taken pains to distinguish *monstre* from *montre* in the 1588 copy, no doubt because they were already close to one another in form. In manuscript he wrote to his printer, "*Montre, montrer, remontrer*, etc., escrives les sans *s* à la difference de *monstre monstrueus*" [write *show, to show*, and *to show again* without *s*, not like *monstrous monster*], notes Charles Beaulieux, "L'orthographe de Montaigne," in *Mélanges Huguet* (Paris: Boivin, 1940), 7. As in the instance of *or*, every time he writes of *montre*, Montaigne forces the weight of the chapter's form and vehicle to sit on both substantive and verb together. What emerges, we can repeat, is that other, unconscious grammar that Michael Riffaterre calls a "paragrammar" common to all poetic structures of discourse (see Introduction, note 7).

21 Watches had a predictable conventional iconography identical to what the text elaborates in this chapter. See J. Drake-Brockman and A. J. Turner, "An Emblematic Watch by Gribelin," *Bibliothèque d'Humanisme et Renaissance*, 36 (1974), 143–50. The workshop at Blois from 1558 to 1635 is furthermore inclusive of the period of Montaigne's acquaintance with that city.

22 The relations that hold between anthropophagia and the Eucharist

are many and figured in the margins of discussions of natives in early New World literature. They are also bound into debates concerning the Wars of Religion that run through both "Coches" and "Cannibales" but would merit extensive discussion elsewhere, as Frank Lestringant demonstrates in "Les Indiens antérieurs (1575–1615)," in Gilles Thérien, ed., "Les figures de l'Indien," *Cahiers du Départment d'Etudes Littéraires* 9 (Montréal: U du Québec à Montréal, 1988), 57–71, especially 67–68.

23 "La lettre O, cy pres deseignee, est aussi large que haulte, & ronde par dehors uniformement en ung Quarre equilateral. Par dedans, elle est ronde en forme de fons de cuve, Cest a dire rond ung peu estandu, & faisant deux coustez ung peu longuets, a la quelle forme interieure & exterieure le Colisee de Rome fut jadis edifie, comme on peut veoir encores aux ruynes qui en restent dedans la dicte Rome (fol. li v^9). [The Letter O, drawn below, is as wide as high, and round on the outside uniformly in an equilateral square. Inside, it is round in the form of the bottom of a basin, that is to say round but stretched, and making two sides a bit longish, to which interior and exterior form the Roman Coliseum was once edified, as we can see still in the ruins remaining in the said Rome.]

24 The impact that writing left in the New World is taken up in Michel de Certeau, "Ethno-graphie: l'oralité, ou l'espace de l'autre: Léry," in *L'écriture de l'histoire*, 215–48. It scarifies, he notes, but it also sets up a system of relays that allow a myth of Western omnipotence to be ingrained in the indigenous imagination. Janet Whatley develops further the relation of writing, colonization, and history in her introduction to her translation of Jean de Léry, *History of a Voyage to the Land of Brazil, Otherwise Called America* (Berkeley: U of California P, 1990), xxxiff.

25 Here is a variant of Montaigne's critique of logocentrism and of "practical" or "clear" stenography that has the limited goal of merely "saying what it means" and no more. The classical ideal of unilateral writing is not far from what, elsewhere, he calls "escrivaillerie" or "quelque simptome d'un siecle desbordé" (946), "scribbling" or a way to make maximum profit from minimal torsions of style, in *escrivaillerie*, the supreme "symptom of an excessive century."

26 The combination figures in what Montaigne calls his own "dictionary" or lexicon of poetic neologisms. *Mechaniques* combines what is mechanical (*mécanique*) with what is nasty (*méchant*), all the while the negotiation for pearls and pepper establishes an allegory of qualities black and white and spherical. The allegorical combination extends the figure of gold within their miniature shape of the globe: *des perles et du poivre*. Whenever Montaigne uses alliteration, the euphony alludes to a more extensive structure of graphic combinations that convey both a poetic and a political charge.

27 *Cause* and *chose* are treated as one throughout the essays, at least if

the reader is to believe the pun on the two words that frames "Des boyteux" (III, ix), an essay that rhymes in size and space with "Coches." In "Montaigne's Gascoigne: Textual Regionalism of the *Essais*," I try to suggest that the amphiboly of *cause–chose–causer* engages a politics through association of writing, space, and the body. The relation of letter, individual and political body also pertains here.

28 In my "Montaigne and the Indies: Cartographies of the New World in the *Essais*, 1580–88)," *Hispanic Issues*, 4 (Summer 1989), 225–62, comparison of Montaigne's text to the French translation of Gómara shows that the allegory of the letter, the world, and prophecy is carefully crafted, so that the overall structure of the essay is reflected even in its most minute aspects.

29 Aristotle because, in the debates between Sepúlveda and Las Casas in 1550–51, the Greek philosopher was marshalled to argue for the inferiority of the native in civilized worlds. Las Casas criticized the efficient use to which such "authorities" were put. See Olive Dickason, *The Myth of the Savage in North America* (Alberta: University of Alberta Press, 1984), 56–57; Marcel Bataillon, *Las Casas et la défense des Indiens* (Paris: Julliard, 1971); Lewis Hanke, *Aristotle and the American Indians: A Study in Race Prejudice in the Modern World* (Bloomington: Indiana UP, 1959), and his *All Mankind is One: A Study of the Disputation Between Bartolomé de Las Casas and Juan Ginés de Sepúlveda in 1550 on the Intellectual and Religious Capacity of the American Indians* (DeKalb: Northern Illinois UP, 1974).

30 Patrick Henry has reviewed the fortunes of the early editions of the *Essais* in respect to papal censure. See *Montaigne in Dialogue* (Stanford: Anma Libri, 1987), ch. 1: "Roman censorship triggered off the practice of defensive writing in the *Essais*" (14). The author's appeal to the synecdoche of a gun shares much with the discussion of warfare in "coches," while some of the history of the subjugation of Indians in the New World is developed in "The Approach of the Europeans, 1497–1600," in Bruce G. Trigger, *Natives and Newcomers* (Kingston and Montreal: McGill-Queen's UP, 1985), 135–63.

Conclusion

1 Montaigne appears to be writing the *Essais* for readers of immemorial time. Our century sometimes loses sight of the notion of long-term planning as known in the early modern age. It has been reported that shortly after 1660, Colbert, Louis XIV's financial advisor, planted a forest of oak trees near Charroux (in the vicinity of Vichy) that were not to be cut before 1990, a time that he declared would be necessary to refurbish the French navy (reported by Professor Michael Nerlich, *seiziémiste* and historian of Charroux). See also Roger Hervé, "Les plans de forêts de la grande réformation colbertienne, 1661–1690,"

in *Sociétés Savantes de la France: Bulletin de la Section Géographique* 73 (1960), 143–71.

2 As they are typified in the Renaissance according to Eric Wolf, *Europe and the People without History*, 82.

3 See chapter 5, note 9. Also: Patrick Lacoste, *Il écrit: une mise en scène de Freud* (Paris: Galilée, 1980); Jean-Michel Rey, *Des mots à l'œuvre* (Paris: Aubier-Flammarion, 1978); Serge Leclair, *Psychanalyser* (Paris: Seuil, 1968); Samuel Weber, *The Legend of Freud*.

4 We can thus surmise that the productive distinction of the *lisible* and the *scriptible* (the readerly and the writerly) that Roland Barthes offered two decades ago in *S/Z* (Paris: Seuil, 1970), 10, is now dated insofar as the notion of the classical text – the *lisible* – pertains only to the seventeenth century and after, at least according to the condition of representation in Foucault's taxonomy of the classical age. We must argue for another category for early modern work since its archaic economies and functions of analogy can be transposed on to our field of writing. The combinations of the rhetoric fold the reader of any age into the contract of their modes of transmission, and make the receiver a virtual writer.

5 *The Political Unconscious* (Ithaca: Cornell UP, 1981). Jameson tends to thematize subjectivity in order to place a Lacanian model of psychogenesis under a higher Marxian order. He effectuates a "strategy of containment" on one level in order to provide the illusion of erasing it from another. In "Capitalizing History," an essay on *The Political Unconscious* in *Institution and Interpretation* (Minneapolis: U of Minnesota P, 1986), Samuel Weber notes that the practice of the letter in a strict analytical sense shows us where and how a material sense of language can help us avoid losing focus in thematic treatments of history or subjectivity.

6 Our account of the sixteenth-century canon in this context might prompt us to articulate in greater detail, or reconsider, Lacan's famous remarks about the unconscious being structured "like a language" and with properties common to rhetoric. The rhetoric may not be Ciceronian but of moving letters and images, what Freud had anticipated in *The Interpretation of Dreams* (SE 4, e.g., 298ff.).

7 The rhetoric is studied in Doris-Louise Haineault and Jean-Yves Roy, *L'inconscient qu'on affiche, essai psychanalytique sur la fascination publicitaire* (Paris: Aubier, 1984), and has many analogues in English. An example of a name as quasi-subliminal montage is *kleenex*. Spelled correctly, as *clean-x*, it puts forward a choice between propriety (*clean*) and maculation (*x*, a stain or a spot). To clean the *x* one reaches for another *kleenex*, which erases an *x*, that persists with the next *kleenex*, and so on …

8 See Mark Crispin Miller, "End of Story," in *Seeing Through Movies* (New York: Pantheon, 1990), 186–246. He notes what Dr. Lewis

Webster Jones, head of the National Conference of Christians and Jews, first said about subliminal writing: "'This approach to human beings strikes me as utterly cynical and directly contrary to the democratic ideal.'" Or: "'Such a weapon could result in the modeling of our population's social and political attitudes and beliefs to the point where democracy would be a mockery and freedom meaningless'" (cited on 186).

9 Miller suggests that the dialectics of the rhetoric may have changed (215ff.). In most film and literature brand-names are inserted into the image or narrative according to fees negotiated between producers and artists. Many films and books could not be produced without income of this kind. Thus art has become almost everywhere an advertisement or a practice of high-speed emblematics that sell substitutes in place of narrative or whatever their genre is traditionally said to purvey.

BIBLIOGRAPHY

Abraham, Nicolas. *L'écorce et le noyau*. Paris: Aubier-Flammarion, 1978.

Ajuriaguerra, J. *et al.* "L'écriture en miroir." *La Semaine des Hôpitaux de Paris* 2 (1956): 80–86.

Arnheim, Rudolph. *The Power of the Center: A Study of Composition in the Visual Arts* Berkeley: University of California Press, 1988.

Auerbach, Erich. *Mimesis*. Tr. Williard R. Trask. New York: Doubleday, 1956.

Aulagnier, Piera. *L'apprenti-historien et le maître-sorcier*. Paris: Presses Universitaires de France, Série 'Fil rouge', 1984.

Un interprète en quête de sens. Paris: Ramsay, 1986.

La violence de l'interprétation. Paris: Presses Universitaires de France, Série 'Fil rouge,' 1975.

Baïf, Jean-Antoine de. *Les amours de Francine*. Ed. Ernesta Calderini. Geneva: Droz, 1966.

Balavoine, Claude. "Une écriture emblématique?" In Frank Lestringant, ed., *Rhétorique de Montaigne*. Paris: Champion, 1985: 59–72.

Baltrušaitis, Jurgis. *Le Moyen Age fantastique*. Paris: Colin, 1955.

Réveils et prodiges. Paris: Colin, 1960.

Barkan, Leonard. *The Gods Made Flesh: Metamorphosis and the Pursuit of Paganism*. New Haven: Yale University Press, 1986.

Bakhtine, Mikkaïl. *Rabelais et le Moyen Age sous la Renaissance*. Paris: Gallimard, 1968.

Barthes, Roland. *L'obvie et l'obtus*. Paris: Seuil, 1982.

S/Z. Paris: Seuil, 1970.

Bataillon, Marcel. *Las Casas et la défense des Indiens*. Paris: Julliard, 1971.

"Montaigne et les conquérants de l'or." *Studi Francesi* 9 (1959): 353–7.

Beaujour, Michel. *Miroirs d'encre*. Paris: Seuil, 1980.

Beaulieux, Charles. *L'histoire de l'orthographe française*. 2 vols. Paris: Champion, repr. 1967.

"L'orthographe de Montaigne." In *Mélanges Huguet*. Paris: Boivin, 1940.

Bellenger, Yvonne, ed. *Ronsard: Discours et derniers vers*. Paris: Garnier-Flammarion, 1979.

Benveniste, Emile. *Problèmes de linguistique générale*. 2 vols. Paris: Gallimard, 1966.

211

Bibliography

Berchtold, J. "Le poète-rat: Villon, Erasme, ou les secrètes alliances de la prison dans 'l'épitre à son amy Lyon' de Clément Marot." *Bibliothèque d'Humanisme et Renaissance* 50.1 (1988): 57–76.

Bersani, Leo. *The Culture of Redemption*. Cambridge: Harvard University Press, 1990.

Bersani, Leo and Ulysse Dutoit. *The Forms of Violence*. New York: Schocken, 1985.

Blanchard, Marc-Eli. *Trois portraits de Montaigne: Essai sur la représentation à la Renaissance*. Paris: Nizet, 1990.

Blanchot, Maurice. *L'entretien infini*. Paris: Gallimard, 1969.

Le pas au-delà. Paris: Gallimard, 1973.

Bloch, R. Howard, *The Scandal of the Fabliaux*. Chicago: University of Chicago Press, 1988.

Boaistuau, Pierre. *Histoires tragiques*. Ed. Richard Carr. Paris: Champion/STFM, 1977.

Bowie, Malcolm. *Freud, Proust, and Lacan: Theory as Fiction and Fiction as Theory*. Cambridge: Cambridge University Press, 1987.

Brunot, Ferdinand. *Histoire de la langue française de ses origines à 1900*, vol. 2. Paris: Colin, 1905.

Bulliet, R. W. "The Camel and the Wheel." In Marc Ferro, ed. *Social Historians in Contemporary France*. New York: Harper, 1972.

Burke, Peter. *Montaigne*. New York: Hill & Wang, 1982.

Butor, Michel. *Essais sur les 'essais'*. Paris: Gallimard, 1968.

Catach, Nina. *L'orthographe française à l'époque de la Renaissance*. Geneva: Droz, 1968.

Cave, Terence. *The Cornucopian Text: Problems in Writing in the French Renaissance*. Oxford: Clarendon Press, 1979.

Certeau, Michel de. *L'écriture de l'histoire*. Paris: Gallimard, 1975.

La fable mystique. Paris: Gallimard, 1982.

Heterologies. Minneapolis: University of Minnesota Press, 1985.

L'invention du quotidien. Paris: Union Générale d'Editions, 1976.

"Lecture absolue." In *Problèmes actuels de la lecture*. Paris: Clancier Guénaud, 1982.

"The Gaze of Nicholas of Cusa." Tr. C. Porter. *Diacritics* 17.3 (Fall 1987): 2–38.

Chartier, Roger. *The Cultural Uses of Print in early Modern France*. Princeton: Princeton University Press, 1987.

"Le passé composé." *Traverses* 40 (1987): 6–18.

Conley, Tom. "*De capsula totae*: lecture de 'Trois commerces.'" *L'Esprit Créateur* 28.1 (Spring 1988): 18–26.

Film Hieroglyphs. Minnesota: University of Minnesota Press, 1991.

"Le jargon d'Orléans." *The New Orleans Review* 12 (1985): 12–26.

"Montaigne's *Gascoigne*: Textual Regionalism of the *Essais*." *Modern Language Notes* 92 (1978): 710–23.

"Montaigne's Hispanic Issues: Cartographies of the New World in the *Essais*." *Hispanic Issues* 4 (Summer 1989), 225–62.

Bibliography

Montaigne en montage: Mapping "De la vanité." *Montaigne Studies* 3 (1992): 208–34.

"Le sonnet-emblème: Scève et Ronsard." *Littérature* 63 (October 1986): 24–37.

Copjec, Joan. "The Orthopsychic Subject:" *Film Theory and the Reception of Lacan. October* 49 (Summer 1989): 53–71.

Cornilliat, François. "La couleur de l'écriture: le débat de peinture et de rhétorique dans *La Plainte du désiré* de Jean Lemaire." *Nouvelle Revue du Seizième Siècle* 7 (1989): 7–23.

"Equivoques moralisées," *Poétique* 83 (September 1990), 281–304.

Cotgrave, Randle. *Dictionarie of the French and English Tongues.* London: Adam Islip, 1611; Columbia: University of South Carolina Press reprint, 1968.

Cottrell, Robert. "Scève's *Blason* and the Logic of the Gaze." *L'Esprit Créateur* 28.2 (Summer 1988): 68–77.

Curtius, Ernst Robert. *European Literature and the Latin Middle Ages.* Tr. Williard R. Trask. Princeton: Princeton University Press reprint, 1971.

Daddesio, Eva. "Le bruissement silencieux de la graphie dans 'Les Fanfreluches antidotées'." *L'Esprit Créateur* 28.2 (Summer 1988): 48–57.

Dassonville, Michel. *Ronsard: étude historique et littéraire.* 3 vols. Geneva: Droz, 1976.

David, Madeleine V. *Le Débat sur les écritures et l'hiéroglyphe aux XVIIe et XVIIIe siècles et l'application de la notion de déchiffrement aux écritures mortes.* Paris: SEVPEN, 1965.

Davis, Natalie Z. *Society and Culture in Early Modern France.* Stanford: Stanford University Press, 1975.

Defaux, Gérard. "Clément Marot: Une poétique du silence et de la liberté." In Jerry C. Nash, ed. *Pre-Pléiade Poetry.* Lexington: French Forum, 1985: 44–64.

Delegue, Yves. *La perte des mots: essai sur la naissance de la "littérature" aux XVIe et XVIIIe siècles.* Strasbourg: Presses de l'Université de Strasbourg, 1990.

Demerson, Guy. "Les calembours de Rabelais." In *Le comique verbal au seizième siècle.* Warsaw: Cahiers de Varsovie, 1981.

Rabelais. Paris: Balland, 1986.

Derrida, Jacques. *La dissémination.* Paris: Seuil, 1972.

L'écriture et la différence. Paris: Seuil, 1968.

"Retrait de la métaphore." *Poésie* 6 (1979); Eng. trans. *Enclitic* 4 (1979): 13–26.

Parages. Paris: Galilée, 1986.

Dickason, Olive. *The Myth of the Savage in North America.* Alberta: University of Alberta Press, 1984.

Dolet, Etienne. *La maniere de bien traduire d'une langue à l'autre. D'avantage. De la punctuation de la langue Françoyse.* Paris, 1540.

Douce, Francis, ed. *Holbein's Dance of Death.* London: Henry G. Bohn, 1858.

Bibliography

Dragonetti, Roger. *La vie de la lettre au Moyen Age*. Paris: Seuil, 1980.

Drake-Brockman, J. and A. J. Turner. "An Emblematic Watch by Gribelin." *Bibliotheque d'Humanisme et Renaissance* 36 (1974): 143–50.

Dubois, Claude-Gilbert. *L'imaginaire de la Renaissance*. Paris: Presses Universitaires de France, 1985.

Le maniérisme. Paris: Presses Universitaires de France, 1979.

"L'impossible à conter et l'inter-dit du silence: problèmes de la profération dans le discours de Ronsard." In Philippe de Lajarte, ed. *Aspects de la poétique ronsardienne*. Caen: Presses de l'Université de Caen, 1988: 41–54.

"Taxionomie poétique: compositions sérielles et des constructions d'ensembles dans la création esthétique au seizième siècle." In Lawrence Kritzman, ed. *Le signe et le texte* (Lexington: French Forum Monographs, 1990): 131–45.

Edgerton, Samuel V., Jr. "From Mental Matrix to Mappamundi to Christian Empire: the Heritage of Ptolemaic Cartography in the Renaissance." In David Woodward, ed. *Art and Cartography: Six Historical Essays*. Chicago: University of Chicago Press, 1987, 10–50.

Ehrenzweig, Anton. *The Hidden Order of Art*. Berkeley: University of California Press, 1971.

Eisenstein, Elizabeth. *The Printing Press as an Agent of Change*. 2 vol. Cambridge: Cambridge University Press, 1979.

Etiemble, René. "Sens et structure dans un essai de Montaigne." *Cahiers de l'Association Internationale des Etudes Françaises* 14 (1962): 263–74.

Febvre, Lucien. *Le problème de l'incroyance au XVIe siècle*. 1942. Paris: Albin Michel, 1968.

Fletcher, Angus. *Allegory: Theory of a Symbolic Mode*. Ithaca: Cornell University Press, 1964.

Foucault, Michel. *Les mots et les choses*. Paris: Gallimard, 1966.

Francastel, Pierre. *La figure et le lieu*. Paris: Gallimard, 1967.

Friedlander, Walter. *Mannerism and Anti-Mannerism in Italian Art*. New York: Columbia University Press (repr.), 1957.

Freud, Sigmund. *The Standard Edition of the Complete Psychological Works of Sigmund Freud*. 24 vols. London: Hogarth Press, 1955.

Furet, François and Jacques Ozouf. *Lire et écrire: l'alphabétisation des Français de Calvin à Jules Ferry*. 2 vols. Paris: Minuit, 1970.

Genet, Jean. *Œuvres complètes*. 4 vols. Paris: Gallimard, 1968.

Gilson, Etienne. *Les idées et des lettres*. Paris: Vrin, 1942.

Glauser, Alfred. *Fonction du nombre chez Rabelais*. Paris: Nizet, 1984.

Le Poème-symbole. Paris: Nizet, 1967.

Rabelais créateur. Paris: Nizet, 1966.

Goody, Jack. *Domestication of the Savage Mind*. Cambridge: Cambridge University Press, 1977.

Goyet, Francis, ed. *Traités de poétique et de rhétorique de la Renaissance*. Paris: Livre de poche, 1990.

Bibliography

Gray, Floyd, "Ambiguity and Point of View in the Prologue to *Gargantua*." *Romanic Review* 56 (1965): 19–25.

Montaigne et la balance: exagium/essai. Paris: Nizet, 1982.

"Rabelais's First Readers." In Raymond C. La Charité, ed. *Rabelais's Incomparable Book.* Lexington: French Forum, 1986: 15–25.

Le style de Montaigne. Paris: Nizet, 1958.

Greenblatt, Stephen. *Shakespearean Negotiations.* Oxford: Clarendon Press, 1990.

Griffin, Robert. *Clément Marot and the Inflections of Poetic Voice.* Berkeley: University of California Press, 1974.

"Title, Structure and Theme of Montaigne's 'Des coches'." *Modern Language Notes* 82 (1967): 285–90.

Guillaume, Jean. "L'escalier dans l'architecture française de la première moitié du seizième siècle." In Jean Guillaume, ed. *L'escalier dans l'architecture de la Renaissance.* Paris: Picard, 1985: 24–47.

Gutwirth, Marcel. " 'Des coches', ou la structuration d'une absence." *L'Esprit Créateur* 15.1–2 (Spring–Summer 1975): 8–20.

Haineault, Doris-Louise and Jean-Yves Roy. *L'inconscient qu'on affiche.* Paris: Aubier, 1984.

Hanke, Lewis. *All Mankind in One: A Study of the Disputation Between Bartolomé de La Casas and Juan Ginés de Sepúlveda in 1550 on the Intellectual and Religious Capacity of the American Indians.* DeKalb: Northern Illinois University Press, 1974.

Aristotle and the American Indians: A Study in Race Prejudice in the Modern World. Bloomington: Indiana University Press, 1959.

Henkel, Arthur and Albrecht Schöne. *Emblemata.* Stuttgart: Metzlersche Verlag, 1967.

Henry, Patrick. *Montaigne in Dialogue.* Stanford: Anma Libri, 1987.

Hervé, Roger. "Les plans de Forêts de la grande réformation colbertienne, 1661–1690." In *Sociétés Savantes de la France: Bulletin de la Section Géographique* 73 (1960), 143–71.

Hodgen, Margaret. *Early Anthropology in the Sixteenth and Seventeenth Centuries.* Philadelphia: University of Pennsylvania Press, 1964.

Hodges, Devon L. *Renaissance Fictions of Anatomy.* Amherst, Mass.: University of Massachusetts Press, 1985.

Hollier, Denis. *Politiques de la prose.* Paris: Gallimard, 1984.

Hotman, François. *Francogallia.* Geneva: I. Stoerij, 1573.

Huchon, Mireille. "Pour une histoire de la ponctuation, 1532–1553." *Nouvelle Revue du Seizième Siècle*, 6 (1988): 15–28.

"Le palimpseste de l'*Abbrégé de l'Art Poétique françois*." In Philippe de Lajarte, ed. *Aspects de la poétique ronsardienne.* Caen: Presses de l'Université de Caen, 1988: 113–28.

"Rabelais et les genres d'ecrire." In Raymond C. La Charité, ed. *Rabelais's Incomparable Book.* Lexington: French Forum Monographs, 1986: 226–47.

215

Huguet, Edmond. *Dictionnaire de la langue française au XVIe siècle*. Paris: Librairie Marcel Didier, 1925–67.

Huizinga, Johan. *The Waning of the Middle Ages. A Study of the Forms of Life, Thought and Art in France and the Netherlands in the XIVth and XVth Centuries*. Tr. Frederick Hopman. New York: Doubleday, 1956.

"L'ivresse." *Corps écrit*. Paris: Presses Universitaires de France, 1984.

Jacob, François. *La logique du vivant*. Paris: Gallimard, 1970.

Jameson, Fredric. *The Political Unconscious*. Ithaca: Cornell University Press, 1981.

Jeffrey, Brian. "The Idea of Music in Ronsard's Poetry." In Terence Cave, ed. *Ronsard the Poet*. London: Methuen, 1973: 208–38.

Jourda, Pierre, ed. *Conteurs du seizième siècle*. Paris: Gallimard-Pléiade, 1965.

Jeanneret, Michel. "Du mystère à la mystification: le sens caché à la Renaissance et dans Rabelais." *Versants* 2 (Winter 1981–82): 3–21.

Des mets et des mots. Paris: José Corti, 1987.

Kelley, Donald. *The Beginnings of Ideology*. Cambridge: Cambridge University Press, 1982.

Kinser, Samuel. *Rabelais's Carnival*. Berkeley: University of California Press, 1990.

Kittay, Jeffrey. *From Telling to Talking: A Study of Style in Rabelais*. Etudes Rabelaisiennes XIV. Geneva: Droz, 1978.

Klein, H. Arthur. *The Graphic Worlds of Pieter Bruegel*. New York: Dover, 1963.

Klein, Robert. *La forme et l'intelligible*. Paris: Gallimard, 1970.

Kline, T. Jefferson. *Screening the Text*. Baltimore: The Johns Hopkins University Press, 1992.

Knecht, Robert. *Francis I*. Cambridge: Cambridge University Press, 1982.

Kritzman, Lawrence D. *The Rhetoric of Sexuality and the Literature of the French Renaissance*. Cambridge: Cambridge University Press, 1990.

Kuhn, David. *La poétique de François Villon*. Paris: Colin, 1967.

La Charité, Raymond C. "Narrative Strategy in Rabelais's *Quart livre*." In Barbara Bowen and Jerry C. Nash, eds. *Lapidary Inscriptions: Renaissance Essays for Donald A. Stone, Jr.* Lexington: French Forum Monographs, 1991: 195–205.

Lacoste, Patrick. *Il écrit: une mise en scène de Freud*. Paris: Galilée, 1980.

Leclaire, Serge. *Psychanalyser*. Paris: Seuil, 1968.

Lemaire de Belges, Jean. *La concorde des deux langages*. Cr. edn. Jean Frappier. Paris: Droz, 1947.

Lestringant, Frank. "Les Indiens antérieurs (1775–1615)." In "Les figures de l'Indien," ed. Gilles Thérien. *Cahiers du Départment d'Etudes Littéraires* 9. Montréal: Université du Québec à Montréal, 1988: 57–71.

"Rabelais et le récit toponymique." *Poétique* 50 (April 1982): 207–25.

Lévi-Strauss, Claude. *La pensée sauvage*. Paris: Plon, 1962.

Bibliography

Du miel aux cendres. Paris: Plon, 1964.

Le regard éloigné. Paris: Plon, 1983.

Lévy, J. M. "L'écriture en miroir des petits écoliers." *Journal de Psychologie Normale et Pathologique* 32 (1935): 443–54.

Lydgate, Barry. "Mortgaging One's Self to the World: Publication and Structure of Montaigne's *Essais,*" *Publications of the Modern Language Association* 96 (March 1981): 210–23.

Lyotard, Jean-François. *Le différend.* Paris: Minuit, 1983.

Discours, figure. Paris: Klincksieck, 1971.

Marin, Louis. *Etudes sémiologiques.* Paris: Klincksieck, 1972.

Portrait of the King. Tr. Martha Houle. Minneapolis: University of Minnesota Press, 1988.

Marot, Clément. *Œuvres diverses: rondeaux, ballades, chants-royaux, épitaphes, étrennes, sonnets.* Ed. C. A. Mayer. London: Athlone Press, 1966.

L'adolescence clémentine. Ed. Frank Lestringant. Paris: Gallimard/ Poésie, 1987.

L'adolescence clémentine. Ed. Verdun-L. Saulnier. Paris: Editions de Cluny, 1958.

Martin, Henry J. and Lucien Febvre. *L'apparition du livre.* Paris: Albin Michel, 1958.

Mathieu-Castellani, Gisèle. *Les commentaires de Muret et de Belleau.* 2 vols. Geneva: Droz, 1985–86.

Emblèmes de la mort: le dialogue de l'image et du texte. Paris: Nizet, 1988.

Montaigne: l'écriture de l'essai. Paris: Presses Universitaires de France, 1988.

"La parleuse muette." *L'Esprit créateur* 28.2 (1988): 25–35.

"Le retour de l'emblème." *Littérature* 78 (May 1990): 3–10.

Mayer, C. A. and D. Bentley-Cranch. "Clément Marot, poete pétrarchiste." *Bibliothèque d'Humanisme et Renaissance* 28 (1966): 32–51.

McGowan, Margaret. *Ideal Forms in the Age of Ronsard.* Berkeley: University of California Press, 1985.

Miller, Mark Crispin. "End of Story." In Mark Crispin Miller, ed. *Seeing Through Movies.* New York: Pantheon, 1990: 186–246.

Molinet, Jean. *Faictz et dictz.* 3 vols. Paris: Société des Anciens Textes Français, 1937.

Montaigne, Michel Eyquem de. *Les Essais.* Ed. Pierre Villey. Paris: Presses Universitaires de France, 1965 (new edn, Série Quadrige, 1988).

O'Neill, John. *Essaying Montaigne.* London: Routledge and Kegan Paul, 1982.

Ong, Walter J., S. J. *Ramus, Method, and the Decay of Dialogue: From the Art of Discourse of the Art of Reason.* Cambridge: Harvard University Press, new edn, 1984.

"From Allegory to Diagram in the Renaissance Mind." *Journal of Aesthetics and Art Criticism* 17 (1959): 423–40.

Bibliography

Panofsky, Dora and Erwin. "The Iconography of the Galerie François Premier at Fontainebleau." *Gazette des Beaux Arts* 52 (1958): 11–113.

Panofsky, Erwin. *Early Netherlandish Painting*. 2 vols. Cambridge: Harvard University Press, 1953.

Renaissance and Renascences in Western Art. Stockholm: Almquist & Wiksell, 1960.

Meaning in the Visual Arts. New York: Doubleday, 1955.

Studies in Iconology. New York: Harper, 1967.

Parker, David. *The Making of French Absolutism*. New York: Saint Martin's Press, 1983.

Parrot, Jean. "L'anamorphose dans les romans de Henry James." *Critique* 383 (April 1979): 330–51.

Poirion, Daniel. *Le poète et le prince*. Paris: Presses Universitaires de France, 1965.

Ptolemy. *Geographia*. Ed. Sebastian Münster (Basle: 1540). Ed. R. A. Skelton, third series, vol. 5, Cleveland and New York: World Publishing, 1966.

Rabelais, François. *Œuvres complètes*. Ed. Jacques Boulenger. Paris: Gallimard-Pléiade, 1955.

Raymond, Marcel. *Baroque et Renaissance poétique*. Paris: Corti, 1955.

Regosin, Richard. *The Matter of my Book*. Berkeley: University of California Press, 1977.

Rey, Jean-Michel. *Des mots à l'œuvre*. Paris: Aubier-Flammarion, 1978.

Richards, I. A. *The Philosophy of Rhetoric*. New York: Oxford University Press, 1959.

Riffaterre, Michael. *Semiotics of Poetry*. Bloomington: Indiana University Press, 1978.

Rigolot, François. "Cratylisme et Pantagruélisme." *Etudes Rabelaisiennes* 13 (1976): 115–32.

"Dichotomie épistémologique chez Rabelais." In *Poétique et onomastique*. Geneva: Droz, 1977.

"Léda and the Swan: Rabelais's Parody of Michelangelo." *Renaissance Quarterly* 38.4 (Winter 1985): 688–700.

Les métamorphoses de Montaigne. Paris: Presses Universitaires de France, 1988.

Poésie et onomastique. Geneva: Droz, 1977.

"Rabelais et la scolastique (*Gargantua* 12)." In Raymond C. La Charité, ed. *Rabelais's Incomparable Book*. Lexington: French Forum, 1988.

"1493: The Rhétoriqueurs." In Denis Hollier, ed. *A New History of French Literature*. Cambridge: Harvard University Press, 1989: 127–32.

Le texte de la Renaissance. Geneva: Droz, 1982.

Rigolot, François and Sandra Sider. "Fonctions de l'écriture emblématique chez Rabelais." *L'Esprit Créateur* 28 (Summer 1988): 38–39.

Bibliography

Ronsard, Pierre de. *Les Amours*. Eds. H. and C. Weber. Paris: Garnier, 1963.

Œuvres complètes. Ed. Gustave Cohen. Paris: Gallimard-Pléiade, 1950.

Œuvres complètes. Ed. Paul Laumonier 20 v. Paris: STFM/Librairie Marcel Didier, 1924–75.

Les Œuvres de Pierre de Ronsard. 1587. Ed. Isidore Silver. Chicago: Published for the Washington University Press by the University of Chicago Press, Librairie Marcel Didier, 1966.

Ropars-Wuilleumier, Marie-Claire. *Le texte divisé*. Paris: Presses Universitaires de France, Série écriture, 1981.

Ecraniques. Lille: Presses de l'Université de Lille, 1990.

Rosolato, Guy. *Eléments de l'interprétation*. Paris: Gallimard, 1985.

"L'objet de perspective dans ses assises visuelles." *Nouvelle Revue de Psychanalyse* 35 (Spring 1987): 143–64.

Rousset, Jean. *La littérature de l'âge baroque en France*. Paris: Corti, 1953.

Roustang, François. "On the Epistemology of Psychoanalysis." *Modern Language Notes* 99 (September 1984): 910–32.

Russell, Daniel. *The Emblem and Device in France*. Lexington: French Forum, 1985.

Sauret, Martine. "Corps et délit dans le *Gargantua* de Rabelais." Unpubl. doctoral dissertation (Minnesota, 1991).

Saussure, Ferdinand de. *Les Mots sous les mots*. Ed. Jean Starobinski. Paris: Gallimard, 1974.

Sayce, R.A. "Baroque Elements in Montaigne." *French Studies* 8 (1954): 1–15.

Schmidt, Albert-Marie, ed. *Poètes du XVIe siècle*. Paris: Gallimard-Pléiade, 1953.

Scott, David. *Pictorialist Poetics: Poetry and the Visual Arts in Nineteenth-Century France*. Cambridge: Cambridge University Press, 1988.

Screech, M.A. *Marot évangelique*. Geneva: Droz, 1967.

Rabelais. Ithaca and London: Cornell University Press, 1980.

"Marot and the Face of the Gospel." In Jerry C. Nash, ed. *Pre-Pléiade Poetry*. Lexington: French Forum, 1985: 75–85.

Schwab, Gabriele. "Genesis of the Subject, Imaginary Functions and Poetic Language." *New Literary History* 15 (Spring 1984): 453–74.

Sébillet, Thomas. *Art poétique françoys* (1548). In Francis Goyet, ed. *Traités de poétique et de rhétorique de la Renaissance*. Paris: Livre de poche, 1990: 37–183.

"Le Silence." *Corps écrit* 12. Paris: Presses Universitaires de France, 1984.

Smith, Pauline M. *Clément Marot, Poet of the French Renaissance*. London: Athlone Press, 1970.

"Clément Marot and the French Language." In P.M. Smith and I.D. McFarlane, eds. *Literature and the Arts in the Reign of Francis I*. Lexington: French Forum, 1985: 145–65.

Bibliography

Souchal, Geneviève. *La tapisserie en France au XVe et au XVIe siècles.* Paris: Catalogue de L'Exposition au Grand Paris, 1976.

Starobinski, Jean. *Montaigne en mouvement.* Paris: Gallimard, 1984.

Les mots sous les mots. Paris: Gallimard, 1974.

Sylvestre, Claude. "Le moment régressif." *Topique* 25 (1980): 27–30.

Terreaux, Louis. *Ronsard correcteur de ses œuvres. Les variantes des "odes" et les deux premiers livres des "Amours".* Geneva: Droz, 1968.

"Le style 'bas' des *Continuations des Amours.*" In *Lumières de la Pléiade.* Paris: Vrin, 1966: 313–16.

Thibaudet, Albert. *Montaigne.* Paris: Gallimard, 1963.

Tory, Geoffroy. *Champ fleury.* (Bourges, 1529). Ed. J. W. Jolliffe. Paris/ The Hague: Mouton and Johnson Reprint, 1970. English translation by George Ives. New York: Grolier Club, 1927; New York: Dover reprint, 1967.

Tournon, André, *La glose et l'essai.* Lyon: Presses Universitaires de Lyon, 1983.

"Palimpsestes, échos, reflets: le dédoublement dans la poétique de Ronsard." In Philippe de Lajarte, ed. *Aspects de la poétique ronsardienne.* Caen: Presses de l'Université de Caen, 1989: 27–40.

Trafton, Dain, A. "Ancients and Indians in Montaigne's 'Des coches'." *Symposium* 27 (Spring 1973).

Trésor de la langue française. Paris: Editions du Centre National de la Recherche Scientifique, 1978– .

Trigger, Bruce G. *Natives and Newcomers.* Kingston and Montreal: McGill/ Queen's University Press, 1985, 135–63.

Whatley, Janet. Tr. and ed. Jean de Léry, *History of a Voyage to the Land of Brazil, Otherwise Called America.* Berkeley: University of California Press, 1990.

Weber, Henri. *La création poétique au XVIe siècle en France.* Paris: Nizet, 1956.

Weber, Samuel. *Institution and Interpretation.* Minneapolis: University of Minnesota Press, 1986.

The Legend of Freud. Minneapolis: University of Minnesota Press, 1982.

Wittkower, Rudolph. "Hieroglyphics in the early Renaissance." *Developments in the Early Renaissance.* Ed. Bernard S. Levy. Albany: State University of New York Press, 1972.

Wolf, Eric R. *Europe and the People without History.* Berkeley: University of California Press, 1982.

Yates, Frances. *The Art of Memory.* Chicago: University of Chicago Press, 1966.

INDEX

Index

Cambridge Studies in French

General editor: MALCOLM BOWIE

Also in the series (* denotes title out of print)

225